PSYCHOLOGICAL STUDIES OF CLERGYMEN:

Abstracts of Research

PSYCHOLOGICAL STUDIES OF CLERGYMEN:

Abstracts of Research

by
Robert J. Menges
and
James E. Dittes

Foreword by
Thomas N. McCarthy, Ph.D.

THOMAS NELSON & SONS
London   NEW YORK   *Toronto*

FOREWORD

This book of abstracts by Robert J. Menges and James E. Dittes is certain to become the basic reference in the field. As a thorough and uniquely organized presentation of empirical studies, the book meets several critical needs.

The researcher working at the frontier of knowledge in a field that has inadequate communication can easily find himself the victim of a kind of myopia. Immersed in staking out a new domain and typically adient about his own exploratory endeavors, he is often subject to a loss of perspective that tends to be intensified when he is not able to exchange information with neighboring prospectors. This has been one of the peculiar characteristics of those who have been engaged in psychological studies of the clergy. Even researchers within the same denomination have found channels of communication woefully inadequate. This work is intended to remedy that deficiency, and the authors have accomplished this task in a way that should be a boon to all who work in the field. They have organized the empirical studies done to date according to the research question that each study has investigated. The net effect should be to facilitate greatly all later research.

One reason for faulty communication in the field of research with clergymen is that the studies have been largely parochial in character. In the main, psychological studies of clergymen of different denominations—Catholic, Jewish, Protestant—have been carried out without reference to one another. Catholic studies have tended to be exclusively Catholic, Protestant studies exclusively Protestant, and so on. It would appear that a tacit assumption has been made that studies of the clergy of different denominations are not relevant to one another. The present work, however, shows clearly the similarity in problems studied, research design, empirical techniques, and even in some conclusions drawn between studies of the clergy of different denominations. This work as a consequence gives unity to a field that has had none up to the present. This alone would make the book invaluable, but the authors have accomplished more.

Much of the psychological research done with the clergy has been in the form of master's and doctoral dissertations or it has appeared in such widely scattered sources and under such a variety of rubrics that researchers have been severely handicapped in assessing work already done. The exhaustive coverage of the literature accomplished by the authors obviates that problem and for the first time provides the researcher with an opportunity to see the field as a whole and to grasp more clearly areas that require further study.

The field of psychological research with the clergy is like Topsy in that it seems never to have been born; it just grew. The authors of *Psychological Studies of Clergy-*

men have provided here a sharply delineated picture of how that growth has occurred and a detailed morphology of the field as it now exists. In doing this they have not only achieved their objective of giving the field an identity, they also have charted a program for its further development.

Thomas N. McCarthy
Past president, American Catholic
Psychological Association

La Salle College
Philadelphia, Penna.
July, 1965

CONTENTS

ABBREVIATIONS

AATS Bull.	*American Association of Theological Schools Bulletin*
Amer. Cathol. Psychol. Newsletter	*American Catholic Psychological Newsletter*
Amer. Cathol. sociol. Rev.	*American Catholic Sociological Review*
Amer. eccl. Rev.	*American Ecclesiastical Review*
Amer. J. Orthopsychiat.	*American Journal of Orthopsychiatry*
Amer. J. Psychiat.	*American Journal of Psychiatry*
Amer. J. Sociol.	*American Journal of Sociology*
Amer. Psychologist	*American Psychologist*
Amer. sociol. Rev.	*American Sociological Review*
Arch. gen. Psychiat.	*Archives of General Psychiatry*
Augustana Seminary Rev.	*Augustana Seminary Review*
Australian J. Psychol.	*Australian Journal of Psychology*
Bull. anc. Élèves Saint-Sulpice	*Bulletin des Anciens Élèves de Saint-Sulpice*
Bull. Guild Cathol. Psychiat.	*Bulletin of the Guild of Catholic Psychiatrists*
Cah. Laënnec	*Cahiers Laënnec*
Cathol. Counsel.	*Catholic Counselor*
Cathol. Educator	*Catholic Educator*
Cathol. Educ. Rev.	*Catholic Educational Review*
Cathol. psychol. Rec.	*Catholic Psychological Record*
Cathol. Univer. Amer. Stud. in Psychol. & Psychiat.	*Catholic University of America Studies in Psychology and Psychiatry*
Crozer Quart.	*Crozer Quarterly*
Dissert. Abstr.	*Dissertation Abstracts*
Duke Divinity School Bull.	*Duke Divinity School Bulletin*
Educ. psychol. Measmt.	*Educational and Psychological Measurement*
Genet. Psychol. Monogr.	*Genetic Psychology Monographs*
Homil. pastoral Rev.	*Homiletic and Pastoral Review*
Iliff Rev.	*Iliff Review*
Int. J. group Psychother.	*International Journal of Group Psychotherapy*
J. abnorm. soc. Psychol.	*Journal of Abnormal and Social Psychology*
J. Bible and Relig.	*Journal of Bible and Religion*
J. clin. pastoral Wk	*Journal of Clinical and Pastoral Work*
J. coun. Psychol.	*Journal of Counseling Psychology*
J. de Psychol.	*Journal de Psychologie*
J. educ. Sociol.	*Journal of Educational Sociology*
Jewish Soc. Stud.	*Jewish Social Studies*
J. Gerontology	*Journal of Gerontology*
Jhb. Psychol. Psychother.	*Jahrbuch für Psychologie und Psychotherapie*
J. Marr. & Fam.	*Journal of Marriage and the Family*
J. nerv. ment. Dis.	*Journal of Nervous and Mental Disease*

J. pastoral Care	Journal of Pastoral Care
J. Psychol. Studies	Journal of Psychological Studies
J. Relig.	Journal of Religion
J. Relig. Hlth	Journal of Religion and Health
J. relig. Instruction	Journal of Religious Instruction
J. scientific stud. Relig.	Journal for the Scientific Study of Religion
J. soc. Psychol.	Journal of Social Psychology
Linacre Quart.	Linacre Quarterly
Lutheran Church Quart.	Lutheran Church Quarterly
Med. J. & Rec.	Medical Journal and Record
Ment. Hyg., N.Y.	Mental Hygiene, New York
Microfilm Abstr.	Microfilm Abstracts
Natl Cathol. Educ. Ass. Bull.	National Catholic Educational Association Bulletin
Natl Cathol. Educ. Ass. Seminary Newsletter	National Catholic Educational Association Seminary Newsletter
Nouv. Rev. Théol.	Nouvelle Revue Théologique
Pastoral Psychol.	Pastoral Psychology
Personnel Guid. J.	Personnel and Guidance Journal
Proc. 8th annu. Convocation of the Voc. Inst.	Proceedings of the Eighth Annual Convocation of the Vocation Institute
Psychiat. Quart.	Psychiatric Quarterly
Psychoanal. Rev.	Psychoanalytic Review
Psychol. Abstr.	Psychological Abstracts
Psychol. Rep.	Psychological Reports
Relig. Educ.	Religious Education
Res. Bull. (ETS)	Educational Testing Service Research Bulletin
Rev. Dioc. Tournai	Revue Diocesaine de Tournai
Rev. Espir.	Revista de Espiritualidad
Rev. Relig.	Review for Religious
Rev. relig. Res.	Review of Religious Research
Rev. Univer. Ottawa	Revue de l'Université d'Ottawa
Rural Sociol.	Rural Sociology
Seminary Quart.	Seminary Quarterly
Sister Formation Bull.	Sister Formation Bulletin
Soc. Forces	Social Forces
Soc. Probl.	Social Problems
Soc. Sci. Abstr.	Social Science Abstracts
Sociol. soc. Res.	Sociology and Social Research
Stud. Psychol. Psychiat. Cathol. Univer. Amer.	Studies in Psychology and Psychiatry, Catholic University of America
Stud. Sociol. Abstr. Series	Studies in Sociology Abstract Series
Suppl. Vie Spir.	Supplément de la Vie Spirituelle
TSI Research Bull.	Theological School Inventory Research Bulletin
Union Seminary Quart. Rev.	Union Seminary Quarterly Review
University of Pittsburgh Bull.	University of Pittsburgh Bulletin
Vie Comm. Relig.	La Vie des Communautes Religieuses

INTRODUCTION

This volume is intended to provide an identity for a field of research which has flourished for over a decade with hardly the awareness, even of those most actively engaged in the research, that they were participating in such a flourishing field. Our purpose is to provide focus, incentive, and guidelines for the many researchers engaged in psychological studies of clergymen.[1] We want them to know, first of all, that they are in an active, identifiable field of research with many co-workers. We hope that discerning here more readily the accumulated work, they can more intelligently plan needed new research and avoid redundant replication. Perhaps most importantly, we hope that with this perspective of the entire field, researchers can more easily discern the points of methodological stalemate and the places where they need to exercise most vigorous and creative research ingenuity. A single researcher facing a baffling methodological problem or disappointing results may become discouraged and abandon his task; paradoxically, we hope, if he sees the research difficulties as commonly shared, he may find in them new challenge.

The abundant and vigorous flourishing of this field is not difficult to demonstrate. This volume contains approximately 700 entries, over 75% of them dated within the last decade. Several of the entries are of book-length research reports (Bowers, Arnold, *et al.*, Fichter, and Bridston and Culver) all published within the last two years. Within the past decade, this research area has been a special topic of meetings of such organizations as the Society for the Scientific Study of Religion and the American Catholic Psychological Association, of several special conferences, and of entire issues of at least one journal, *Pastoral Psychology*. The topic has received the special attention of diverse educational and religious agencies, and one organization, The Ministry Studies Board, was formed five years ago solely to foster research in this area.

But neither is it difficult to demonstrate the relative isolation of researchers within this field. In an informal poll of a small but relatively sophisticated sample of researchers whose own work is represented in this volume, we asked two questions. "How many pieces of psychological research on clergymen are you personally acquainted with?" The median answer to this question was less than a dozen. "How many pieces of psychological research on clergymen do you suppose can be found by a thorough search of the literature?" The median answer was in the range 50-75. This compares with our answer of 700, which may still be too low. Regrettably and more significantly,

---

[1] Not the least sign of the field's ambiguous identity is the lack of a single term to represent the object of study. "Clergymen" is an inexact approximation, used here to refer to all those who serve, with or without ordination or vow, in the professional employ of religious institutions.

11

examination of almost any of the research reports abstracted here supplies unfortunate evidence of the relative isolation in which each worker has proceeded. This problem is especially acute among Protestant and the rare Jewish researchers; Catholics' work has tended to cluster around a few research centers and to show corresponding continuity from one worker to another. Authors who, incidental to other purposes (Roe, Argyle), have undertaken to provide definitive review of research on clergymen have drawn their conclusions from a bare half-dozen scattered and relatively primitive reports. Dissertation writers, who have often felt special responsibility and opportunity for "surveying the field" before proceeding with their own research, have typically developed sparse and scattered findings. Such difficulties in viewing the field as a whole are understandable in light of considerations we shall come to shortly.

In the next few paragraphs we wish to discuss some of the factors which seem to account for the increasing flood of research and some of the factors which have kept researchers isolated and have deprived the field of a clear identity.

Background of research

One in the clergy or in a religious order is, by calling and training—if not also by temperament—inclined to be introspective. The affairs of the inner life assume a primary importance and the affairs of his own inner life are apt to assume special importance and to invite scrutiny in at least two respects. First, the circumstances of his calling to clerical or religious life are intense, intimate, sometimes dramatic, never entirely unequivocal, always requiring some degree of reappraisal and test. (This type of question corresponds to category **A** in the classification scheme we have adopted for our entries. An explanation of the categories is found in the User's Guide, which follows this Introduction.) Second, the effectiveness or adequacy of performance in response to his call is necessarily subject to excruciatingly personal appraisal. Clear, objective criteria and the guidance of superiors and supervisors go only so far in helping a person to determine the faithfulness with which he is fulfilling his religious vocation. It is, finally, a matter of subtle individual conscience and reflection. (This corresponds to our category **B**.)

To point out that such concerns of the clergy and the religious are intimate and personal does not necessarily mean that they are private. Educators, supervisors, and other counselors have always felt some responsibility—both on behalf of the individual clergyman or religious and on behalf of the institutions they represent—to assist clergy and religious in assessing these questions, to test their call and to evaluate the adequacy of their vocational performance. But even though shared and to some degree public, these considerations remain intimate and subjective.

Through the centuries, these questions, although remaining essentially religious, have been considered with a variety of vocabularies and with the aid of many conceptual schemes. In our century, it is no surprise that they, like other personal introspective concerns and insights, have induced the more formal and systematic observations of maturing psychological research methods.

The present level of psychology's conceptual and technical sophistication for tackling such problems was gained largely during World War II and has since been applied to similar problems in many professions, including psychology and psychiatry themselves.

This growing readiness and eagerness of behavioral science to address such problems has coincided, since World War II, with several influences which have called the researchers' services into urgent demand.

One concern has been with the supply of clergymen and religious workers. The postwar church boom has created an increased need for clergymen but has by no means stimulated a proportionate increase in decisions for religious vocation. Organized religion has experienced increased recruiting competition from secular and scientific appeals and from attractive secular service occupations, such as the Peace Corps. Institutional officials have found themselves concerned, sometimes urgently, with questions of the *quantity* of clergymen and religious, and have asked researchers for help in studying processes of recruitment and vocational decision-making. (This concern corresponds with our category **A**.)

Increased attention to the *quality* and effectiveness of clergy performance has developed from many sources, including a more serious theological concern with the church and increased sensitivity, as in "pastoral psychology," to the opportunities and the pitfalls in a clergyman's pastoral relations with his parishioners. Certain intense training situations, such as clinical training or postseminary training institutes, have tended to raise questions and to provide norms. Public scrutiny has been given to the adequacy of clergymen's reactions to social crises, such as school integration. The popular cultural concern for mental health has also found a target among clergymen, and there has been considerable journalistic discussion of "the mental health of ministers," some of which may have generated significant research on the personalities of clergy. Educators and officials have wondered whether they could improve the general quality of clergy functioning by improving selection and training procedures. (The research questions related to these practical concerns generally fall in our category **B**.)

Both the concerns for quantity and for quality have received a special urgency from the contemporary mood in many church quarters of reappraisal and search for relevance. Dissatisfaction with many of the conventional patterns of church and of ministry have raised for many clergymen, educators, and church officials particularly insistent questions about the effectiveness of ministerial activities. And for the prospective candidate, they have underscored all the more his own dilemmas of decision.

One other confluent strand has to do with the development of the broad field of what may be regarded as the psychology of religion. Those with sophisticated interests jointly in psychology and religion have, during the decades, found many different occasions for exploring their joint interest. But these seem to have clustered around a progression of themes. In the early decades of this century, the concerns of religious education provided a focus. In the immediate postwar years, the activities of personal counseling became dominant. New liturgical interest may beckon psychologists. But it may now be that for a time attention to the person, the calling, and the functions of the clergymen and religious may provide a focus for exploration and expression of the many more general issues in the relationship of psychology and theology.

On the dispersion of research

Perhaps the very multiplicity of influences fostering research has been responsible for its dispersion. Because of the varying interests which have prompted research, its results have been reported in all levels of popular and technical publications in psychology, pastoral psychology, education, theological education, religious education, theology, religion, and ecclesiology.

Oddly enough, there has also been a great deal of excellent research left in fugitive form: in unpublished dissertations, in privately printed or mimeographed reports, and in collections of papers on diffuse themes. Perhaps a topic that is rooted in so many concerns and disciplines has difficulty finding lodging in any one. Or perhaps the seeming presumption of doing psychological research on persons following a religious vocation still meets enough barriers of social disapproval to impede some publication.[2]

This dispersion is both symptom and cause of what seems to us a research stalemate which we hope this volume will help to remedy. The general level of research reflected in this volume can be described, at best, as preliminary. Scouting parties have ventured out on almost all fronts and have reported. But the difficulty has been the lack of any main army to report to, to consolidate the reports, to plan the strategy of major campaigns. Research has not accumulated as it ought to in science, allowing one worker to build upon another. Research has not generated nor been derived from increasingly sophisticated conceptual models. One scouting party after another has reported bucking against major methodological obstacles—most notoriously and anguishingly the problem of criteria on effectiveness. But the report of the obstacle has been the last word and has not typically generated a strategy around it. It has been left there for the next researcher to stumble on and to report anew. One of us has written in detail elsewhere concerning the methodological state of this field (see **H**: Dittes 1962).

History of this volume

In the light of this abundantly flourishing but diffuse research, in the spring of 1963, two different agencies sensed simultaneously the need for a reference publication that would provide greater cohesion and focus to the research. The Board of Theological Education of the Lutheran Church in America and the executive of the Board in charge of psychological services, Victor Benson, commissioned Menges to compile a

[2] Undoubtedly, much misunderstanding and distrust of such research may still exist in many quarters. However, we have not felt ourselves called upon in this place to address ourselves to it. Even if this task had not already been well done in many publications we have abstracted, particularly in categories **H** and **I**, a field vital enough to produce 700 publications hardly needs an apology for its being. We have felt our aim to be more like that of helping provide an identity for this vital, yet perhaps still adolescent, field of research, and not that of serving as midwife or godparent to an infant.

set of abstracts of reports concerning psychological evaluation of prospective and or-dained clergymen. The Research Council of the Ministry Studies Board asked one of its members, Dittes, to compile an up-to-date bibliography of behavioral science re-search on clergymen. Inevitably, our paths soon crossed, and, we think wisely, merged, although the combined path is not that which either originally intended. The scope of the present coverage, psychological studies of clergymen, is less than planned by Dittes, in excluding sociological studies except as relevant to our particular categories. But the scope is broader than originally planned by Menges and Benson; psychological evaluation, as such, is limited largely to categories **A1, B2, F,** and **I** of this work. We have continued with the Lutheran Church in America's ambitious plan of abstracting, not simply listing works. But following the Ministry Studies Board's plans, we have tried to meet bibliographic responsibilities of accuracy and comprehensiveness and of matching the comprehensiveness with useful systems of categorizing and indexing the entries.

Consistent with our original separate intentions, Menges has written a large majority of the abstracts, and Dittes has assumed more of the responsibility for seeking com-plete coverage of the field and for devising the systems for categorization and indexing. But we have checked and revised each other's efforts in these respects to the point of making the work truly collaborative. Menges' work has been supported from the begin-ning by the Board of Theological Education. Dittes' work, especially in searching the literature, was capably aided at various points by Mrs. Carole Carlson, Mrs. Jane I. Smith, Paul Capra, and James Vaughan. In the final editing processes, the project has benefited from the careful work of Mrs. Fawn Hewitt, especially in checking the accuracy of our citations, working at the task of indexing, and conscientiously retyping the entire material for the printer, without introducing more errors than she corrected.

Insofar as this volume has a predecessor, it is derived from a bibliography prepared in 1958 by the Ministry Study of the Educational Testing Service, directed by Fred-erick B. Kling. We have also profited from the bibliographic work of others: most notably Paul D'Arcy, who has compiled lists of reported research, especially among Roman Catholic samples; the bibliographic search completed by Morris Taggart and John Vayhinger in 1961 for the Research Planning Workshop of the Religious Edu-cation Association; annual bibliographies edited by Walter Houston Clark for the Society for the Scientific Study of Religion; abstracts of dissertations assembled by Helen F. Spaulding and Edward E. Thornton and published periodically in *Religious Education* and *Pastoral Psychology*; *Bibliography of American Doctoral Dissertations in Religious Education, 1885-1959* by Lawrence C. Little, published by the Uni-versity of Pittsburgh Press in 1962; and *Annotated Bibliography in Religion and Psychology* by W. W. Meissner, published by the Academy of Religion and Mental Health in 1961. We are especially grateful for the permission Father Meissner and his publishers have given us to quote several abstracts of foreign publications which we have not had an opportunity to consult directly. Of course, research reports which we have consulted have occasionally helped us with their own set of references.

Unpublished dissertations have, of course, presented a special difficulty for us, because they have not all been readily accessible. For dissertations listed in *Dissertation Abstracts* with an apparently accurate and adequate summary, we have relied on this source, unless the work seemed of unusual significance. We have also benefited greatly from the care and generosity of John D. Shand, who has shared with us his notes on several dissertations consulted by him for another purpose. Considerably more than half of the doctoral dissertations abstracted have been personally consulted by one of us.

When Menges completed an earlier stage of this work, he prepared several hundred abstracts in mimeographed form, and these were distributed by the Board of Theological Education and by the Ministry Studies Board to several dozen researchers and authorities in this field. Helpful comments were received from Gordon W. Allport, George C. Anderson, William C. Bier, Gotthard Booth, Clifford E. Davis, Robert A. Embree, Robert C. Leslie, Thomas H. McDill, Edgar W. Mills, Samuel Southard, and Robert G. Torbett. Others freely shared with us their notes, unpublished papers, and knowledge of the field. We wish to thank B. Evans, M. Freihage, W. G. Jamison, and T. N. McCarthy. Our final search of the literature for this volume was done in early 1965.

We anticipate that users of this volume will bring other omissions and corrections to our attention, perhaps for inclusion in a subsequent supplement.

Principles of inclusion

The principal audience we have in mind is the researcher, not the consumer or sponsor of research. Therefore, the abstracts are categorized according to alternative research questions (although as we have shown above, we believe these categories correspond closely to the practical problems raised by consumers of research); the abstracts tend to emphasize procedures somewhat over results; and we have had primarily the researcher in mind in determining what to include and what to exclude.

"Studies" in our title refers primarily to systematic empirical collection of data following customary canons of science. Case studies and other general observational techniques have not been excluded, where these have followed canons common to these methods of investigation. Speculative writing has been welcomed for inclusion where such speculations have seemed to us couched in terms relevant to and suggestive for empirical research. We have tended to be generous in defining this criterion. Especially have we included, mostly in category **B1**, speculative and even normative discussions of the nature of clergy functions which seem to us suggestive of empirical criteria of effectiveness. But we have excluded normative analyses and recommendations for recruiting, theological education, or the conduct of ministry which were clearly neither based on nor suggestive of empirical research. So much for the second word of our title.

Categories **E** and **I** include some items which may appear an exception to our criterion of research relevance. In these cases the first word of our title may have carried precedence over the second. We have included normative and practical suggestions for clinical work with clergymen—therapy in the case of category **E** and testing in the case of **I**.

As for the third word of our title, the area of research represented is well defined, however somewhat inaccurately represented, by the word "clergymen." The clearly defined population for researchers and the group of distinct concern to the consumers of research are those selected and employed by religious institutions in a professional capacity. This includes those who are ordained as clergymen, but also those who serve in religious orders and also those who serve, without ordination or vow, in full-time religious employment, for example, as education workers in a church or parochial day school or in a foreign area. No general word is satisfactory for covering this group of persons who are selected and employed by religious organizations. "Clergymen" is general enough to refer to the majority of populations studied, and we have been content with it.

Our category **G**, of course, represents an exception but a topic of active research relevant enough to our topic to warrant inclusion, so long as discretely segregated.

The first word of our title has perhaps been most arbitrarily employed. Our definition of psychology is perhaps best seen by consulting the categories we have used and the discussion of these categories which follows this paragraph. When we have encountered studies that might be called more sociological in nature, we have almost always included them, usually in categories **A2**, **B3**, and **D**, sometimes in **B1** or **C**. But we have not made a determined effort to survey sociological writing as we have psychological. We suspect, however, that little important sociological research has been omitted, and perhaps the volume could make the more pretentious claim to represent behavioral science.

We suspect a sociologist would have wanted a separate category on the topic of roles of clergymen. However, it has seemed to us that this concept has been used so variously as to be relevant to many different categories in our scheme, depending on the particular usage and particular research. We have accordingly distributed the studies, but have conscientiously collected them in the topical index under "role."

THE CATEGORIES: A USER'S GUIDE

To be of optimal use to a researcher, a bibliography or collection of abstracts must be arranged in categories corresponding closely to the researchers' definitions of research problems. Ideally, a researcher should be able to find within one category all the studies relevant to his particular research problem and only studies which are relevant. It is just as cumbersome to have to work through too broad and general topical categories as it is to work with too restricted and narrow groupings. We have chosen to risk error on the side of too precise an anticipation of researchers' definitions of their task. We have been bold to specify, in devising our categories, the particular type of question which we think will—or perhaps we mean, should—most likely be asked. We feel some confidence that competent researchers will be able to find studies relevant to their own research concern within one of our categories, and that most of the entries in that category will be relevant.

However, in case we are wrong about the categories, we have attempted to safeguard ourselves and users of this volume with elaborate indices which cover methods, samples, and topics, and cut across the categories by which we have arranged the entries.

Our decision about good or likely *research questions* is reflected in categories **A** through **D**, including their subcategories: ten groupings in all.

Three groupings—categories **E, F, G**—are *topical* categories, which have seemed warranted because of the number of publications, of varying or no design, focused on these particular topics.

Two other categories—**H** and **I**—refer to more general *surveys*.

We will now attempt to explain the conceptions of research which lie behind our categorization.

Research question categories. Virtually any research reduces, in its bare outline, to an attempt to determine the relationship between two "variables": an *independent variable* (usually earlier in time and more or less thought of as a "*cause*" or as a "*predictor*") and a *dependent variable* (usually later in time and more or less thought of as an "*effect*" or "*consequence*," or as a "*criterion*").

Each of our first four categories brings together studies whose authors purport to answer one particular question. Those questions and the variables they imply follow: **A**: What factors produce a vocational decision to become a clergyman or a religious worker? Here the dependent variable is "decision" and the independent variable is the "factor," such as personality profile. **B**: What factors produce effectiveness in clergymen? Here the dependent variable is "effectiveness" and the independent variable is the "factor," which again could be personality profile. **C**: What

18

factors produce other differences in theological position? Here the dependent variable is the specified difference, such as "theological position," and the independent variable is the "factor," such as personality profile. **D**: What consequences does the decision to become a clergyman produce? Here the dependent variable is the "consequence," such as personality profile, and the independent variable is "decision."

The practical concerns behind the first question are related to the quantity of clergymen and religious and to problems of recruiting. The simplest criterion for research purposes is to ask, What factors distinguish someone who is a clergyman (or religious) from someone otherwise just like him who is not a clergyman?

The practical concerns behind the second question relate to the quality of clergymen and to problems of selection and training. The prototypical form of this question is to ask, What factors distinguish someone who is effective in performing his clerical or religious duties from someone who is otherwise just like him but less effective? But this question requires prior solution of the more vexing question of defining the criterion of effectiveness, for which the researcher needs the help of his clients and sponsors.

Elsewhere (see **H**: Dittes 1962) one of us has argued in greater detail about the importance of distinguishing these two criteria from each other. Popular thought often confuses them, and this leads both to ambiguous and unproductive research designs and also to popular mistrust and misunderstanding of such research. When, for example, a writer mixes discussion of factors producing a decision for ministry with factors producing effective ministry or healthy ministers, he may easily seem to imply that bases of decision themselves become predictors of effectiveness or health, and hence that some bases of decision are better or more valid than others. Another example of confusion arises from suggestions that screening for effectiveness (our category **B**) is best done by matching candidates with existing clergymen (our category **A**).

(It might be proposed as a researchable theory that there is an important relationship between these variables; for example, that the processes of selection or determination of vocation do tend to produce the most effective practitioners. However, it should be pointed out that the test of this contention comes not in any overlap between the criterion indicators, but rather in overlap among the predictors or independent variables. If it turns out empirically that on the variables predictive of becoming a clergyman, the most extreme scores are obtained by persons who become effective clergymen, this kind of evidence would be decisive. But this design presupposes precisely the rigorous distinction between the two criteria, for which we here argue.)

We will now discuss in more detail the operational definitions of these categories which we have acknowledged in arranging the entries. It should be noted that the "*factors*," the "predictors," the independent variables, are arranged under each of these categories as subcategories.

A: Unique characteristics of clergymen and religious. This criterion implies a comparison between some sample of those who have made a vocational decision (active clergymen or religious, students, candidates, or perhaps those who have expressed "an interest") with a control group of those who have not made such a decision. The degree of matching of control groups may vary from the use of general population norms on standardized tests to relatively close matching for such variables as age, sex, social class, education, church experience, values, etc. One researcher's control variables are, of course, another researcher's experimental variables.

A common control procedure is to compare those who persist in their education or vocation with those who drop out after an initial "interest" or some degree of commitment. This assumes that the decision to drop out is comparable to a delayed decision against a religious vocation and that the factors which separate the persisters from the drop-outs are critical and representative and not incidental. (Alternatively, it might be supposed that drop-outs and persisters are similar to each other and different from the general population—for having made the initial decision—and that they differ only on relatively incidental factors, such as academic aptitudes.) We have classified in this category all studies which use drop-outs as a criterion, even in the few instances in which this criterion was regarded by the researcher as evidence of "failure" or "ineffectiveness." Drop-out studies can be located through the index.

Another type of criterion classified here has been the quasi-longitudinal study comparing groups at different stages of training, in which the author has argued or demonstrated that a major difference between the groups is the drop-out of a sizable proportion. More commonly, however, this type of design has been intended to demonstrate the effects of training and has, therefore, been categorized under **D**. Studies using this criterion can be found through the index category, "Length of training."

A1: Personality. Personality characteristics which are researched as characteristic of those making vocational decisions range as widely as the use of this term in contemporary psychology and include, for our purposes, motivational, ability and intelligence, and interest variables. All variables inferred by the experimenter in terms other than those directly reported by the subject are included here, as is the use of all independently standardized and validated instruments.

A2: Background. This category includes data directly reported by subjects: biographical and demographic data, environmental influences, conscious considerations in making vocational decisions, etc. Typical instrument is a self-report questionnaire, which has not been independently validated or standardized.

A3: Recruiting, screening, training, guidance **procedures.** This category includes variables and conditions which are more or less under the control of officials in church and school and which are studied with some more or less systematic variation. That is, the report by a student that a recruiting procedure had been effective would be categorized under **A2**. Independent access by the researcher to recruiting procedures, if not actual manipulation and variation, would make the research categorized here.

A4: Miscellaneous. A few variables which do not appear clearly to fall into one of the above three categories are included here. This most commonly includes assessment of *attitudes*, which does not appear to us to belong strictly under the category of personality, and which is measured by instruments somewhere between the standardized measurements categorized under **A1** and the direct report questionnaires of **A2**.

B: Effectiveness is the term we have used to cover a wide range of evaluative criteria. We do not mean to imply that we believe all these evaluative criteria are necessarily correlated and form a single factor, nor that all bear adequate evidence of validity. Quite the contrary. A major decision by a researcher is his choice of a relevant criterion, and a major responsibility is his demonstration that his criterion may be validly generalized to as broad a range of effectiveness as he wishes to claim. For example, grades or faculty ratings may or may not be representative of and predictive of effective performance in the ministry.

Commonly used criteria are academic success in seminary, evidence of mental health and emotional adjustment, judgment of effective performance of vocational functions. These may be obtained by self-report, by judgments of others, by various objective indices. Criteria may be gross and general or they may be specific. They may assume a single dimension of effectiveness or they may suppose many uncorrelated dimensions. They may involve molar categories in which, for example, judges are asked to define and assess broad terms, such as "effectiveness"; or they may use more molecular and precise categories.

Among the subcategories, **B2**, **B3**, and **B4** represent independent variables exactly as defined in **A1**, **A2**, and **A3**.

B1: Definitions. We have categorized separately those publications which primarily address themselves to solving the vexing problem of determining valid indices of effectiveness. This includes various empirical attempts at measurements, including the report of reliabilities and validity of rating scales and other measures, and of interrelationships among them. This category also includes those theoretical and normative analyses of the general category of what is here called effectiveness, which seem to us to promise help in devising empirical measures.

B2: Personality. See **A1**.

B3: Background. See **A2**.

B4: Procedures. See **A3**.

Where a publication has been primarily concerned with the methodological problem of identifying or defining one of the independent variables, we have classified this under one of the relevant categories **A1-A4** or **B2-B4**, even though the publication has not explicitly made the effort to relate the independent variable to one of the dependent variables.

C: Differences among clergymen other than differences in effectiveness. Some research studies have been concerned with a dependent variable other than that covered by one of the above two major categories. They have, for example, compared, as the dependent variable, clergymen of liberal and conservative theology, or persons who have chosen different specialties within the profession. The use of clergymen or religious as a sample has sometimes been incidental to the original purpose of the researcher who was concerned primarily with the criterion variables themselves, for example, liberal or conservative theology. These studies have used a wide range of independent variables. We have grouped them all under this single category.

D: Consequences of being a clergyman. The above three categories focus on some aspect of vocational decision or status as the *dependent* variable. This fourth category covers those studies which focus on some aspect of the vocational decision or status as the *independent* variable. These research studies ask such questions as, What are the effects of vows of celibacy, of community living, of seminary education, of peculiar vocational stresses and demands? Research in this category tends to ignore, or to deny by assumption, differences of the kind implied by research under category **A**.

Topical categories. Three particular topics have attracted research and other publication to a degree to warrant separate listing. These have commonly followed designs somewhat varying from that implied in the above category system.

E: Counseling and therapy with clergymen and religious. These reports, on the basis of clinical experience or other research, suggest special theoretical and practical considerations in connection with the therapy, or the referral to therapy, of clergymen and religious. These discussions often imply a theoretical analysis relevant to our categories **A** or **D**. They may concern some assessment of typical problems occasioning therapy or they may concern typical reactions and resistances to therapy.

F: Mental health and illness among clergy and religious. This category includes research attempting to establish relative incidence of illness as well as discussions of peculiar and typical factors productive of health or illness. It often includes theoretical analysis relevant to our categories **A** or **D**.

G: A limited number of projects have done research with **wives** of clergymen, covering problems and designs as varied as those implied by our categories **A** through **F**. We have also included here the few studies of clergymen which focus primarily on relations with wife and children.

General surveys

H: Surveys of research and research methodology. This category includes attempts at summarizing findings or making general methodological appraisals. We have also included here bound publications which include a variety of papers; the individual papers have been categorized under one of the above appropriate categories.

I: Surveys of psychological testing of seminarians, clergy, and religious. This category includes general introductions to psychological tests, and reports or recommendations concerning their interpretation and utilization in making decisions concerning candidates.

UNIQUE CHARACTERISTICS: PERSONALITY

ABRAMS, R. H.
Psychic satisfactions of the clergy.
J. abnorm. soc. Psychol., 1936, *30*, 423-430.

Biographical sketches of ministers from *Who's Who in America* (1932) are surveyed. Suggested as sources of psychic satisfaction are statistics, preaching, family origin, travel, war records, etc. The types of examples chosen suggest a possible satirical intent on the part of the author.

ALOYSE, M.
Evaluations of candidates for religious life.
Bull. Guild Cathol. Psychiat., 1961, *8*, 199-204.

Procedure: MMPI, Otis, autobiographical sketch, and interview are used to screen out psychologically unfit candidates.
Results: Over a 6-year period of blind use of the tests, 93% of those classified as unfit dropped out; 76% of those classified as doubtful dropped out. Only 14 MMPI items, all from the depression scale, differentiated the drop-outs successfully.

ARGYLE, M.
Religious behaviour.
Glencoe, Ill.: Free Press, 1959.

Chap. 9, pp. 109-112: Summary of the speculative literature on mental disorder among religious leaders.
P. 105: Tabular summary of 6 personality studies of theological students: **A1** and **B2**: Cockrum; **A1**: Johnson 1943; **A1**: Kimber; **A1**: McCarthy 1942; **A1**: Peters; **A1**: Sward.

BAKER, O. H.
Profile of the American Baptist pastor: summary of a study.
Ministers and Missionaries Benefit Board of the American Baptist Convention, 1962.

A descriptive account based on 200 individual interviews with Baptist ministers, additional group interviews, and general observations.

BARRY, W. A.
An MMPI scale for seminary candidates.
M.A., Fordham University, 1960.

Sample: All seminary candidates who took Bier's MMPI from 1949 to 1958, divided into good (persevered) and poor (drop-out) groups.
Procedure: The seminary scale, derived from an item analysis of results from half the subjects, was cross-validated on the other half. Norms were then constructed from all scores.
Results: The Seminary Candidate Scale, consisting of 81 items, proved to have adequate validity and reliability. According to the derived norms, no one in the good group and 28% of the poor group scored above the critical score. It is concluded that the scale is fruitful when used in conjunction with other MMPI scales and other tests in a battery.

BENKO, A., & NUTTIN, J.
Examen de la personnalité chez les candidats à la prêtrise.

Louvain: Publ. Univ. de Louvain, 1956.

Sample: Experimental group—181 students in theology or philosophy and 79 candidates for religious orders; control group—university students and soldiers.

Procedure: MMPI, translated into French and Dutch.

Results: Critical scores of the L, F, and K scales are calculated for each group tested.

BERTNESS, H. J.

An analysis of the interests of Lutheran ministers as measured by the Strong Vocational Interest Blank. (Volumes I and II.)

Ph.D., University of Minnesota, 1955.

Dissert. Abstr., 1955, *15,* 2094-2095.

Sample: 995 Lutheran ministers in the American Lutheran conference selected by stratified random sampling. 905 responded.

Results: Subjects differed considerably from men in general, but their interests were not adequately represented by the minister scale. Two new keys for Lutheran ministers, General and Rural, were constructed and found to have acceptable reliability and low overlapping. A third key, Urban, needs further study.

BLANEY, H. J. S.

The attitudes of Nazarene ministers toward their profession.

Th.D., Boston University School of Theology, 1960.

Dissert. Abstr., 1960, *21,* 686.

Sample: Nazarene ministers (N not reported in abstract).

Procedure: Questionnaire.

Results: All report a personal experience of conversion. 41% had transferred into the Nazarene Church, 14% are seminary graduates, 58% are college graduates. 43% favor more active ministerial recruitment, 27% favor compulsory college education for ministers, 81% favor the inclusion of pastoral counseling in ministerial training.

BROWN, C. B.

Theological students today: a student's perspective.

Union Seminary Quart. Rev., 1959, *14*(3), 32-36.

A graduating B.D. student at Union describes his fellow students in terms of introspectionism and activism, Biblical and cultural preoccupation, and ecumenicity and denominational tradition.

CAHEN-SALABELLE, R.

Vocation et affectivité.

Cah. Laënnec, 1950, *10*(4), 3-30.

An extended discussion of emotional and psychological aspects of religious vocation. The influence of unconscious motivation is discussed under the rubric of the "law of double motivation." (Abstract by Meissner.)

CHRISTENSEN, C. W.

Religious conversion.

Arch. gen. Psychiat., 1963, *9,* 207-216.

Sample: 22 men, each with a history of religious conversion: seminarians, ministers, religious educators or missionaries. All were treated in private practice.

Results: From anecdotal case material, the following predisposing factors were identified: unconscious conflict, adolescence, fundamentalist religious background. In most cases the precipitating factor was attendance at a religious meeting. Religious conversion experiences are special instances of the acute confusional state described by Helen Carlson. Explanatory hypothesis: religious conversion experience is an ego phenomenon functioning to reintegrate the ego.

COCKRUM, L. V.
Personality traits and interests of theological students.
Relig. Educ., 1952, *47*, 28-32.

Sample: 93 male ministerial students at Austin Presbyterian Theological Seminary over a 2-year period; 53 counseling students and 48 education majors.
Procedure: Kuder, Guilford-Martin Inventory (GAMIN), Guilford's Inventory STDCR.
Results: For ministerial students the Kuder scale scores agreed with clergy norms except for lower literacy scores. On the GAMIN the seminarians were within the normal range of healthy adjustment. The STDCR showed them in the middle range between impulsiveness and overcontrol.

COLWELL, C. A.
Motivations for choosing the Christian ministry as a vocation.
B.D., Union Theological Seminary, 1952.

Available from the author: Congregational Church, Morris, Connecticut.

D'ARCY, P. F.
Constancy of interest factor patterns within the specific vocation of foreign missioner.
Ph.D., Catholic University of America, 1954.
Stud. Psychol. Psychiat. Cathol. Univer. Amer. 1954, *9*(1), ix. 54 pp.

Sample: 300 foreign-mission priests, all members of the Maryknoll Society. Younger group of 134 with mean age of 15.8; older group of 166 with mean age of 24.7.
Procedure: Scores were analyzed for 10 variables on the Kuder and 15 scales on the SVIB plus Lhota's Diocesan Priest Scale and the new Missionary Priest Scale.

Results: There were significant differences between groups on 17 of the variables. The SVIB Minister Scale did not differentiate these priests from men in general. The Missionary Priest Scale was more effective than the Diocesan Priest Scale in detecting the interests of missionary priests.

DAVIS, C. E.
Guide for counseling prospective church workers.
Pittsburgh (616 N. Highland Ave.): The United Presbyterian Church U.S.A., Board of Christian Education, Office of the Church Occupations Counselor, 1963.

Information for counselors of ministerial students in the United Presbyterian Church, U.S.A. Discussions are given of Kuder (forms C and D), SVIB, GZTS, MMPI, "Z" (Zulliger test), SORT Rorschach. Norms are included for Kuder (form D) and "Z" (N = 675 male seminary students).
Supplement I: SVIB norms for 200 seminary men, 100 seminary women, 100 national missions men, 100 national missions women, 100 ecumenical missions men, and 100 ecumenical missions women.
Supplement II: The MMPI is discussed. Norms for the 6 populations listed above and for the general population are presented for the usual MMPI scales and for the following auxiliary scales: Academic Achievement, College Achievement, Iowa Manifest Anxiety, Delinquency, Dominance, Escapism, Emotional Maturity, Ego Overcontrol, Ego Strength, Graduate School Potential, Hostility Control, Honor Point Ratio, Intellectual Efficiency, Impulsivity, Leadership, Positive Malingering, Neurotic Overcontrol, Neurotic Undercontrol, Originality, Prejudice, Pharisaic Virtue, Social Responsibility (revised), Rigidity (male and female), Role-playing, Self-sufficiency, Social Desirability (re-

vised), Social Participation, Social Status (revised), Sexual Deviation, Tolerance, Teaching Potentiality, Underachievement, Homosexuality.

DICK, W. W.
Vocational self-concept in terms of the vocational interests and values of seminarians and ministers.
M.A., University of Ottawa, 1964.

Sample: 59 students in the two Mennonite Biblical Seminaries in Indiana, 45 Mennonite ministers.
Procedure: SVIB, A-V Study of Values, ranking of preference among pastoral, missionary, teaching, administrative, or other ministry.
Results: Seminarians reporting first preference for pastoral ministry scored similar to ministers and significantly higher than other seminarians on Minister and Social Welfare scales of the SVIB. The A-V Study of Values did not so discriminate.

For 17 seminarians retested at the end of school and for 19 ministers who had taken the SVIB while in seminary, there was a significant increase in score on the Minister Scale from first to second testing.

DITTES, J. E.
Vocational guidance of theological students: a manual for the use of the Theological School Inventory.
Dayton, O. (1810 Harvard Blvd.): Ministry Studies Board, 1964. 128 pp.

The TSI was developed by the Educational Testing Service to serve as a guidance instrument for entering theological students. The student's self-report of his motivation for the ministry yields scores on 12 scales, referring to different characteristics of motivation, and different appeals of the ministry. Additional sections elicit biographical reports of background of decision and expressions of confidence in

meeting 10 characteristic roles. The manual presents suggestions for interpretations of the scores and norms, based on administration to 2,300 students in 53 schools. Validity data are reported as research supplements to the manual; see **A1:** Kling; **A1:** Dittes; **B2:** Dittes; **D:** Dittes.

DITTES, J. E., & DEWIRE, H.
Face impression study: correlation of TSI scores with student self-report of motivation and with interviewer ratings.
TSI Research Bull. #2. Dayton, O. (1810 Harvard Blvd.): Ministry Studies Board, 1963. 14 pp.

Sample: 272 students from 18 theological schools tested in the fall of 1961.
Procedure: After taking the TSI, but before its interpretation, each student ranked descriptions of the 7 motivations measured by section 2 of the TSI. A faculty interviewer also ranked the 7 motivations as he thought they appeared in the student, and also rated him on over-all motivation, fitness, emotional problems, growth capacity. Factor analysis.
Results: Students' self-ranking and faculty ranking were well correlated with rankings yielded by TSI scores. Each scale tended to define a separate factor. Intellectual concern and evangelistic witness were most easily discriminated. No substantial correlation between TSI scales and 4 faculty ratings.

DODSON, F. J.
Personality factors in the choice of the Protestant ministry as a vocation.
Ph.D., University of Southern California, 1957.

Sample: 50 seminarians from 3 interdenominational Protestant seminaries in southern California matched individually with 50 graduate students from 3 southern California universities.

Procedure: The following tests were administered on a group basis: personal data sheet, disguised test of authoritarianism, Rosenzweig, word association, Sentence Completions Test, Gregory Religious Beliefs.

Results: Data suggest that seminarians are more guilt-ridden, show more discomfort with sexual and hostile feelings, and are more intropunitive in handling hostility and aggression than controls. Seminarians are not more authoritarian or emotionally disturbed as a group. The most conservative seminarians are more authoritarian but not more emotionally disturbed than the most liberal seminarians.

DONOVAN, J. D.

The American Catholic hierarchy: a sociological profile.

Amer. Cathol. sociol. Rev., 1958, *19,* 98-112.

Sample: 133 (72%) of the United States bishops and archbishops, as of 1957.

Procedure: Questionnaire. Some comparative data from 1897 and 1927 are included.

Results: Social background: these men are predominantly second- and third-generation Americans tending to come from upwardly mobile Catholic families. Parochial education and religious vocations occur frequently in the families.

Career patterns: Bishops frequently hold an earned degree, have held a variety of administrative positions, and entered the hierarchy at age 47 (average).

ECK, DOCTEUR & LARÈRE, P. CH.

Psychasthénie et vocation.

Cah. Laënnec, 1955, *2,* 3-17.

Psychasthenia and vocation.

In P. Flood (Ed.), *New problems in medical ethics,* Volume III. Westminster, Md.: Newman, 1956. Pp. 149-163.

28 of 50 religious patients were diagnosed as psychasthenic (56%). The security of the religious life is the chief attraction to the psychasthenic. He was already a psychasthenic before becoming a priest or religious, but if ill-directed or ill-counseled, he will find in the religious life all the circumstances which favor his condition. Various types of psychasthenia require various degrees of caution. The importance of the supernatural call should never be forgotten.

EGGERT, C. M.

Personality trends in seminarians.

M.A., Catholic University of America, 1948.

Sample: 163 students in a preparatory seminary; 172 male Catholic college students.

Procedure: Mental Health Analysis Test. (Thorpe and Clark, California Test Bureau.)

Results: Trends, not significant, were found toward higher scores for the seminary group and increase in critical ratios among the upper classes in the seminary.

ERNST, P.

Option vitale—contribution à une psychologie ascétique de la vocation.

Nouv. Rev. Théol., 1947, *69,* 731-742; 1065-1084.

A testing procedure was developed for evaluating the affective dispositions. The *option vitale* is a conscious direction of one's life course. On the basis of the results, the author feels that this occurs at about 16 years of age. The occurrence of previous *options* in adolescence or even childhood is discussed as a source of later difficulty in vocational choice. His hypothesis is that the *option vitale* is fundamentally an affective disposition in regard to a certain climate of life required for the profound development of our personality and that rational motivation for vocational choice is secondary. . . . (Abstract by Meissner.)

ESTADT, B. K.
The relationship of interest development, ego strength, and intelligence to realism of vocational choice in minor seminarians.
M.A., Catholic University of America, 1963.

EVELY, L.
Psychologie et vocation sacerdotale.
In *Psychologie et pastorale.* Louvain: Nauwelaerts, 1953, 158-174.

FEHR, R. C.
An inventory and projective personality study of a religious and lay group.
Ph.D., Fordham University, 1958.

   Sample: Matched groups (each N = 45) of religious (under vows for 5 years) and lay college students at the same coed university.
   Procedure: Bier's MMPI, SCT, Rorschach (Beck's scoring).
   Results: Contrary to previous research, the lay group obtained the more deviant scores. Only one difference between groups was found on the MMPI (Pd) and one on the SCT (attitude toward stress). Only 3 of 4 tests for difference on the Rorschach were significant (.05). Similarity between groups is discussed in terms of their similar environments and the fact that the religious group was at the beginning of its religious life.

FRIEDL, FRANCIS P.
Vocational interests of successful and unsuccessful seminarians in a foreign-mission society.
M.A., Catholic University of America, 1952.

   Sample: 534 seminarians in 11 foreign-mission seminaries. 178 drop-outs matched for age with 356 continuing.
   Procedure: SVIB, including D'Arcy's Missionary Priest Scale and the Diocesan Priest Scale.
   Results: A significant difference between drop-outs and perseverers was revealed by the Missionary Priest Scale but not by the Diocesan Priest Scale. Accuracy was not great enough for *individual* prediction.

GÉRAUD, J.
Itinéraire médico-psychologique de la vocation.
Paris: Editions Xavier Mappus, 1958.

   A brief discussion of the role which psychological factors involving emotionality, character, qualities of will and intelligence, etc., play in determining and selecting priestly vocations. (Abstract by Meissner.)

GILBRIDE, T. V.
A study of personal and vocational integration of students for the priesthood at different levels of training.
M.A., Catholic University of America, 1960.

   Sample: 4 groups of 20 students at each of 4 levels in minor or major seminary.
   Procedure: Q-sort with 100 self-referent items. 4 sorts: self-concept, ideal self-concept, vocational self-concept, vocational ideal concept.
   Results: The hypothesis that there is a progressive increase in integration (i.e., increasing intercorrelations among sorts for each level) was not confirmed. The framework may have been too global, not allowing for highly personalized variables present at different phases of educational development.

GODFREY, R. J.

Predictive value of the MMPI with candidates for the religious brotherhood.

M.Ed., Marquette University, 1955.

Sample: 149 candidates from one teaching order, members of 5 annual novitiate classes 1951-55.

Procedure: All took MMPI before admission to novitiate. Groups of perseverers (N = 91) and nonperseverers (N = 58) were formed according to the student's status in 1955. Students were divided into highly, moderately, and poorly successful groups by a faculty rating scale.

Results: High Ma and Pd scores indicate small likelihood of perseverance. Only the Ma scale, and that in a limited way, showed value in predicting degree of success.

GONZALES, A.

A study on Mexican minor seminarians.

M.A., Catholic University of America, 1956.

Sample: 150 seminarians in their first 3 years from 3 seminaries; 150 high school boys in the same years. Both groups Mexican.

Procedure: Mental Health Analysis Test (Thorpe and Clark, California Test Bureau).

Results: Wide differences between groups included lower scores for seminarians on "feelings of inadequacy," close personal relationships, interpersonal skills, and social participation.

GORMAN, J. R.

Adjustment and interests of fourth year minor seminarians studying for the diocesan priesthood.

M.A., Loyola University (Chicago), 1961.

See also **A1**: McDonagh.

Sample: 188 minor seminarians in the senior year of high school.

Procedure: MMPI, Kuder, Mooney, and a faculty rating scale.

Results: The MMPI showed this group to be better adjusted than college males except on Sc. 82% of the group were judged by the faculty to be well accepted. When the MMPI was used to divide the group into adjusted and nonadjusted, these subgroups could not be distinguished by the other instruments except for clerical or artistic interests.

HASS, SISTER MARY G.

A comparative study of critical thinking, flexibility of thinking, and reading ability involving religious and lay college seniors.

Ph.D., Fordham University, 1963.

Dissert. Abstr., 1963, *24,* 622-623.

Sample: 282 sisters and 272 lay students from 10 colleges.

Procedure: Watson-Glaser Critical Thinking Appraisal, Guilford Alternate Uses Test, Nelson-Denny Reading Test, Otis.

Results: No real differences between groups in critical thinking, flexibility of thinking, or reading ability.

HICKMAN, F. S.

A psychological study of the conviction that one's choice of a religious vocation is a divine imperative.

M.A., Northwestern University, 1921.

This discussion aims to describe the psychological forces and processes related to the choice of a vocation. Preliminary to Hickman 1923.

HICKMAN, F. S.

A psychological study of the conviction which leads to the choice of a religious vocation.

Ph.D., Northwestern University, 1923.

A wide-ranging discussion of the psychological implications of the call and religious vocation. The hope is expressed of laying the foundations for a "religious vocational analysis technique," although no attempt is made to develop the technique empirically.

HOLLAND, J. B., & LOOMIS, C. P.
Goals of life of rural ministers.
Sociometry, 1948, *11*, 217-229.

> *Sample:* 29 ministers from "conservative" Protestant denominations at a summer session; 403 college students.
> *Procedure:* Goals of Life Inventory (Cooperative Study in General Education).
> *Results:* Ministers showed a consistent pattern of sentiments as reflected in the most highly chosen and rejected goals. A "Service to Others" motif was highly rated; Security and Getting Ahead were frequently rejected. The groups differed significantly in their choices, the differences largest in the rejected category. Some differences may be due to the factors of age and occupation.

HOSTIE, R.
The discernment of vocations.
New York: Sheed and Ward, 1963.

> Following a distinction between internal and external vocations, theological and psychological criteria of each are discussed. Consultation with psychological specialists is suggested for doubtful cases; psychological testing is briefly referred to. Occasional case descriptions serve as illustrations.

HUDSON, W. S.
The Protestant concept of motivation for the ministry.
Pp. 33-44 in **H:** Southard.

> Historical survey of the subject of individuals and groups within Protestantism.

JALKANEN, R. J.
The personality structure of seminarians: the use of available MMPI norms for diagnosis.
M.A., Roosevelt University, 1955.

> *Sample:* 100 Lutheran seminarians.
> *Procedure:* Compared these 100 profiles with established MMPI norms for male college students, limited data on Roman Catholic seminarians, adult males, and graduate students in various fields.
> *Conclusion:* Because seminarians achieve a highly elevated profile on the MMPI clinical scales and on K, separate norms for seminary students should be established.

JOHNSON, ELEANOR H.
Personality traits of workers in the field of religion.
Relig. Educ., 1943, *38*, 325-329.
Also in *Amer. J. Orthopsychiat.*, 1942, *12*, 317-323, under title Personality and religious work: results of the Bernreuter Personality Inventory given to students in religion.

> *Sample:* 150 seminary students enrolled in the author's course and counseled by her; 150 successful insurance salesmen already tested by their company.
> *Procedure:* Bernreuter.
> *Results:* Although no trait characterized the seminary students as a whole, the salesmen were higher on dominance. Suggestive results are discussed.

JOHNSON, G. K.
Personality patterns peculiar to theological students.
M.A., University of North Dakota, 1947.

> *Procedure:* Bernreuter, SVIB, MMPI.
> *Results:* Personality patterns followed a normal trend with only a few barely reliable deviations. Bernreuter: tendency

toward self-sufficiency and dominance. SVIB: strong interest in social work.

JOHNSON, G. K.
Psychological testing at the seminary.
Augustana Seminary Rev., 1952, *4*(2), 18-20.

Explanation, for laymen, of the 5-year-old Augustana Seminary testing program. Test results indicate that students are a cross section of an average congregation of the church, that individual quality has not decreased with rising enrollment, and that the average seminarian has little insight into his own personality and its problems. The most serious problems are struggles with guilt and incapacity for emotion.

JUDY, M. T.
The Christian clergy—their vocational concepts and performance observed in a theological dimension.
In S. W. Cook (Ed.), *Research plans.* New York (545 W. 111th St.): Religious Education Association, 1962. Pp. 200-205.

A research proposal directed toward an understanding of the ideal self-image of the clergy, the concept of the minister's intimate objectives of how he serves God and people, and the minister's theological position. Checklists, questionnaires, and Q-sort instruments will be developed. Worldwide sampling is proposed.

KENNEDY, E. C.
A comparison of the psychological test scores of successful and unsuccessful major seminarians in a foreign mission seminary.
M.A., Catholic University of America, 1958.

Sample: 81 candidates for foreign mis-sionary priesthood: 48 ordained and 33 dropped out during their major seminary years.
Procedure: SVIB and Kuder scores when seniors in college and 6 years later when either successful (ordained priests) or unsuccessful (in other vocations). Other terminal tests: MMPI, Thurstone Temperament Schedule, CTMM, faculty ratings.
Results: No significant differences were found between the groups on the objective standardized tests, but 7 areas of significant difference emerged from the ratings.

KENNEDY, E. C.
The relationship of self-perception to expressed motivation for occupational choice.
Ph.D., Catholic University of America, 1962.
Dissert. Abstr., 1963, *23,* 3468.

Sample: 127 seminarians who had chosen foreign missioner as an occupation; 50 male college students, at the same grade level, as control.
Procedure: Q-sort to measure self-concept. Motivation was measured by ranking statements derived by Hammond.
Results: Negative; groups not distinguished by either measure.

KENNEY, C. E.
Differential vocational interest patterns of successful and unsuccessful foreign mission seminarians.
Ph.D., Loyola University (Chicago), 1959.

Sample: 125 matched pairs of foreign missionary seminarians: successful (completed at least 8 months of novitiate) and unsuccessful (drop-out).
Procedure: SVIB and Kuder.
Results: Although the 2 groups can be

differentiated on several SVIB keys and the Kuder literary scale, there is too much overlapping to approach individual prediction. Unsuccessfuls were more heterogeneous in interests but groups differed more in intensity than in kinds of interests. Foreign-mission seminarians were shown to differ from diocesan seminarians, clergymen, and typical liberal arts college students.

KIMBER, J. A. M.
Interests and personality traits of Bible Institute students.
J. soc. Psychol., 1947, *26*, 225-233.

> *Sample:* 274 students at one Bible Institute in 4 consecutive entering classes took the ACE. 140 students took the CTP, MMPI, Kuder.
> *Results:* The group placed at the 25th centile of ACE norms. These students had higher social standards, higher sense of personal worth, and a higher number of nervous symptoms. The prevailing interest was in social service. Low scores were obtained on community relations, computations, and clerical interest.

KIRK, J. P.
A study of the interests of brother candidates and professed brothers on the Strong Minister and Clerical Interest scales.
Ph.D., St. John's University (New York), 1959.

> *Sample:* 484 brothers: 150 high school seniors, 134 junior brothers, 100 non-professed brothers, 100 professed brothers.
> *Procedure:* SVIB Minister Scale and Lhota's Clerical Interest Scale.
> *Results:* On both scales the nonprofessed brothers obtained the highest scores, followed by the professed and then the juniors. All three groups differed significantly from the high school seniors.

The Clerical Interest Scale was able to discriminate more effectively than the Minister Scale between only the older levels. The diocesan, religious, and missionary seminarians and priests tended to exhibit interests that were similar throughout all levels of training. Results are compared with findings from other studies.

KLING, F. R.
The motivations of ministerial candidates.
Res. Bull. 59-2. Princeton, N. J.: Educational Testing Service, 1959.
Available from the Ministry Studies Board, 1810 Harvard Blvd., Dayton, O.

> Describes the method of analysis and theoretical framework underlying the Theological School Inventory.
> *Sample:* 500 ministers from 8 denominations (Assembly of God, American Baptist, Southern Baptist, United Lutheran, Lutheran Church-Missouri Synod, Methodist, Presbyterian U.S., and Presbyterian U.S.A.).
> *Procedure:* Content analysis of statements obtained from ministers regarding their motivation for entering the ministry at that time and their present evaluation of that motivation.
> *Results:* 2 theoretical structures derived from the analysis are described and are illustrated from the statements. The construction of the TSI, some practical implications of the findings, and hypotheses suggested by the data are discussed.

KNOTT, T. G.
Motivational factors in selected women candidates for the Master of Religious Education degree.
Ph.D., Boston University, 1964.
Dissert. Abstr., 1964, *25*, 3140.

> *Sample:* 31 women who were enrolled for the MRE at Boston University School

of Theology from September, 1959, through September, 1962.

Procedure: Autobiographical statements, Edwards Personal Preference Schedule, Theological School Inventory, open-ended questionnaires (N = 25), interviews (N = 8), vocational status as of September 1, 1963.

Results: Factors related to perseverance in the vocation are formation of strong ego ideal, higher scores on Acceptance by Others, Witness, and Order (TSI), and lower scores on Heterosexuality (EPPS). Differences with college norms are noted. No support for the belief that escape from personal problems or husband-seeking are important motives. Strong motivating factors include need Understanding, unconscious need Basic Trust, religious devotion, and service to others.

KOBLER, F. J.
Screening applicants for religious life.
J. Relig. Hlth, 1964, *3,* 161-170.

Sample: 3 groups of religious totaling 390 (67 females, 323 males, average age 19). MMPI means also reported for 658 additional men religious, 104 additional women religious, and 5,035 college men.

Procedure: MMPI, SCAT, Kuder, and Mooney. 102 subjects were designated as "highs" for mean MMPI scores of 58 or more and for one peak of 70 or more. Faculty rated emotional adjustment.

Results: High MMPI scorers were not distinguished by SCAT or by faculty ratings, checked more but not different problems on the Mooney, and on Kuder showed less feminine interest and fewer pronounced peaks.

KOLB, A.
Vocational interests of the Brothers of the Sacred Heart.

M.A., Catholic University of America, 1952.

Sample: 136 teaching brothers, average age 34.

Procedure: SVIB data were used to develop a scale to measure the interests of teaching brothers (split-half reliability of .912). No scores are given on other SVIB scales.

KREMP, B.
Study of tested differences of interest and personality variables between continuing and discontinuing Franciscan seminarians.

B.A., Duns Scotus College (Detroit, Mich.), 1961.

Procedure: 227 GZTS and 185 Kuder profiles were grouped according to what stage of religious training the examinee was in when he took the test.

Results: No single score on either test emerged as an adequate basis for discrimination, although the use of a weighted formula should not be overlooked. Variations shown on the test were probably due to the vocational difficulties rather than vice versa. There was increasing moodiness, shyness, and seclusiveness when subjects were tested before a time of decision (e.g., taking vows), but the picture was almost reversed for those tested *after* profession.

LAURIER, B.
The relation of introversion-extroversion to vocational preference.
M.A., Catholic University of America, 1942.

Sample: 114 French-speaking twelfth-grade students; 33 religious brothers.

Procedure: General intelligence test of the Institut Canadien D'Orientation Professionnelle, MacNitt's Personality and Vocational Guidance Test, questionnaire.

Results: Brothers had higher introversion scores and lower IQ's. In general there were no significant relationships between IQ and introversion-extroversion, or vocational interest scores and introversion-extroversion.

LESLIE, R. C.
A discussion of Gotthard Booth's article and paper.
Pp. 110-117 in **H:** Southard.
Also pp. 86-96 in **H:** Oates.

Sample: 18 older (ages 25-43) students from 2 small interdenominational seminaries.

Procedure: Subjects were classified into 10 categories (**C:** Gustafson) of theological students (coerced, disturbed, manipulating, resistant, sheltered, zealous, skeptical, humanitarian, searching, and maturing) on the basis of test battery results, admission papers, autobiography, and interview.

Results: All fell into the last five categories above—those not distinguished by unconscious motivation. Concludes that commitment around high ideals, or conscious motivation, is as important a factor as unconscious motivation.

LHOTA, B.
Vocational interests of Catholic priests.
Ph.D., Catholic University of America, 1948.
Abstract published by Catholic University of America Press: *Stud. Psychol. Psychiat. Cathol. Univer. Amer.,* 1948, 7(1).

Sample: 262 diocesan priests, 208 diocesan theological students, 190 minor seminarians, 133 Catholic high school students.

Procedure: Developed scoring weights for a SVIB scale to measure the interests of diocesan priests. Scores on this scale correlated .85 with scores on the SVIB Minister Scale.

Results: 73% of the items effected a significant differentiation between priests and Strong's men in general. A cross-validation affirmed this Clerical Interest Scale on a sample of 208 diocesan major seminarians. The scale differentiated minor seminarians from Catholic high school students.

LINDER, IRENE C.
Some factors influencing women to choose church-related vocations: a study in occupational sociology.
Ph.D., State University of Iowa, 1956.
Dissert. Abstr., 1956, *16,* 1733-1734.

Sample: 98 women training for church-related vocations; 61 women entering other vocations.

Procedure: Questionnaire for background data; 20-statement test to measure personality.

Results: The church-related group had significantly more religious and fewer family self-concepts. They were less aware of social class, more likely to be from lower-class families, and more downwardly mobile. One subgroup of the church-related group was from unstable and unhappy family backgrounds; religion became the means of adjustment in such stressful conditions.

LOGSDON, LAURA L.
The controlled association responses of religious and lay women as measured by the Loyola Language Study.
M.A., Loyola University, 1961.

Sample: Matched groups of 50 "older" nuns and 50 "older" lay women.

Procedure: Took the Loyola Language Study, a type of controlled word-association test which asks for common responses to stimulus words. Comparisons were made with other data on younger religious and lay women.

Results: Older but not younger religious and lay women were distinguished, although not at a level which would permit individual prediction. The test is not recommended as a screening device.

LUCAS, J. P.

An evaluation of Strong's Minister Scale applied to the Roman Catholic clergy.

M.A., University of Ottawa, 1946.

MAFFIA, L. A.

Measured interests of priests, seminarians, and former seminarians in the selection of seminary applicants.

Ph.D., University of Oregon, 1954.

Sample: 100 ordained priests, 108 seminary drop-outs, and 117 present seminarians.

Procedure: SVIB, several rating scales, Lhota's Clerical Interest Scale (**A1:** Lhota). 50 priests and 50 drop-outs were used to select differentiating items. These items formed the Seminary Priest Scale. The scale was cross-validated on the remaining 50 priests and 58 drop-outs.

Results: The validation groups were distinguished at the .01 level. Differences were also found between the priests and the seminarians and between the drop-outs and the seminarians. This scale differentiated the groups more effectively than did the Lhota scale.

MARY OF THE REDEMPTION, SISTER

Psychologie des religieuses.

In *Directoire des prêtres chargés de religieuses.*

Paris: Editions du Cerf, 1954. Pp. 119-138.

McCABE, S. P.

The self-concept and vocational interest.

Ph.D., Catholic University of America, 1958.

Washington, D.C.: Catholic University of America Press, 1958.

Sample: 100 seminarians, homogeneous with regard to sex, age, IQ, and vocational objective.

Procedure: Semantic differential ratings of "myself," "my ideal self," and occupational titles. SVIB taken with usual instructions and with instructions to simulate a particular interest type.

Results: The similarity of self-perception and occupational perception does not appear to be a primary factor in responding to an interest test. Subjects demonstrated ability to simulate an interest even when their measured interest in that occupation is very low and their perception of it shows no relation to their self-perception.

McCARTHY, T. J.

Personality traits of seminarians.

Stud. Psychol. Psychiat. Cathol. Univer. Amer., 1942, 5(4).

Sample: 85 major seminarians, 144 minor seminarians.

Procedure: Bernreuter, Bell, A-V Study of Values, Otis, ACE. 3 faculty members rated each.

Results: 2 general factors: (1) schizoid, (2) general fitness for continuance in seminary life. Compared with high school norms on Bell, seminarians showed slight neurotic tendency, greater self-consciousness, below average total adjustment. On Bernreuter, introversion and sociability were average, submissiveness higher. On A-V, religious interest was significantly higher and dominant.

McCARTHY, T. N.

The relationship of vocational interests to personality traits.

M.A., Catholic University of America, 1952.

Sample: 94 male liberal arts college students, 50 of whom were aspirants to the religious life.

Procedure: Kuder, Cattell 16 Personality Factor Questionnaire, SVIB.

Results: Hypotheses were confirmed that interests are related to personality traits, that certain of these relationships may be generalized from one occupational group to another, and that there are relationships which are unique to a particular occupational group. There was no effect from age or from educational level.

McCARTHY, T. N.
Evaluation of the present scientific status of screening for religious vocation.
In W. C. Bier and A. A. Schneiders (Eds.), *Selected papers from the American Catholic Psychological Association meetings of 1957, 1958, 1959.* New York: American Catholic Psychological Association, Fordham University, 1960. Pp. 35-43. (a)

Studies are reviewed which indicate the typical personality of those who enter religious life. Some personality deviations are characteristic of religious. Suggestions are made for needed research in the areas of effectiveness of prediction, drop-outs and defections, and on a theory of vocational choice.

McCARTHY, T. N.
Psychological assessment in the religious vocation.
Unpublished paper. Philadelphia: Author, LaSalle College, 1960. (b)

The psychologist can go a step further than personality investigation by studying the religious motives or intention. By limiting himself to *natural* motives, the psychologist can legitimately and profitably explore the motives of the candidate without doing violence to the fact that grace may be a critical ingredient of the candidate's behavior. Possibilities and cautions in an assessment program are discussed.

McCARTHY, T. N.
The psychological investigation of the personality in the examination of religious vocations.
Suppl. Vie Spir., 1960, *13,* 340-350. (c)

McCARTHY, T. N.
Psychological assessment in recruiting for religious vocations.
Unpublished paper. Philadelphia: Author, LaSalle College, 1962.

Summarizes findings from research on selecting the most promising candidates for teaching brothers. Personality comparisons are made of college men with candidates and of perseverers with non-perseverers. Some Kuder and SVIB results are described. Better criteria of success should be derived and these results should be cross-validated.

McDONAGH, A. J.
A study of adjustments and interests of first year college seminarians for the diocesan priesthood.
M.A., Loyola University (Chicago), 1961.

Parallel design to **A1**: Gorman with a different population. Very similar results.

Sample: 135 first-year college seminarians.

Procedure: MMPI, Kuder, Mooney, faculty ratings.

Results: MMPI: this was a better-adjusted seminary population than other college and seminary populations, although Pt was high. Kuder: coincided with national clergy norms. Mooney: this population had fewer problems than comparable college populations. Faculty ratings: most of the group was acceptable to seminary authorities.

McGann, Sister John R.
Interests of a group of women religious on the Strong Vocational Interest Blank.
Ph.D., St. John's University (New York), 1963.

Sample: (A) 290 sisters enrolled in the novitiate college of a teaching community and judged "adjusted"; (B) 290 Catholic college women (control group for A); (C) 100 sister students from the same novitiate college tested later than A as a cross-validation sample; (D) 125 professed sisters in the same congregation as A and C but with a mean teaching experience of 6.6 years.

Procedure: Strong Vocational Interest Blank.

Results: Since none of the welfare or uplift scales (social worker, social science teacher, YWCA secretary) reflected a pattern of interests which would characterize these women religious, the Religious Scale was developed on A as a criterion group. Their score (M = 101.95, S.D. = 68.24) was highest of the 4 groups. Despite the rather large variance, this religious group seemed to differ from the lay group and from Strong's women in general by a preference for nonleadership roles, a tendency to reject activities of a creative nature, and less interest in intellectual activities. Group C's score was second highest (M = 89.13, S.D. = 46.80). Group D received the third highest score (M = 69.0, S.D. = 33.75). Group B was fourth (M = 30.18, S.D. = 46.37), significantly different from A. Caution in the use of the scale is advised because of the percentage of overlap in the responses of the groups.

Morse, P. K.
The Strong Vocational Interest Blank and Minnesota Multiphasic Personality Inventory as measures of persistence toward the ministry as a vocational goal.
Ph.D., University of Michigan, 1962.
Dissert. Abstr., 1963, *23,* 3239-3240.

Sample: 701 white Presbyterian men who had declared in writing an interest in the ministry. 503 achieved ordination (persisters) and 198 were apparently not going to be ordained because of a change of interest (nonpersisters).

Procedure: Data on SVIB and MMPI, accumulated between 1950 and 1954.

Results: (1) Persisters differed from men in general on both tests. (2) Neither test distinguished the persisters and the nonpersisters. (3) Suggests that the SVIB norms should be revised and that MMPI K-corrections be re-examined. (4) Pattern analysis of the SVIB was not superior to the analysis of single scale scores.

Murray, J. B.
Training for the priesthood and personality and interest test manifestations.
Ph.D., Fordham University, 1957.

Sample: 400 Catholic college-level men: 100 college students, 100 minor seminarians, 100 major seminarians, 100 ordained priests.

Procedure: Bier's MMPI, SVIB, GZTS.

Results: MMPI: the more training a group had, the higher its scores were, although all groups had a similar pattern.

SVIB: similar pattern for all groups. Both Minister Scale and Clerical Interest Scale differentiated major seminarians from collegians.

GZTS: groups did not follow similar patterns. More significant differences were found in the groups with more training.

Murray, J. B.
Personality study of priests and seminarians.

Homil. pastoral Rev., 1958, *49*, 443-447.

Summary of Murray 1957. Work by Bier and Lhota is reviewed. Lhota's Diocesan Priest Scale (Clerical Interest Scale) for the SVIB is termed "the best single instrument for selecting candidates with positive signs for religious training."

NIEBLING, H. V.
Self concepts of diocesan and missionary seminarians.
M.A., Catholic University of America, 1961.

Sample: Matched groups of 15 diocesan and 15 missionary seminarians.
Procedure: A 99-statement Q-sort was constructed for the study.
Results: The average intercorrelation within each of the two groups, as well as the average correlation between the two groups, was barely beyond the range of chance. Among the seminarians tested there were large variations in self-concept.

NISI, W. F.
A study of dependency as a dominant personality factor in ministerial students and its implications for theological education.
M.A., Princeton Theological Seminary, 1962.

Sample: 50 randomly selected students from the 300 male B.D. students at Princeton Theological Seminary.
Procedure: EPPS; interview to determine occupational certainty.
Results: Compared with Edward's college norms, subjects scored slightly lower on exhibition and higher on intraception. No other distinctive characteristics emerged. There was a negative correlation between certainty of vocational plans and high dependency needs.

NODET, C.-H.
Considérations psychanalytiques à propos des attraits névrotiques pour la vocation religieuse.
Suppl. Vie Spir., 1950, *4*(14), 279-306.

The knowledge of unconscious motives can help in understanding the spirit. Unconscious motives are often furnished by the isolation, security, and withdrawal from sexuality of religious life.

PETERS, SISTER RICHARDA
A study of the intercorrelations of personality traits among a group of novices in religious communities.
Stud. Psychol. Psychiat. Cathol. Univer. Amer., 1942, *5*(7).

Sample: 148 novices in several religious communities, with a mean age of 21.
Procedure: Bernreuter, Bell, ACE, A-V Study of Values, controlled interview, personality rating scale.
Results: The sample showed the same results in general as the published norms for students. Factor analysis suggested 3 groups: (1) undesirable traits: sulkiness, anxiety, etc.; (2) dominated by will: sense, capacity to adjust, etc.; (3) sociability: leadership, dominance. (1) and (3) as well as (1) and (2) have negative correlations suggesting 2 mutually exclusive types of trait organization.

PLÉ, A.
Peut-il exister des attraits inconscients à la vie religieuse?
Suppl. Vie Spir., 1950, *4*(14), 269-278.

Unconscious motives for entering religious life are discussed. The psychic life is constituted by analogous levels in which the unconscious level of the instincts underlies the others. Underlying the desire to enter religion there may be a mixture of sadism in the sexual instinct; superiors must be aware of this possibility. (Abstract by Meissner.)

PLÉ, A.
Unconscious attraction to the religious life.
In *Vocation*. London: Blackfriars, 1952. Pp. 101-113. (Religious Life Series, II.)

Unconscious motives for entering religious life are discussed. They may be understood or removed through psychological treatment. No psychological process can evaluate the supernatural side of a vocation.

POULAT, E.
Notes sur la psychologie religieuse des prêtres ouvriers.
J. de Psychol., 1957, *54,* 51-66.

PUGH, T. J.
A comparative study of the values of a group of ministers and two groups of laymen.
J. soc. Psychol., 1951, *33,* 225-235.

Sample: 220 Negroes in three groups: 64 male ministers, 90 male and female lay church members, 66 male and female lay nonchurch members. Predominantly Baptist.
Procedure: A-V Study of Values and a personal data sheet.
Results: Ranking of values: (1) ministers: religious, political, economic, theoretical, social, aesthetic. (2) church members: religious, theoretical, social, economic, political, aesthetic. (3) nonmembers: religious, social, economic, theoretical, political, aesthetic.

REINDL, MARY O.
The relationships between attitudes toward obedience and personality characteristics measured by the A-S Reaction Study and the Gordon Personal Profile.
M.A., Fordham University, 1957.

Sample: 50 third- or fourth-year girls each in 3 types of high schools: coed, all-girl, and aspiranture.
Procedure: A-S Reaction Study, Gordon Personal Profile, obedience attitude scale.
Results: Aspirants tend to have a greater supernatural motivation for obedience; the other 2 groups obey more frequently from naturally good motives. Religious aspirants are higher on responsibility but lower in ascendance and sociability.

RICE, P. J.
An MMPI study of religious seminarians.
M.A., Loyola University (Chicago), 1958.

Sample: 79 presumably well-adjusted members of one religious order.
Procedure: MMPI, compared with general norms and with Bier's norms.
Results: Differences were found between each of the groups to the extent that author concluded each seminary and religious order should develop its own MMPI norms since there is no one identifiable "seminarian profile" for the MMPI.

ROE, ANNE
The psychology of occupations.
New York: John Wiley, 1956.

In author's classification scheme, clergymen are classed at level 2 (with columnists, editors, and teachers) in group 7: general culture. 5 studies on clergymen are reported (**A1**: Cockrum, **A1**: Johnson 1943, **A1**: Kimber, **A1**: McCarthy 1942, **A1**: Peters). The conclusion is that this group often "as a whole, shows some dominance of verbal over non-verbal abilities, a generally more feminine attitude, and some tendencies toward low dominance. . . . In the religious groups there is a fairly high degree of neuroticism."

ROUSSET, SUZY

Motives for entering the coenobitic life.

In *Communal Life*. Westminster, Md.: Newman, 1957. Pp. 251-265. (Religious Life Series, VIII.)

The interaction of unconscious motivation with motives of religion and charity is discussed.

SANDRA, MOTHER M. ELAINE

Degree of adherence to the Catholic religion as related to selected personality indices.

Ph.D., Fordham University, 1957.

Sample: 5 groups of 150 women each: 3 at different stages in a teaching order, 1 of Catholic college women, 1 of Protestant college women.

Procedure: Bier's MMPI, SCT, DAP.

Results: All 5 groups deviated from general population norms. They followed similar patterns although the magnitude of deviation differed. The author concludes that the deviant profiles are attributable to training in the religious life and even more to the personality characteristics of those attracted to the religious life. Catholic background appeared to exert little influence on these deviations. Deviations did not increase with time.

SAUNDERS, D. R.

Evidence bearing on the use of the Myers-Briggs Type Indicator to select persons for advanced religious training: a preliminary report.

Res. Bull. 57-8. Princeton, N. J.: Educational Testing Service, 1957. 18 pp.

Sample: 5 small samples: 9 active and 7 inactive ordained Protestant ministers; 108 entering Yale Divinity students; 42 female candidates for training in religious education (see **B2**: Fairbanks); 177 students at Southern Baptist Theological Seminary; 13 Rockefeller Theological

Fellows (students at a seminary but not firmly committed to the ministry).

Results: Among the 16 types provided by the Myers-Briggs instrument, clergymen cluster in the ENFJ type (except for ESFJ at the more conservative Baptist seminary), and other types tend to drop out of the ministry. In the female sample, those in ENF types received better criterion ratings as directors of religious education.

SCHEUERMAN, E. L.

Use of the Bernreuter Personality Inventory in a seminary program of personality appraisal and guidance.

Natl Cathol. Educ. Ass. Bull., 1958, *55,* 93.

Sample: 45 successful minor seminarians (completed studies) and 45 dropouts.

Procedure: Bernreuter.

Results: The successful group was significantly higher on Bernreuter scale B2-S showing greater self-sufficiency. Other differences (not significant) favored successes on emotional stability, dominance, and adjustment to environment.

SCHROEDER, C. E.

Personality patterns of advanced Protestant theology students and physical science students.

Ph.D., Michigan State University, 1956.

Dissert. Abstr., 1958, *18,* 154-155.

Sample: 55 divinity students: University of Chicago, Oberlin, Anderson School of Theology. Control group of 45 Michigan State science students.

Procedure: Group Rorschach, Monroe Checklists, A-V Study of Values.

Results: Significant differences in personality factors and values were found between the scientific and divinity groups. No difference in adjustment level was found. The behavior of theological students tended to be marked by passivity and conformity as a reaction formation of deep-seated feelings of hostility and rebellion.

SHEERIN, SISTER MARY T., &
BARRETT, SISTER MARY N.
Assessment of the personalities of sister teachers.
Mimeographed report to the Public Health Service on Research Project MH 07199-01. Weston, Mass.: Authors, Regis College, undated (about 1964). 15 pp.

Sample: 67 candidates for sister teacher in the congregation of the Sisters of St. Joseph of Boston.
Procedure: MMPI, supervisor rating, record of persistence or drop-out. MMPI scores were analyzed in a 2 × 2 classification of adjustment and persistence. Profile and code analysis.
Results: Factor analysis of MMPI scales (excluding K) showed significant difference between persisting and dropped subjects, but analysis of interaction between persistence and MMPI scales indicated no single scale could account for the differences. Codes 94 and 49 were found significantly more often among persisting students. Persistence found unrelated to age, amount of formal schooling, or OSUPE scores.

SIEGELMAN, M., & PECK, R. F.
Personality patterns related to occupational roles.
Genet. Psychol. Monogr., 1960, *61,* 291-349.

Sample: 16 chemists, 16 ministers, 16 military officers.
Procedure: A personality model was devised for each occupation based on job-role requirements. Data gathered by activities index, SCT, interview, and biographical data sheet.
Results: Each group manifests different and distinct personality patterns. Need patterns of the individual coincided with the job requirements of the occupation.

SKRINCOSKY, P.
A comparative study of the standard form of the MMPI and a modified form of the same adapted for a seminary group.
M.A., Fordham University, 1953.

Sample: 100 minor seminarians.
Procedure: MMPI, Bier's MMPI.
Results: (1) Mean profiles were similar in pattern although Bier's form was generally higher. (2) 5 clinical scales were significantly different: D and Ma (.05); Pd, Mf, and Sc (.01). (3) These differences disappeared when the modified items were not included in the analysis.

SOUTHARD, S.
Faithful commitment to the ministry.
Pastoral Psychol., 1963, *14*(139), 31-36.

A lack of continuing interest in the ministry does not make a candidate "faithless." A "faithless" candidate would be one who drifts toward the ministry without inner motivation. Several cases are described. Several research projects are cited.

STERN, G. G.
Personality assessment and the prediction of academic success.
Amer. Psychologist, 1952, *7,* 324.

Preliminary report of Chapter 8 in Stern 1956.

STERN, G. G., STEIN, M. I., &
BLOOM, B. S.
Methods in personality assessment.
Glencoe, Ill.: Free Press, 1956.

Chap. 4: An analytic study of personalities of theological students. (See **B1:** Stern) Chap. 8: Empirical studies of graduate students: a comparison of theology, education, and physics students. Using methods similar to **B1:** Stern, the following results were obtained: (1) All three groups were alike on goal orientation. (2) Theologians and teachers were higher than physicists on interpersonal relations and conflict over impulse control. (3) Physicists only were high on independence, impulse freedom, lack of spontaneity.

STÉVAUX, A.

Problèmes psychologiques de la vocation. *Rev. Dioc. Tournai,* 1954, *9,* 558-562.

The relation of vocation to the religious life, affectivity, unconscious motivation and psychological maturity is discussed. The place of psychological examinations in the selection of candidates is briefly noted. (Abstract by Meissner.)

STRIKE, D. J.

Self concept as a factor in choices between the priesthood and a non-teaching brotherhood.

M.A., Catholic University of America, 1961.

Sample: 100 boys preparing for the priesthood and 100 boys preparing for the brotherhood, all at secondary school level.

Procedure: 100% return of questionnaire using yes-no-doubtful items.

Results: Differences between the groups are very slight. They do not form a personality syndrome.

STRUNK, O., JR.

Interest and personality patterns of preministerial students.

Psychol. Rep., 1959, *5,* 740. (a)

Sample: 60 preministerial students and 50 business majors attending same liberal arts college at the same time. Matched on sex, age, ACE percentile, race.

Procedure: SVIB and Bell were administered to both groups at the beginning of the freshman year.

Results: (1) Personality: Preministerial students showed more aggressiveness in social contacts. Difference (.01) in the area of social adjustment, yet both groups are in the "average" category defined by the Bell norms. (2) Occupation: There were significant differences in 22 of 45 areas. Preministerial students showed interest in the following in decreasing order: minister, city school superintendent, psychiatrist, architect, musician, lawyer, YMCA physical director, author-journalist, psychologist, vocational counselor, YMCA secretary. . . . Business students: purchasing agent, pharmacist, junior accountant, sales manager, office worker, banker. . . . Preministerial students were significantly higher on M-F Scale, showing more feminine interests, and on specialization level.

STRUNK, O., JR.

Men, motives, and the ministry.
Relig. Educ., 1959, *54,* 429-434. (b)

Qualitative interpretation of data from another study (**A2:** Strunk 1958). Altruism and call are the most frequently reported motives. About one third reported a definite religious experience which played a decisive part in their decision. Some indicated doubt as to whether stated motives are the real motives.

SUTTER, C. R.

A comparative study of the interest and personality patterns of major seminarians.

Ph.D., Fordham University, 1961.
Dissert. Abstr., 1961, *22,* 328.

Sample: 1,693 major seminarians with at least 2 years in the major seminary.

Procedure: Kuder, GZTS, questionnaire on 7 environmental variables.

Results: Significant differences on all Kuder interest scales except artistic were found between seminarians and men in general. The direction of these differences was seen as appropriate to the performance of priestly duties. Significant differences were found on all 10 GZTS scales. Most influential environmental variables were area of the country, density of population, socio-economic status.

SWARD, K.

Temperament and religious experience.

J. soc. Psychol., 1931, *2,* 374-396.

Sample: 80 students in a Catholic seminary.

Procedure: Self-ratings on the Heidbreder scales for "introversion" and "inferiority complex."

Results: Greater introversion and inferiority attitudes among seminary students than among college students, professors, and businessmen. Finds support for James and Leuba in that emotionality in the form of inferiority attitudes and introversion may be regarded as a condition which predisposes an individual toward the religious life.

SWEENEY, R. H.

Testing seminarians with the MMPI and Kuder: a report of ten years of testing.

M.A., Loyola University (Chicago), 1964. (a)

Sample: Of 461 men tested while in seminary, 126 persevered to perpetual profession and 335 dropped out.

Procedure: MMPI scores on all. Kuder profiles for a sample of 40 perseverers and 77 drop-outs. Faculty members made retrospective ratings of seminarians; the 50 rated with a poor chance of persevering were compared with a sample of 50 successful seminarians.

Results: All scores fell within the normal ranges. MMPI scores on Sc, Pt, and Pd were higher for drop-outs. No satisfactory cutting points for use in screening could be found. Scores on the Kuder could not distinguish between successful and unsuccessful candidates. Insufficient time had elapsed to assess adequately the effectiveness of the faculty ratings. A questionnaire was voluntarily administered to 65% of those tested. Half of them indicated that their answers to the test had been spontaneous; the rest did not. If testing is voluntary, the MMPI and Kuder hold value for use in counseling (rather than screening).

SWEENEY, R. H.

The morality of psychological testing of vocation prospects.

Natl Cathol. Educ. Ass. Bull., 1964, *60,* 370-380. (b)

Since psychological tests are not designed to be screening devices for emotional suitability of vocation candidates, a question is raised as to the morality of their use in this capacity. Results of the Notre Dame testing program (1953-64) are given to illustrate the limitations of psychological tests:

Sample: 461 religious life candidates, of whom 335 have dropped out and 126 have been successful, selected from more than 1,000 candidates in the Notre Dame program.

Procedure: Battery of tests included the OSUPE, MMPI, and Kuder.

Results: Drop-outs scored significantly higher on Sc, Pt, and Pd of the MMPI.

THORNDIKE, R. L., & HAGEN, ELIZABETH
Ten thousand careers.

New York: John Wiley, 1959.

Chap. 11:

Sample: 33 clergymen among 10,000 men followed up in 1955-56 among 17,-

000 air force cadets given aptitude tests in 1943.

Data: Reported occupation in 1955. Scores on battery of aptitude tests and biographical data blank in 1943.

Results: In general on the aptitude tests, "clergymen showed a rather flat profile falling close to the average." On biographical data, "responses to a number of items suggest verbal, musical, and dramatic talents and/or interests . . . some indication of a deficit in mechanical activities . . . they were words-and-persons oriented rather than a thing-oriented group. . . ."

URSCHALITZ, M. ODELIA

Measurement of general interests and interests relevant to vocation aim among religious women.

M.A., Fordham University, 1956.

Sample: 299 sisters from 9 communities, primarily teachers, divided into 3 groups according to length of community membership.

Procedure: Used the Kuder and a specially developed Checklist of Religious Interests to measure and differentiate three motivational commitments: to the apostolate, to her own spiritual perfection, to an integration of the two.

Results: Sisters differed most from women in general on the persuasive and clerical (lower) and the social service and musical (higher). The general interest pattern remained stable over a 13-year period. Greatest gain in the integration of vocational aims occurred during the first 5 or 6 years.

VASSE, D.-H.

Survey on the relations between psychopathology and religious vocation.

Doctoral dissertation, University of Marseille, 1960.

VAUGHAN, R. P.

A psychological assessment program for candidates to the religious life.

Cathol. psychol. Rec., 1963, *1,* 65-70.

Sample: 218 men, 18-30, who entered a religious order over a 5-year period.

Procedure: MMPI, SCT, and reports to the major superior. Scores of 55 drop-outs were compared with scores of those who remained.

Results: MMPI: no prediction could be made on the basis of the scales. However, those who left had profiles tending to center around Hy-Pd and Pd-Ma peaks. SCT: effectively predicted failure in about one fourth of the cases. Psychological reports: not statistically significant in predicting success or failure. The author concludes that these psychological evaluations were useful only when used with other sources of information.

VERSTYNEN, R. J.

A study of perseverance in relation to vocations to the priesthood.

M.A., Catholic University of America, 1948.

Sample: Rectors from 27 of the 42 minor seminaries listed in the 1938 survey of the National Catholic Welfare Council.

Results: The average seminary lost 6 of 10 entering students, ranging from 40% to 95%. 4 of 10 listed as reason for leaving "loss of desire." Other reasons include inadequate mental ability, sickness, transfer, discipline.

WAGONER, W. D.

Bachelor of divinity: uncertain servants in seminary and ministry.

New York: Association Press, 1963.

A discursive essay, based on various experiences and observations of the author, touching personality characteristics of theological students, problems of theological education, and problems of church organization.

WALSH, F. A.
Personality estimation of seminarians.
Amer. eccl. Rev., 1937, *97*, 337-346.

1,000 students were observed over a 25-year period in order to "pass judgment on the fitness of students both to enter the classes of philosophy in seminaries and to be ordained priests." Comments are made in such areas as physical appearance, intelligence, drop-out rate, and background.

WEISGERBER, C. A.
Survey of a psychological screening program in a clerical order.
Pp. 107-148 in **B2:** Arnold *et al.* 1962.

Sample: 211 men entering the novitiate in the early 1950's.
Procedure: A psychologist's global rating at the time of entrance on "suitability for the religious life from the standpoint of mental health" based on Bier's MMPI, faculty ratings, and some background data. Psychologists interviewed "doubtful" cases.
Criteria: (1) 141 remained in order, 70 left, 48 of them during the novitiate. (2) The author's ratings of mental health, based on the record of the candidate and on reports of at least 2 superiors or teachers.
Results: (1) Significant relation between psychologist's judgment and perseverance: 70% initially judged satisfactory, and 55% judged doubtful or unsatisfactory persevered. (2) A profile of high scores on Mf and Ma, and to a lesser degree Pd, of MMPI discriminated drop-outs from perseverers. No single scale score so discriminated. (3) Initial judgments were correlated, but not significantly, with criteria judgments of mental health.

WEST, F. E., & KEW, C. E.
Clergymen's resistances to training in pastoral counseling.
Pastoral Counselor, 1963, *1,* 11-24.

Discussion of inhibitions to learning observed by a supervisor of individual sessions with students and in group supervisory situations. Direct supervision of the students' counseling is the most meaningful learning process. The psychoanalytic training of clergy requires an intensive exposure of at least 3 years.

WHEELIS, A.
The quest for identity.
New York: Norton, 1958.

Pp. 207-210 offer, as analogy to "some psychoanalysts," a psychological interpretation of career choice and crises common among clergymen who have been seen as psychiatric patients. The ministry is perceived by the adolescent as providing decisive resolution of conflicts over impulse control: it offers partial vicarious gratification but also provides many strengths against temptation. Experience in the parish reopens ambiguity of moral issues, and the conflict over impulse control. Reactions at this point may include more rigid refuge in dogma, abandonment of those absolutes of profession which once provided resolution, or a creative new resolution.

WHITLOCK, G. E.
The relationship between passivity of personality and personal factors related to the choice of the ministry as a vocation.
Ph.D., University of Southern California, 1959.
Dissert. Abstr., 1959, *20,* 2392.

Sample: 25 male candidates for the ministry, randomly selected, either in college or recent graduates.

Procedure: Passivity of personality was measured by a clinical rating, SCT, 2 scales of the CPI. Passivity rankings were correlated with ranking on Christian and Vocational Decision Index, rating of work orientation, Scale of Religious Beliefs, 3 SVIB scales.

Results: The study recognizes the variety and individuality of contemporary motivations and indicates the importance of examining ego structure rather than the genetic origin of motivation. The passive ministerial candidate tends to be unrealistic in his vocational goal.

WHITLOCK, G. E.
The choice of the ministry as an active or passive decision.
Pastoral Psychol., 1961, *12*(112), 47-53.
J. coun. Psychol., 1962, *9*(1), 88-90.

An article drawn from Whitlock 1959.

WHITLOCK, G. E.
Role and self concepts in the choice of the ministry as a vocation.
J. pastoral Care, 1963, *17,* 208-212.

A treatment of the data in Whitlock 1959 limited to the relationship between passivity of personality and the role and self concepts of individuals choosing the ministry as a vocation. The more passive the subject, the lower he scores on the Occupational Level Scale and the higher he scores on the Ministry Scale.

YOUNG, D. R.
Counselor responses in marriage counseling: a comparison of minister and nonminister trainees.
Ed.D., University of Pennsylvania, 1962.
Abstracted in *Relig. Educ.,* 1963, *58,* 528; 537.

Sample: 16 ministers and 15 nonminister professionals in training between 1955 and 1960.

Procedure: Interview data were analyzed.

Results: The groups began from a similar point of readiness. Ministers made themselves more available to supervision than nonministers near the end of training. Sexual adjustment in marriage was difficult for both groups to work with. The sizable differences between the groups which were expected were not found.

ZAX, M., COWEN, E. L., & PETER, SISTER MARY
A comparative study of novice nuns and college females using the response set approach.
J. abnorm. soc. Psychol., 1963, *66,* 369-375.

Sample: 40 novice nuns and 40 female university psychology students.

Procedure: Ratings on 21 semantic differential scales of 10 Rorschach inkblots. Ratings (by 28 of each group) of the social desirability of 209 traits.

Results: "Nuns generally rated the inkblots toward the more positive extreme of the evaluation scales and at times toward the more potent extreme of the potency scales." On social desirability ratings, nuns rated positive adjectives more positively and negative adjectives more negatively than college females. Nuns showed greater variability in rating neutral adjectives. Authors conclude a "generalized tendency to respond in an extreme manner, once given the possibility of positive or negative responses. In the absence of such a frame of reference more variable behaviors may be expected."

ZIRKELBACH, I.
An interest profile for Franciscan seminarians.

B.A., Duns Scotus College (Detroit, Mich.), 1956.

Sample: 78 Franciscan seminarians at Duns Scotus.

Procedure: Kuder.

Results: The group had very high social service scores which tend to increase with time in training. The same is true, but in an opposite direction, for the clerical scale. Scores on computational, persuasive, and clerical scales varied with the time of testing.

FURTHER REFERENCES

For further references on Unique Characteristics: Personality, see also: **A2:** Judy; **B1:** Santopolo; **B2:** Ashbrook 1964; **B2:** Bier 1948; **B2:** Bier 1956; **B2:** Maehr; **B4:** Wise; **C:** Gustafson; **C:** Vaughan; **C:** Whitesel; **D:** Calpin; **D:** Grünewald; **D:** Mastej; **D:** Murphy; **E:** Bowers 1958; **E:** Bowers 1963a; **F:** McAllister; **F:** William; **I:** Bier 1960b.

UNIQUE CHARACTERISTICS: BACKGROUND

ALAIMO, P.

Factors influencing ministers' vocational choice.

M.A., Northwestern University, 1940.

    Sample: 30 theological students; 30 non-theological students.

    Procedure: Case study analysis through extensive interviews.

    Results: Family, social, church, and college influences are examined in detail but without reference to statistical analysis.

BARRETT, MARY M.

A study of the influences of Catholic high school experiences on vocational decisions to the sisterhoods.

Ph.D., Catholic University of America, 1961.

Washington, D.C.: Catholic University of America Press, 1960.

    Sample: 200 first-year professed sisters graduated from Catholic high schools not previous to 1955; 250 postulants graduated in 1958; 420 senior girls attending the same school.

    Procedure: Questionnaire.

    Results: Most decisions are made in the last year of high school after several years of consideration. The greatest influence for or against the religious life comes from contact with sisters. Giving up one's family and the fear of not being suited to the life are the greatest deterrents for girls in accepting a religious vocation. Annual retreats, daily masses, and films about the work of religious orders make great impressions on girls.

BENNETT, T. R.

Some sociological considerations on motivation for the ministry.

Pp. 136-146 in **H:** Southard.

    Discusses conceptual models, especially with reference to typologies; denominational polity and problems of authority; and the "minister-producing environment," as posing research problems.

BITTINGER, E. F.

Realism and vocational expectations: a study of the changes in the patterns of vocational expectations and other characteristics of 32,056 seventh through twelfth grade boys and a sample of 1,729 boys who selected the ministry in the Washington, D.C. metropolitan area with respect to the hypothesis of increasing realism with advancing age.

Ph.D., University of Maryland, 1964.

Dissert. Abstr., 1964, 25, 3155.

    Sample: "Universe": all public high school boys (N = 29,644) and a sample of 2,414 seventh- and eighth-grade public school boys in the Washington metropolitan area. "Ministerial sample": 1,729 boys from the universe who had selected the ministry on a vocational expectation test. Subjects were classified into high and low socio-economic status and 3 age categories (seventh and eighth grades, ninth and tenth grades, eleventh and twelfth grades).

Results: "Significant support was given to the general hypothesis of increasing realism in occupational expectations through advancing age groups, especially as measured by increasing congruity of expectations with the occupational structure." Some support was found for changes over time in the following variables among those who continue interest in the ministry: education of parents, plans to graduate from college, membership in groups, religious activities, intelligence, passivity.

BLANCETTE, SISTER LEO CLARE
Study of the environmental factors of vocations to the Sisters of St. Joseph of Carondalet, St. Paul Province.
M.A., Catholic University of America, 1954.

Of 1,055 questionnaires, 734 (70%) were returned. Background factors are tabulated.

BOHI, A.
Der Spätberufene Priester: Eine psychologish-pädagogische Studie seines Werdeganges.
Freiburg: Universitätsverlag Freiburg Schweiz, 1956.

Sample: 300 priests whose calling for the priesthood came later than usual.
Procedure: Questionnaire.
Results: Report of family, religious, educational and motivational backgrounds, and special problems faced in their seminary training. The findings are discussed in terms of their practical implications for the training of future priests with similar backgrounds.

BOSSART, D. E.
Leaving the campus ministry: critical factors in vocational change.
Ph.D., Boston University, 1963.

Sample: Questionnaires were mailed to 168 ministers. 122 finally qualified as full-time, ordained, male campus ministers who had served at least 5 years and left the profession between 1950 and 1962. 75 of the 122 (62%) replied with valid questionnaires. No control group.

Results: Tendencies toward the following pattern seem to characterize this group: they express lack of sufficient opportunities to preach, teach and work with the faculty. They move to the parish or to full-time teaching. Most stated reasons reflect a "pull" from without rather than a "push" from within. They tend not to indicate difficult relationships as an important reason for their leaving.

BOWDERN, T. S.
A study of vocations: an investigation into environmental factors of vocations to the priesthood and religious life in the U.S. from 1919 to 1929.
Ph.D., St. Louis University, 1936.
Microfilm Abstr., 1940, *2*(2), 32-33.

Reported in Bowdern 1942; see also Bowdern 1941.

BOWDERN, T. S.
Vocations.
America, 1941, *65,* 410.

A letter to the editor reporting some of the findings of Bowdern 1936.

BOWDERN, T. S.
How vocations grow.
Rev. Relig., 1942, *1,* 364-375.

Reports dissertation, Bowdern 1936; see also Bowdern 1941.
Sample: 2,500 men and 5,000 women in seminaries and religious orders in 1930 replied to a questionnaire.
Results: Discussed are age of vocational choice, meaning of vocation, and motivation.

BRIDSTON, K. R., & CULVER, D. W.
Latest reports on the continuing study on
the Protestant seminarian.
Seminary Quart., 1964, *5*(3), 1-3.

Preliminary report on Bridston 1965.

BRIDSTON, K. R., & CULVER, D. W.
Pre-seminary education.
Minneapolis: Augsburg Publishing House,
1965.

Part Two, pp. 157-252, presents results
of the Lilly Endowment Study of preseminary education.
Chap. 5: "Seminarian Questionnaire."
Sample: 17,565 (83% of the total
population) students in 125 Protestant
seminaries in 1962-63.
Procedure: Questionnaire.
Results: 56 tables tabulate data on background, development of vocational decision, education, and attitudes toward education and the ministry. The seminarian is
seen as a person with a relatively narrow
"religious" background in regard to both
family origins and education.
Chap. 4: "Baccalaureate Origins of
Seminarians."
Sample: Total population of students
enrolled in 1960-61 in member schools of
the American Association of Theological
Schools. 17,565 Protestant seminary students in 1962-63 (see above).
Results: Tabulation of colleges attended
by seminary students is given in 4 lengthy
tables.
Chap. 3: "Consultations and Opinions"
summarizes opinions of 250 educators and
265 ministers concerning theological education.
Chap. 2: "College Catalogs, Presidents,
and Teachers."
Sample: 572 (55% response) college
and university teachers in 70 schools.
Procedure: Questionnaire.
Results: 16 tables tabulate attitudes to-

ward ministry and theological and pre-
theological education.
Part One discusses various issues in
theological and pretheological education.

BRIDSTON, K. R., & CULVER, D. W.
Theological Education, 1961, *1*, 137-184.

Special issue on *Preseminary Education*
by K. R. Bridston and D. W. Culver. Re-
ports by Liston Pope, Robert E. Cushman,
A. Roy Eckardt, Frederick Sontag, A. B. B.
Moore, Theodore O. Wedel, Terrelle B.
Crum, Thomas C. Campbell, and John M.
Vayhinger.

BROWN, W. A.
The education of American ministers.
Volume I. *Ministerial education in
America: summary and interpretations.*
New York: Institute of Social and Re-
ligious Research, 1934.

Summary of conclusions of 5-year study
sponsored by the Conference of Theological Seminaries and the Institute of Social
and Religious Research. More detailed results are presented in **B4:** May and **A2:**
May 1934a. Instruments and statistical
tables are presented in **A2:** May 1934b.
Discussion of the function and institutional context of the Protestant clergyman,
and detailed attention to characteristics of
Protestant seminaries, their faculty, students, curriculum, and education practices.
Discussion of problems in theological education, and recommendations to churches,
colleges, and seminaries.

BURNS, MARY S.
A comparative study of social factors in
religious vocations to three types of
women's communities.
Ph.D., Catholic University of America,
1957.
Abstract published by Catholic Univer-

sity of America Press: *Stud. Sociol. Abstr. Series,* 1957, *12.*

Sample: All members of a major pontifical cloister, a minor pontifical cloister, and a noncloistered community were surveyed. 1,573 (93.8%) of the questionnaires were returned.

Results: Certain "social types" are predominant in religious communities of women. Although contemplative orders follow the general pattern substantially, they differ from it so consistently on certain points as to imply a distinct "contemplative type."

CANTWELL, P. J.

A study of sociological and religious factors in the backgrounds of students in three diocesan seminaries of Australia.

M.A., Catholic University of America, 1960.

336 students (83%) from the 3 seminaries returned the questionnaire.

CARPER, E. G.

The recruitment and conservation of the ministry in the Church of the Brethren. (Volumes I and II.)

Th.D., Boston University School of Theology, 1962.

Dissert. Abstr., 1962, *23,* 1807-1808.

Sample: 2,621 Brethren pastors, and 54 who had withdrawn from the pastoral ministry.

Procedure: Questionnaire, interview.

Results: Suggest that the Brethren pastor has peculiar problems due to the transition from a "sect-type" to a "denomination-type" church. Pastors are key persons in the recruiting process; certain small churches under part-time pastors apparently produce the kind of environment needed to recruit young men. The three most frequently suggested reasons for pastoral withdrawals relate to appeal of other professions, questioning of their own beliefs, and dissatisfaction with methods of ministerial placement.

CASPER, ALICE E.

The social background factors in vocations to the Sisters of Charity of Nazareth, Kentucky.

M.A., Catholic University of America, 1956.

439 sisters (89%) from a random sample of the Sisters of Charity completed the questionnaire.

CASSADY, M. L.

A comparative study of two generations of theological graduates in Union Theological Seminary, New York.

Ph.D., Columbia University, Teachers College, 1935.

Sample: 296 male graduates 1888-1900 and 275 male graduates 1919-1929. Some comparative data from Yale Divinity School and Princeton Theological Seminary are reported.

Procedure: Mailed questionnaire; return of about 50%.

Results: The most important determinant of the character of the background of graduates was the occupation of the father. Students were not selected by the seminary in terms of background factors; instead students with certain backgrounds were attracted to the seminary.

COXON, A. P. M.

Interim report to theological college principals and students on the November 1962 sociological questionnaire, administered to a 30% random sample of Anglican ordinands at Church of England theological and pretheological colleges.

Mimeographed paper. Leeds, England:

Department of Social Studies, Leeds University, 1963. 17 pp.

Sample: A 30% stratified sample of all Church of England theological and pre-theological colleges. 494 (92%) completed the questionnaire.

Results: Who becomes a priest? Mainly middle- and professional-class, public- and grammar-school-educated men, older than in most other professions (due to bi-modal age of entering training: after university, and after time in other occupations), influenced chiefly by other clergy. Ordinands were "quite" interested in political activities; the greatest number (36%) tended to sympathize with the Conservative Party. With regard to vocational plans, there is a demand for specialization and for pastorally and clinically oriented training. 3 preferred specializations: overseas missionary work; group and urban ministry; teaching and chaplaincy. A feeling of insufficiency was reported for all subjects but church history.

DⅮ'ARCY, P. F.
Study of dropouts in Maryknoll Seminary.
Unpublished faculty study, No. 29. Glen Ellyn, Ill.: Maryknoll Seminary, 1954.

Sample: All students (N = 3,121) who have entered Maryknoll seminaries (age 12 and up) from the time records began and including all those who were dismissed (18%), who resigned (65%), or who were finally ordained (17%) to the priesthood by the winter of 1952-53.

Procedure: Analysis of various sociological background factors of entering students and various categories of drop-outs.

DARLING, H. W.
A comparative study of persisting and non-persisting ministerial candidates in evangelical colleges.
Ph.D., Purdue University, 1958.

Dissert. Abstr., 1959, *20*, 586.

Sample: 229 persisting and 28 non-persisting ministerial candidates.

Procedure: Questionnaire, GZTS.

Results: Significantly more persisting candidates had a "call" to the ministry.

Persisters had a significantly higher score on thoughtfulness and scored higher on all but 2 of the GZTS traits.

DENNIS, R.
A la recherche des vocations de frères enseignants, hospitaliers et auxiliares.
Suppl. Vie Spir., 1956, *9*, 149-164.

DESMOND, SISTER ELLEN M.
Study of the social background factors in vocations to the Sisters of Charity of St. Elizabeth, Convent Station, New Jersey.
M.A., Catholic University of America, 1955.
501 questionnaires were returned.

DeWire, H. A.
Motivation for the ministry.
Unpublished mimeographed paper. Dayton, O. (1810 Harvard Blvd.): Author, undated. 12 pages.

Sample: 168 preministerial college students in Evangelical United Brethren colleges, 163 male college students preparing for other vocations, 113 men entering United Theological Seminary.

Procedure: Questionnaire on history of vocational plans and attitude toward ministry.

Results: Family and persons in the profession were influential for both ministerial and nonministerial students. Ministerial students valued ministers higher and teachers lower as "helping" professions than did nonministerial students. Ministerial students showed highest motivation in concern for emotional and spiritual health of persons.

DOLAN, M. J.

A study of the social backgrounds of vocations to the brotherhood in the Society of the Divine Word, Eastern and Western Provinces.

M.A., Catholic University of America, 1960.

102 of the 128 American-born brothers completed the questionnaire.

DOUGHERTY, J. M.

Factors contributing to the choice and development of sacerdotal vocations.

M.A., Catholic University of America, 1929.

ELSEN, R. MARIE

A study of the entrance age and social backgrounds of the vocation subjects of the School Sisters of Notre Dame, Milwaukee Province.

M.A., Catholic University of America, 1963.

358 of the 366 sisters in the 20% sample completed the questionnaire.

EMBREE, R. A.

A factor analytic investigation of motivations and attitudes of college students with intentions for the ministry and a comparison of the performance of persisters and non-persisters on the Theological School Inventory.

Ph.D., University of Denver, 1964.

Sample: 196 male college students, 100 freshmen and 96 seniors, who had expressed intentions to enter the ministry.

Procedure: All subjects completed the TSI in the fall. 167 subjects completed the following in the spring: Dean's Alienation measures, Wilson's Extrinsic Religious Values Scale, ESDS, Marlowe-Crowne's Social Desirability, Broen's Religious Attitude Inventory (fundamentalism only), Armatas' Q-sort of God concepts, modifications of measures of Machiavellianism, superego sentiment, sadism erg, self sentiment, career sentiment of Cattell, and a 10-point self-rating scale of commitment to the ministry. Factor analysis.

Results: 16 factors were derived and interpreted; TSI scores loaded significantly on 7 of them. Two major patterns, motivational tendencies and secondary God concept factors, accounted for about 47% of the total variance. A natural leading-special leading factor accounted for 3.2% of variance and was associated with social desirability. Definiteness scale showed some correlation with later measure of commitment.

EVANS, P.

An investigation into the origins of vocations to the teaching brotherhoods.

M.A., Catholic University of America, 1948.

Data on age and other circumstances of vocational decision were collected from application forms to the Xaverian Brothers Community and from a questionnaire. Replies are analyzed according to length of time since vows.

FELTON, R. A.

New ministers: a study of 1,978 ministerial students to determine the factors which influence men to enter the ministry.

Madison, N. J.: Drew Theological Seminary, 1949.

Sample: 1,978 ministerial students from 20 Protestant denominations and 57 theological schools and church-related colleges.

Procedure: An 83-item questionnaire on the influences on their decision for the ministry.

Results: The pastor is the chief influence on young men to enter the ministry. Wholesome religious life at home and an interested pastor will do most to recruit new pastors. The call is usually conceived of as a continuing educational process. The modal age of decision is in high school. The percentage responses to questions are tabulated in detail.

FICHTER, J. H.
The religious professional.
Rev. relig. Res., 1959, *1,* 89-101.

A review of research. Covers such areas as meaning of vocation, occupational choice, age of entrance into the profession, motivating reasons for occupational choice, and social status of religious professionals.

FICHTER, J. H.
Religion as an occupation: a study in the sociology of professions.
Notre Dame, Ind.: University of Notre Dame Press, 1961.

From the orientation of sociology of occupations, the author summarizes surveys and discusses the background and selection of candidates, their professional training and education, the roles they perform and problems they meet during their careers, and the structural and organizational forms in which they are encapsulated.

FICHTER, J. H.
Priest and people.
New York: Sheed and Ward, 1965.

Sample: 2,183 (47% of 4,560 originally contacted) diocesan parish priests and 2,216 adult Catholics nominated as "modal" or "nuclear" parishioners by approximately 1,500 of the parish priests. *Procedure:* Questionnaire; interviews in 21 cities throughout the U.S.
Results: Analysis is given of the kinds of parishioners with whom the priest associates, their relations with him and attitudes toward his work, educational and social class background, sentiments of anticlericalism, and variations in attitude with age. Chapters are devoted to the special groups of converts, liberal and conservative Catholics, and small-town Catholics.

The concluding chapter on role expectations deals with a series of images of the parish priest: executive, insolvent businessman, overburdened professional, spiritual leader, and personal friend.

FLUMERFELT, MARY J.
The social backgrounds of vocations to the Dominican Sisters of the Congregation of Our Lady of the Sacred Heart, Grand Rapids, Michigan.
M.A., Catholic University of America, 1957.

640 of the 740 (87%) sisters and novices of the congregation completed the questionnaire.

FOLEY, E. C.
A study of some socio-religious factors in the home backgrounds of a vocational family group and a non-vocation family group.
M.A., Catholic University of America, 1953.

Sample: 20 families with priests as sons and 50 families without a religious, all from the same parish.
Procedure: Interview.
Results: The vocation family is larger, more likely to have two Catholic parents, more likely to have religious among the relatives, more likely to have Catholic education. Differences are very slight in the area of religious obligatory observances.

GALLAGHER, AGNES
The social backgrounds of vocations to

the Sisters of Charity of Providence of the Sacred Heart Province.
M.A., Catholic University of America, 1950.

> 379 of the 430 Sisters of Charity (88%) responded to the questionnaire.

GARESCHÉ, E. F.
Congenial soil for vocations.
America, 1942, *66*, 511-512. (a)

> Summary of replies to a questionnaire given by "many" sisterhoods. Motives and influences determining vocations are discussed.

GARESCHÉ, E. F.
The influence of schools on religious vocations.
Cathol. Educ. Rev., 1942, *40*, 193-198. (b)

> Some results of a survey of communities for women in the U.S. are reported. Good influences on vocations are: (1) Teachers who are happy, congenial, and competent; (2) adequate explanation and understanding of the religious life; (3) immediate entrance from high school to the novitiate.

GARESCHÉ, E. F.
Influences in our schools unfavorable to religious vocation.
Cathol. Educ. Rev., 1942, *40*, 286-291. (c)

> Unfavorable influences include emphasis on worldly careers, emphasis on intellectual development over moral development, too much social life, incomplete picture of the religious life (emphasis on sacrifices rather than joys).

GARLAND, MARY
Certain domestic factors in the choice of a religious vocation among women.
M.A., Catholic University of America, 1950.

> 156 professed religious and 310 high school girls replied to the questionnaire.

GASPAR MISSION SOCIETY
Where do priestly vocations come from?
Shield, 1953, *32*(6), 16; 26.

> *Sample:* 6,314 students in 94 major U.S. Catholic seminaries.
> *Procedure:* Questionnaire.
> *Results:* (1) 74% were from cities of more than 10,000. (2) Age at which the students began considering the priesthood as a vocation ranged from 11 to 46, with mode of 14. (3) 75% were trained in Catholic elementary schools, and 50% of those attending high schools went to Catholic high schools. (4) Other common characteristics: family stability, father in a managerial office position, and 4 or more children in the family.

GILBERT, J.
What makes boys seminarians?
Priest, 1958, *14*, 1034-1038.

> *Sample:* About 2,000 students from 8 minor seminaries.
> *Procedure:* Questionnaire.
> *Results:* The most frequent attraction to the priesthood was, "I wanted to say mass," and next, "I wanted to help others." Half of 1,577 boys had opposition in going to the seminary. Results are reported on other questions including influences to enter seminary and study habits before entering.

GLASS, V. T.
An analysis of the sociological and psychological factors related to the call to Christian service of the Negro Baptist minister.
Th.D., Southern Baptist Theological Seminary, 1952.

HAGAN, J. R.

Some factors in the development of religious vocations of women.

J. relig. Instruction, 1945, *15,* 621-628; 712-718; 794-800.

Sample: 2,120 sisters in 11 communities in two Midwestern dioceses.

Procedure: Questionnaire data were analyzed according to the date of first profession, covering 1885-1943.

Results: About 80% came from large cities. The percentage of parents of American birth rose gradually until the last decade when it took a sharp upturn. These religious came from families larger than the typical Catholic family and their chances of becoming a religious decrease with the decrease of their rank in the family. Home backgrounds were usually piously Catholic.

Chances of becoming a religious decreased with increasing non-Catholic education. The 8th grade, followed by the 7th and 6th, was most frequently mentioned as the time of greatest influence toward the religious state; 55% had considered it by age 10 and typically had made a final decision by age 18. There is a recent tendency to enter at an earlier age.

Few sermons on vocations were reported to have been heard by the sisters. Other sisters most often were the chief influence toward the vocation. In general, sisters tended to enter the community to which their schooling had exposed them. 40% reported that they had been effective in bringing others into the convent.

HARTE, T. J. (Ed.)

A study in comparative family size.

Unpublished report. Washington, D.C.: Catholic University of America, Department of Sociology, 1951.

Sample: Random sample of religious and lay summer students at C.U.A. in 1951.

197 of 200 religious replied and 104 of 200 lay persons.

Procedure: Questionnaire.

Results: The mean number of children in vocation families was 6.2; for nonvocation families, 4. Other variables are examined and the results compared with other studies.

HARTE, T. J. (Ed.)

Prestige ranking of religious groups of men and women.

Unpublished report on a project conducted by the 1956-57 departmental seminar. Washington, D.C.: Catholic University of America, Department of Sociology, 1957.

Chap. I: Summarizes the descriptive research on background of religious vocations in the U.S. Based on statistical averages, it can be said that the typical vocation-producing family is relatively large in size, is a religious family, will probably produce more than one vocation. It is most likely second-generation American in a large or medium-size city. Although the head of the household is in manual work, his family enjoys a certain measure of stability and economic security.

Chap. II: "Implications of social status and role as applied to religious functionaries."

Chap. III: "The ranking of religious communities according to Canon Law."

Chap. IV: "Prestige ranking of religious groups of men and women."

Sample: 102 lay and 66 priests, nuns, and seminarians; a 5% sample of students at Catholic University of America in fall, 1956.

Procedure: Questionnaire asking for ranking of groups and reasons for ranking.

Results: Most important factor in rankings is "respect them through personal experience." Next come other nonspiritual reasons: practical efficiency, adaptability, and actual accomplishment. There is a positive correlation between the size of the group ranked and its selection as one of the best in its category.

HARTSHORNE, H., & FROYD, M. C.
Theological education in the Northern Baptist Convention.
Philadelphia: Judson, 1945.

Sample: Every sixth church in the Northern Baptist Convention.

Procedure: Usable questionnaires were returned by 415 ministers; interviews at seminary, testing of seminary seniors (Cooperative General Culture, vocabulary, opinion ballot).

Results: In addition to a report of test results, information is given on background factors, activities of ministers, and seminary curricula.

HAWKINS, C.
Changes in ministers' religious zeal in the Church of the Nazarene.
M.A., University of Chicago, 1956.

Sample: 38 ministers and students training for ministry in the Church of the Nazarene.

Procedure: Two-hour unstructured interview emphasizing (1) data on age, family background, college career, date of first pastorate, size of church, and (2) information on motivation. After the first four interviews, a 13-item questionnaire was conducted. From these items, a numerical index of "charismatic motivation" was derived; one with a high index (high religious zeal, great deal of confidence in self) would have answered that he felt a distinct call to the ministry, that he felt more effective than most men in the ministry, that Nazarene schools should not let "outsiders" into their student bodies, etc.

Results: Given in three stages corresponding to steps in development of ministry:

(1) Origin or background: Greater charismatic motivation is demonstrated in those ministering in the Nazarene Church who were converted from other backgrounds, in those subjects falling into the category of "younger boy" rather than in "oldest boy or only child" when sibling position is considered, and in those making a decision for the ministry when older, i.e., after completing high school.

(2) Training for ministry: The level of charismatic motivation decreases with more education, as the number of years between training and first pastorate increase, and is higher for students than for men already in the vocation stage.

(3) Vocational life: Church size and length of experience are directly related to charismatic motivation. Men leaving the pastorate to enter college teaching show a lower charismatic motivation index, as do pastors identifying themselves with teaching.

HEMPHILL, A. T.
A study of social background factors in vocations of seminaries of the Eastern Province of the Society of the Divine Word.
M.A., Catholic University of America, 1960.

101 of the 112 seminarians replied to the questionnaire (90%).

HEPPLE, L. M.
The church in rural Missouri.
Columbia, Missouri: Agricultural Experiment Station Bulletin #633C, December, 1958.

Sample: 345 of 405 clergymen serving in 99 sample rural townships of Missouri in 1953 completed a questionnaire.

Results: Extensive information is presented on family and educational background, salary, tenure, age, wives, and children. Principal reasons for entering the ministry: call to preach, home influence, desire to serve people; chief satisfactions: doing God's work, helping people. A poll of 88 ministers revealed the following "preferred type of clergyman": trained in a theological seminary after completing college, devote all of his time to the ministry, receive a cash salary of at least $3,000, participate in community activities, spend at least 28 hours per week in the role of a student, 25 in the role of pastor, and 4.6 in the roles of priest and prophet.

HERMAN, A. P.
Motivating factors entering into the choice of the ministry: a case study of ministerial students.
Ph.D., University of Chicago, 1930.

  Sample: 50 ministerial students selected by faculty and students to be most representative of the student body.
  Procedure: Extended interviews.
  Results: Factors giving rise to favorable attitudes toward religion and the church are classified under home, church, college, personal. Home and church factors are presented as most important. In addition, the following "plus" factors are cited as necessary for sufficient motivation in making the choice: early identification with the role of the minister, commitment to the ministry in response to recruiting efforts, implantation of the idea of the ministry by parents and friends, "reorganization of life" about religion culminating in a decision for the ministry, positive conception of the church and ministry, appeal and challenge of opportunity for *service* which the ministry offers, appeal of public-speaking opportunities of the ministry, the church and religion representing the individual's most satisfying experiences and achievements.

HERTZBERG, A.
Conservative rabbinate—a sociological study.
In J. L. Blau (Ed.), *Essays on Jewish life and thought.* New York: Columbia University Press, 1959. Pp. 309-332.

  Sample: 45 (58% of 78) who had been students in the Rabbinical School of the Jewish Theological Seminary in 1943; 118 students in the School in 1955. (These 2 samples comprise about 20% of the entire population of the Conservative rabbinate.)
  Procedure: Questionnaire on family background.
  Results: Older sample tended to come from orthodox families and to be first-generation American or foreign-born. Decision for Conservative rabbinate represented social mobility and relaxation of religious observances. Younger sample typically had Conservative parents, at least one of them American-born. Decision for rabbinate represented an acceptance of "greater burdens of the Law."

HESKAMP, C. A.
A study of social background factors in vocations to the priesthood in the Society of the Divine Word.
M.A., Catholic University of America, 1959.

  111 of the 146 white, American-born priests of the Society working in the U.S. returned questionnaires (76%).

HIGDON, E. K.
New missionaries for new days.
St. Louis: Bethany Press, 1956.

  A description of 12 years of the missionary selection program of the United Christian Missionary Society, a board of the Disciples of Christ. Much of the clinical work was done by Dr. Jules Masserman. (See I: Masserman 1955 and I: Masserman 1961 for more systematic and technical accounts of the selection procedures.) Information is given on the background of missionaries as well as suggestions for specialized training and counseling for prospective missionaries.

HOLDBROOK, G. W.
Factors associated with the attitudes of high school girls toward religious life.
M.A., Catholic University of America, 1947.

> *Sample:* 1,281 girls from 8 Catholic high schools in a Midwestern state.
> *Procedure:* Questionnaire and some interviews.
> *Results:* The attitude of the girls toward religious life seemed favorable and most of them had considered religious life at some time. Girls seemed to fail both to depend enough upon spiritual help in choosing their vocation and to seek counsel from nuns outside of class.

HUNTINGTON, H. S.
Where do ministers come from?
Eugenics, 1928, *1*(3), 22-28.
Soc. Sci. Abstr., 1929, *1*, #3653, 554.

> Of 104 of the most eminent ministers in this country, nearly two fifths were sons of ministers. Of those who were not sons of ministers or lay preachers, 39 were the sons of church officers. Only 21 came from homes where the father (or mother) was neither a minister, lay preacher, nor church officer.

JACKELS, R.
A study of social background factors of seminarians of the Western Province preparing for the priesthood in the Society of the Divine Word.
M.A., Catholic University of America, 1959.

> 65 of the 71 clerical seminarians of the Society of the Divine Word returned the questionnaire (91%).

JAMES, W. R.
A comparative study of attitudes toward vocation to the priesthood of 8th, 9th, and 12th grade boys.
M.A., Catholic University of America, 1961.

> *Sample:* 200 boys in each of eighth, ninth, and twelfth grades in Catholic schools.
> *Procedure:* A 125-item, Thurstone-type scale was constructed.
> *Results:* Over 3 times as many boys in the eighth and ninth grades wanted to be priests as in the twelfth grade. 15% of those tested said that they had a vocation to the priesthood but didn't know what to do about it.

JAMIESON, H. M., JR.
Factors which have influenced men to enter the ministry of the United Presbyterian Church.
M.A., University of Pittsburgh, 1952.

JOHNSON, R. M.
Relation between the religious needs of theological students and the provisions made for their religious development in theological seminaries.
Ph.D., Yale University, 1932.

> *Sample:* 1,771 students in 31 seminaries (see **A2:** May 1934a).
> *Procedure:* Items on religious experience of the student data blank of the study of theological education. Additional questionnaire on religious life completed by officials of 63 seminaries.
> *Results:* 48% report an outstanding religious experience of conviction of sin and pardon, associated with decision for the ministry. They tend to come from Midwest, rural, or lower-class backgrounds.

Students' understandings of their own religious needs are tabulated, and the resources provided by schools. "On the whole students indicate that they are helped least by those activities regarded by the faculty members as most important, and vice versa. The students believe that many of their religious needs are unmet. Specifically, they believe that they are neither known nor treated as individuals . . . that, while intellectual processes are being reconstructed, it is difficult to retain positive faith."

JOSEPHINA, SISTER
Factors in fostering religious vocations: questionnaire data.
Sponsa Regis, 1961, *32,* 182-187.

> *Sample:* 65 postulants in two different religious communities.
> *Procedure:* Questionnaire.
> *Results:* 75% graduated from parochial school. 69% of fathers and 75% of mothers had completed or gone beyond high school. Median family size was 4. Teachers were influential in arousing interest in vocations.

JUDY, M. T.
Why preach?
Dallas, Tex.: Author, Perkins School of Theology, 1961. 107 pp.

> *Sample:* 306 students in author's class at Perkins in 4 successive years.
> *Procedure:* Essay on "My call to the ministry," MMPI, biographical data.
> *Results:* Influences reported in the following approximate rank order: ministers, church activities, other persons, parents. Niebuhr's categories of call ranked as follows: call to be a Christian, secret call, providential call, ecclesiastical call. MMPI had virtually no correlations with other variables. Factor analysis yielded 8 factors, labeled by the author as follows: home-church, college failure and recovery, mission and reason, the urban-older, the

young youth-organization participant, the procrastinator, the doubter (composed mainly of MMPI scales), the rational scholar.

KAUFFMAN, J. F.
A study of the Unitarian ministry with special emphasis on motivational and environmental factors related to choice of vocation and persistency.
M.A., Northwestern University, 1951.

> *Sample:* 195 Unitarian ministers; 20 drop-outs.
> *Procedure:* Questionnaire.
> *Results:* Economic problems, family models and influences, and motive to serve world needs are most directly related to choice and persistency.

KAUFFMANN, M.
Apropos d'une enquête sur les vocations religieuses masculines en France.
Suppl. Vie Spir., 1956, *9,* 319-334.

KEIGHTLEY, C. E.
Factors related to persistence in vocational choice with particular reference to the Methodist ministry.
M.A., Northwestern University, 1947.

> *Sample:* 158 questionnaire replies (male) were analyzed: 58 from drop-outs (most of whom changed their intention during college years before beginning graduate work) and 100 from persons engaged in or preparing for full-time religious work. Nonprobability sample, predominantly Methodist.
> *Results:* Analysis of differences between the two groups indicates that persisters more often feel a "distinct and divine call," more often indicate the following factors in their choice of the ministry: regular family prayers, the religious faith and personality of parents, a college teacher or Wesley Foundation director or friend, and

regular family attendance at prayer service. Reasons for dropping out include the problem of getting people to follow the leadership which the minister provides, weakening of faith at college, financial difficulties, and politics in the church. Differences are noted in personal, family, and occupational background of the 2 groups.

KELLEY, SISTER MARY W.

Family background and some related factors of the members of the California Institute of the Sisters of the Most Holy and Immaculate Heart of the Blessed Virgin Mary.

M.A., St. Louis University, 1954.

KELLY, R. L.

Theological education in America: a study of one hundred sixty-one theological schools in the United States and Canada.

New York: George H. Doran Company, 1924.

A survey of the history and existing status of theological schools, including discussion of facilities, programs of study, students, finances, and problems. Descriptions are given of 100 seminaries. Data on students based on 9,000 seminary enrollees and 2,700 questionnaire respondents, and include educational, geographical, denominational background, occupation of father, reports of nature of call, and vocational plans.

KENNEY, R. D.

A study of the social background of priests and seminarians in the American Province of the Oblates of St. Francis de Sales.

M.A., Catholic University of America, 1954.

76% of the priests and 88% of the

seminarians replied, all Oblates of St. Francis de Sales.

LEIFFER, M. H.

A study of retirement and recruitment in the Methodist ministry.

Chicago: Methodist Publishing House, 1944. 30 pp.

A tabulation, by age, of all Methodist ministers in the period 1942-1944. "The present age distribution . . . is definitely weighted toward the older years . . . more than one third of all ministers now in service will die or retire within 10 years." Absolute numbers of ministerial candidates and seminary graduates are increasing since 1900; the rate of new ministers, in proportion to church membership, is steadily declining.

LEIFFER, M. H.

Influence of denominational appeals upon motivation for the ministry.

Pp. 83-96 in **H**: Southard.

Sample: 532 male students in 5 schools (Bethany Biblical Seminary, McCormick Theological Seminary, Associated Mennonite Biblical Seminaries, Garrett Biblical Institute, College of the Bible). Somewhat over 50% return.

Procedure: Questionnaire asking subjects to rank 13 factors influencing decision for ministry.

Results: Pastors, parents, youth camp, ranked in that order, were most prominent influences. Formal vocational guidance, through conferences and literature, appeared to have slight effect.

LENSKI, G. E.

The religious factor: a sociological study of religion's impact on politics, economics, and family life.

Garden City, N. Y.: Doubleday, 1961.

Sample: 146 Protestant and Catholic

clergy, the head pastor of every third church whose members were in the larger Detroit sample of this study (656 Detroiters selected as a cross-sectional sample).

Procedure: Interviews were completed with 127 of the clergy (87%): 49 Catholic, 57 white Protestant, and 21 Negro Protestant clergymen.

Results: Chiefly presented in Chap. 7, "The Clergy," pp. 256-287. Social backgrounds of the three subgroups are compared: Catholic clergy are similar to their laity in social class but differ ethnically (more often Irish); Protestant clergy resemble laity ethnically, but white Protestant ministers are disproportionately recruited from middle-class families and are mobile geographically. Data on theological commitments are summarized, and on relations between and attitudes towards other faith groups. Attitudes of the clergy groups are compared in detail with each other and with those of their laymen on such issues as intellectual autonomy and freedom of speech, relative value of economic job security or chances for advancement, political preferences, civil rights, moral questions such as gambling, drinking, and Sunday business, foreign affairs, and foreign relief. In general, clergy are more liberal than laymen on broad issues, less so on more personal issues such as child training. Most differences between groups of clergy and between clergy and laymen could be attributed to the preponderant middle-class background of Protestant clergy. "Protestant churches tend to develop in their adherents beliefs, values, and behavior patterns which facilitate upward mobility." "Catholic and Protestant churches pull their adherents in opposite directions on the question of freedom of speech."

LEPAULMIER, O.
Une enquête sur les vocations femmines.
Suppl. Vie Spir., 1958, *11*, 106-119.

MALONEY, D. J.
Age differences in the perceived influence of personal factors on vocation choice.
M.A., Catholic University of America, 1963.

MARTIN, S. H.
A twenty year survey of the functional aspects of Methodist theological education.
Ph.D., Boston University, 1954.

Sample: All graduates of Methodist seminaries, 1927-1947, were sent questionnaires. 1,510 (20%) were returned.

Results: Respondents indicated that many educational and social responsibilities gave little satisfaction and that schools had not trained their graduates to meet the personal and social needs of the community. Their major task was considered to be pastoral work by 29%, preaching and evangelism by 20%, teaching by 20%, administration by 20%, and leading worship by 11%. There was urging for increased curricular attention to clinical training, field work, and the arts.

MASSON, J.
Vocations to the priesthood and environment: an enquiry in the Belgian Congo, Ruanda, and Urundi.
Lumen Vitae, 1958, *13*, 120-145.

A questionnaire was used in 5 of the 6 major seminaries in these areas. Fecundity grows with the population but only to a certain limit. Two thirds of seminarists come from villages. 85% come from monogamous families. 67% of fathers and 68% of mothers are Christian. Lower classes have a lower proportion of vocations than their numbers would suggest.

MATEO, L. G.
A study of the problems of the third, fourth, and fifth year minor seminarians

in the diocesan seminaries in the Philippines.

Ph.D., Fordham University, 1964.
Dissert. Abstr., 1964, *25,* 1750.

Sample: 740 Filipino minor seminarians from 22 of 23 seminaries and accounting for 97% of the total third-, fourth-, and fifth-year minor seminary population.

Procedure: Checklist of 143 items.

Results: Designated as important background factors: Catholic schooling, encouragement from mother rather than from father, service as an altar boy, having a benefactor. Combined score on academic, social, spiritual, health, and recreational problems, and study habits showed fourth year with highest mean score and fifth year with lowest.

MAY, M. A.
The education of American ministers. Volume III. *The institutions that train ministers.*

New York: Institute of Social and Religious Research, 1934. (a)

A study of 176 theological institutions in the United States, including seminaries, graduate and undergraduate departments of religion, and Bible schools. Detailed data on seminary curricula, policies of admission and graduation, teaching procedures, libraries, faculty, field work, religious life of students, and administrative and financial relations with the churches.

Findings are summarized in **A2:** Brown. Detailed data and instruments are reported in **A2:** May 1934b. Part 3, p. 253-398, reports on "The Student Body." Chaps. 11, 12, and 13 summarize **A2:** Zerfoss, including data on backgrounds of students and history of vocational decision (N = 1,776 students).

Chap. 14 summarizes **A2:** Sadler and reports an additional study, "A comparison of the mental abilities of freshmen entering the ministry with those entering other professions."

Sample: 11,995 freshmen entering 62 colleges in 1930.

Procedure: Brief questionnaire asking for occupational decision or preference, ACE intelligence test.

Results: General tendency for low intelligence among those anticipating ministry. Additional data on vocations alternatively considered by theological students, background of preseminary training, and student opinions on theological education.

Chap. 18 is on the physical and mental health of students.

Sample: 1,776 students (see above and **A2:** Zerfoss).

Procedure: Questionnaire items on health, habits, and awareness of solved or unsolved personal problems.

Conclusion: Physical, personal, and social aspects of ministerial training "are left largely in the hands of the students."

Part 4, "The Seminary as the Center of Corporate Religious Life," was written by R. M. Johnson.

Sample: 1,771 students (see above, **A2:** Johnson, and **A2:** Zerfoss).

Procedure: Observation and interview in 3 seminaries; questionnaires.

Results: Agreement on importance of personal religious experience, but wide variation as to reported nature. Summary of types of religious problems experienced by students, the degree to which resources for help were found in the seminary, and the nature of such resources. Students suggest means for improvement of the spiritual life. "A considerable number of students are about to leave the seminary with unsolved problems of personal religious living."

MAY, M. A., & SHUTTLEWORTH, F. K.
The education of American ministers. Volume IV. *Appendices.*

New York: Institute of Social and Religious Research, 1934. (b)

Instruments, characteristics of samples, detailed statistical reports, excerpts from questionnaire responses, and 2 extended case summaries, supporting the results reported in **A2:** May 1934a, and **B4:** May, and summarized in **A2:** Brown.

MCCARRICK, T. E.
An analysis of the social factors affecting vocational supply to the diocesan priesthood in the Archidocese of New York, 1928-1958.
M.A., Catholic University of America, 1960.

Describes information from seminary records on 772 seminarians from New York who studied at the major seminary, St. Joseph's, Dunwoodie, and the preparatory seminary, Cathedral College in New York City.

MCCARRICK, T. E.
The vocation parish: an analysis of a group of high vocation supplying parishes in the Archdiocese of New York to determine the common characteristics of the vocation parish.
Ph.D., Catholic University of America, 1963.
Dissert. Abstr., 1963, *24,* 2611.

Sample: 6 parishes in New York State which produce high frequency of vocations.
Procedure: These parishes were analyzed in detail using community survey data, parish records, and a questionnaire to priests who had served in them. An ideal type of "vocation parish" was constructed and its distinctive characteristics were checked through an analysis of three low vocation parishes.
Results: The "vocation parish" was characterized by a significantly higher proportion of foreign stock (especially Irish-American), a more stable population, and a large middle-income group of residents.

The parishioners identified closely with it, and its social system served to a high degree as a uniting value.

MCDADE, SISTER MARY T. F.
A study of the factors in the home and in two types of high schools, coeducational and all-girls, which influence the young woman at the time of her making her religious vocational decision.
In S. W. Cook (Ed.), *Research plans.* New York (545 W. 111th St.): Religious Education Association, 1962. Pp. 206-211.

Candidates who entered one religious congregation between 1949-58 will be given questionnaires and rating scales now being developed.

MCMAHON, MIRIAM D.
An investigation of the religious vocational concepts of high school girls.
Ph.D., Fordham University, 1955.
See also McMahon 1957.

Sample: 600 girls (age 12-19) at a New York City Catholic high school were divided into 3 groups according to scores on the Otis.
Procedure: All subjects completed investigator's Religious Vocational Checklist, a 63-item multiple-choice questionnaire.
Results: 94% had at some time considered the religious life for themselves and 62% had not yet abandoned that consideration. 90% admitted they would like to live a life of greater perfection. Several recommendations favorable to recruitment are made.

MCMAHON, SISTER MIRIAM D.
Religious vocational concepts revealed by survey.
Lumen Vitae, 1957, *12,* 326-341.

Report of McMahon 1955. Reprinted in

Lumen Vitae studies in religious psychology. I: Research in religious psychology speculative and positive, 1959, 130-145.

MIRSE, R. T.

The self-image of the Methodist minister in Indiana.

Th.D., Boston University School of Theology, 1962.

Dissert. Abstr., 1963, *23,* 1811.

Sample: 861 (87%) of 926 ministers in Indiana returned questionnaires.

Procedure: The 99-item questionnaire, "Ministerial Resources Study," constructed for the study, was supplemented by personal interviews and Annual Conference reports.

Results: Typical of the Indiana minister is a rural, middle-class background, small churches, low salaries, and frequent moves. The task of the minister is described as falling within five roles: preacher-prophet, pastor, priest, teacher, and administrator. There is a strong emphasis on "building the church" with major effort directed toward an improved statistical record. The desire for approval is seen as a strong motivating factor.

MORGAN, CATHERINE B.

Study of the social factors in the background of vocations to the Sisters of St. Joseph of Chestnut Hill, Pennsylvania.

M.A., Catholic University of America, 1954.

750 questionnaires sampled the 2,000 sisters in the order. 551 responded.

NEVINS, A. J.

A questionnaire on vocations.

Homil. pastoral Rev., 1946, *46,* 502-511.

Results of a survey in "a large national seminary" on age of decision, religious background, and relations with parish priest. Several campaigns to foster vocations are discussed and suggestions to increase the number of vocations are made.

O'BRIEN, MOTHER PATRICK

A study of the attitudes of high school girls toward religious vocations.

M.A., Catholic University of America, 1957.

Sample: 2,063 girls from 11 Catholic high schools.

Procedure: Questionnaire.

Results: Confusion on how to know one's vocation was evident. 90% admitted at one time considering the religious life; 60% did not consider the possibility of a personal religious vocation frightening. The amount of prayers said by religious was seen as the greatest difficulty in living up to the life of a nun.

OLIVER, W. R.

A study of social background factors in vocations to the Sisters of the Holy Family of New Orleans, Louisiana.

M.A., Catholic University of America, 1959.

175 of a possible 300 questionnaires from this Negro community were completed.

PATTERSON, H.

A study of student mortality at St. Anthony's Seminary and suggestions for improving the situation.

M.A., Catholic University of America, 1942.

The rate and causes of mortality at this preparatory school for aspirants to the priesthood were analyzed through a study of school records. Comparable data from 5 other seminaries fail to show any general consistent pattern of mortality. Causes of mortality at St. Anthony's include lack of desire to become a priest (39%), poor mental fitness (34%), and poor moral fitness (17%).

PIPES, J. C.
Motivation for entering the ministry among mountain preachers.
Pp. 16-24 in **H:** Southard.

The author describes his own dramatic call to the ministry and supplements this with written reports by five other North Carolina ministers.

POPE, L.
Millhands and preachers: a study of Gastonia.
New Haven: Yale University Press, 1942.

Procedure: Interview and observation. "Ministers and Social Classes" (pp. 107-116) gives data and discusses the education of ministers and the implications of this in terms of social and denominational status. Other references to the situation of the minister in a community in transition are made throughout the book.

ROBINSON, F. J.
A study of social background factors of Negro vocations in the Society of the Divine Word, Southern Province.
M.A., Catholic University of America, 1959.

64 of the 72 Divine Word missionaries returned the questionnaire (88%).

ROMAN, MARY
Negro vocations and religious communities.
Rev. Relig., 1964, *23*, 129-134.

Of 5 communities surveyed, only 1 reported Negro members. "Racial prejudice manifest by our religious groups is not the defect of the discipline but of us, the members."

ROSILDA, M.
A comparative study of the religious vocations of women from various types of schools.
M.A., Creighton University, 1954.
See Rosilda 1955 for report.

ROSILDA, SISTER M.
Religious vocations among women—a comparative study of schools and places they come from.
Cathol. Educ. Rev., 1955, *53*, 296-305.
See also Rosilda 1954

Sample: 2,100 communities of women replied to a questionnaire.
Results: Rural elementary schools produce vocations at a significantly higher rate than do urban elementary schools, but there is no difference on the secondary coed level. Rural academies produce at a higher rate than urban academies.

ROTZ, H. W.
A study of the recruitment, training, support, and performance of church leaders in three Protestant denominations in the Philippine Federation of Christian Churches.
Ph.D., Cornell University, 1955.

Sample: 651 church leaders in Baptist, Methodist, and United Church of Christ, 60% of whom are ordained and 20% are seminary trained.
Procedure: Questionnaire.
Results: Detailed descriptions are given of the work and characteristics of several types of leaders: women, seminary trained, ordained.

RYAN, E. J.
Some psychological implications of the vocational survey: natural factors affecting vocations to the priesthood.
Natl Cathol. Educ. Ass. Bull., 1956, *53*, 57-63.

Results of a questionnaire sent to major Roman Catholic seminaries in 1951. Students from 100 institutions replied. Discussed are family factors, environmental factors, preseminary education, geographical distribution, and entrance age.

SADLER, M. E.

A comparative personnel study of ministerial, medical and law students.

Ph.D., Yale University, 1929.

Sample: 1927 and 1928 entering classes at Yale Divinity (N = 93), medical (N = 103), and law (N = 176) schools. 24,074 graduates of 6 New England colleges (Yale, Middlebury, Williams, Harvard, Trinity, University of Vermont) between 1904 and 1926.

Procedure: Records in registrar and alumni offices. Chapman, Anderson & Burr Psychological Test (speed and accuracy of thinking), Thorndike CAVD (general intelligence).

Results: Divinity students were distinguished from medical and law students in being older, more likely married, coming from central and southern states, church colleges, and in having fathers not in business or professions (except ministry). Divinity students had better college grades; they scored significantly lower on 2 intelligence tests. 2% of graduates of the 6 New England colleges entered the ministry (compared with 6% medicine, 14% law). Ministry and law drew a greater percentage of honor graduates than medicine and far greater than business.

ST. PETER, M.

La recherche des vocations de religieuses.

Suppl. Vie Spir., 1956, *9,* 165-174.

SCHERER, R. P.

Ministers of the Lutheran Church–Missouri Synod: origins, training, career lines, perceptions of work and reference.

Ph.D., University of Chicago, 1963. (a)

Abstracted in *Relig. Educ.,* 1963, *58,* 522.

Sample: 572 respondents (75% return of 14% random sample of population of ministers of Lutheran Church–Missouri Synod).

Summary of data on social origins, training, motivation, reactions to entrance into ministry, patterns of career, especially mobility and promotion, perception of pressures and influences on them, and their opinions of these. Distinctions are found among teachers, executives, pastoral specialists, and parish ministers in different size parishes.

SCHERER, R. P.

The Lutheran ministry: origins, careers, self-appraisal.

The Cresset, 1963, *26*(3), 9-17. (b)

Reprinted in *Information Service,* 1963, *42*(9), 1-8.

Summarizes data in Scherer 1963a.

SCHMELLING, W. D., & FALK, L. L.

Ministers and laymen of the Evangelical United Brethren Church: environmental influences and beliefs.

Dayton, O.: Authors, United Theological Seminary, 1958. 16 pp.

Sample: 178 E.U.B. ministers (38% return from a random 10% sample of population) and 1,094 laymen nominated by respondent ministers.

Procedure: 24-item questionnaire of apparent environmental influences on decision for the ministry (ministers only) and 24-item questionnaire of theological beliefs.

Results: More decisions gradual than related to a single experience. Chief influential person was pastor, followed by father, church workers, friend, mother, wife. Most decisions in late teens. Authors find seemingly large proportion of death of family members associated with decision (no data given). Other data on social and family background provided. Ministers tend to be more liberal than laymen on questions such as biblical infallibility; ministers stress personal belief, laymen stress ethical conduct as Christian criteria.

SHEA, FRANCES T.
A study of the social factors in the vocational backgrounds of the Sisters of Charity of Leavenworth, Kansas.
M.A., Catholic University of America, 1951.

The 785 members of the society were studied by means of a mailed questionnaire (68% return) or a search of records.

SHERMAN, I. E.
Military service as a factor in vocational choice of the Methodist ministry.
M.A., Northwestern University, 1947.

Sample: "30% of all the Methodist servicemen who said at one time that they were interested in entering the ministry."
Procedure: Questionnaire.
Results: If the decision to enter the ministry was made before entering the service, the likelihood of perseverance is greater. Those who persevered are more emotionally stable than men whose vocational interests have declined or ceased.

SMITH, J. O., & SJOBERG, G.
Origins and career patterns of leading Protestant clergymen.
Soc. Forces, 1961, *39,* 290-296.

Sample: 297 clergymen (88% respondents from random sample of 335) listed in *Who's Who* (26% pastors, 22% church officials, 30% educators).
Procedure: Mailed questionnaire.
Results: Although the clergymen studied generally came from high-status families,

certain evidence points to a broadening of the recruitment base in more recent times. In their career patterns, clergymen show considerable diversity in background and training. Most have married advantageously and have sons who are relatively successful. Family members are most influential in the decision. Divine call, service, influence of family and pastor were the three most common "reasons" for entering the ministry. Low rates of parental divorce (2.7%) or death (.7%) before adulthood.

SMITH, L. M.
The clergy: authority structure, ideology, migration.
Amer. sociol. Rev., 1953, *18,* 242-248.

Sample: 12 Episcopal and 12 Congregational clergymen from a metropolitan area, from 5 to 35 years beyond ordination.
Procedure: Open-ended interviews averaging 1 hour and 45 minutes.
Results: Clergy of both denominations moved more frequently during the early than the later years of their careers. During later years Congregationalists continued to move whereas Episcopalians settled down. Also discussed are reasons for entering ministry, social relationships, institutional control, success goals, and reasons for moving.

SMITH, R. O.
Factors affecting the religion of college students: a study of personality and cultural factors affecting the religion of college students.
Ann Arbor, Mich. (Lane Hall, University of Michigan): Author, 1947. 194 pp.
Psychol. Abstr., 1949, *23,* 4466.

Sample: 140 men at Yale Divinity School during 1944-45.
Procedure: Informational questionnaire.

Results: Attempts are made to isolate the factors which caused the men to enter religious work. Most frequent are sensitivity to the need, personal influence of friends and leaders, activities of friends and religious groups, influence of family, development of a strong faith in Christian life and belief. Data are reported in detail on family background; college experiences; religious knowledge, attitudes, beliefs, and practices; and vocational history. Suggestions are made for changes in college religious environment.

SMITH, R. O.
Personality and cultural factors affecting the religion of one hundred and forty divinity students.
Relig. Educ., 1948, *43,* 106-111.

Summary of Smith 1947.

SMYTH, J. P.
Parental understanding of adolescent psychology in view of religious vocations.
In *Proc. 8th annu. Convocation of the Voc. Inst.* Notre Dame, Ind.: Notre Dame Press, 1955. Pp. 68-81.

A discussion of adolescent psychology in light of Allport's personality theory. The adolescent must make 5 major adjustments: physical growth, emotional independence, sex attitudes, occupational choice, philosophy of life. The relationship of parents and adolescents in the area of occupational choice is discussed in some detail.

STRUNK, O., JR.
Theological students: a study in perceived motives.
Personnel Guid. J., 1958, *36,* 320-322.

Sample: 76 first-year theological students, predominantly Methodist.
Procedure: A written class assignment was given: "Motives for entering the ministry." Category analysis revealed 12 frequent motives. 6 weeks later the 12 statements were distributed to the same students and they rated them according to "entering motive" and "present motive."
Results: Altruism, call, and reform were clearly highest on both ratings. One clear shift in rank was monetary, from eleventh (entering) to ninth (present).

STRUNK, O., JR.
The preministerial student's education.
Relig. Educ., 1961, *56,* 351-354.

Sample: 45 students, mostly Methodist, who had served parishes while in college.
Procedure: 39 replied (87%) to a mailed questionnaire.
Results: Most of these students reported that they were carrying a regular full academic load and pastoring a full-time circuit in order to gain financial aid and experience. 79% said they would do it over again, while 46% said they would not advise a young preministerial student to do full-time pastoring as a student. Implications for education are briefly discussed.

SUNDAY SCHOOL BOARD, SOUTHERN BAPTIST CONVENTION
Research and Statistics Department.
Church related vocations study.
Nashville: Sunday School Board, Southern Baptist Convention, 1960. 16 pp.

Sample: 809 usable replies from 9,997 young people who had signed a church-related vocations commitment card at a camp or assembly in 1949 or 1959. 34% were males, 66% females. 56% had persisted in commitment, 44% had since changed to a nonchurch vocation.
Procedure: 2-page questionnaire, including open-ended questions on conversion, call, and change to another vocation.
Results: Tabulation, separately by sex and separately for those persisting and changing, on preferred activities, school subjects, hobbies, sports, musical instru-

ments, books, and on attendance at church activities, offices held, part-time jobs, and size of home town. Other family variables are analyzed.

TAGGERT, P. J.
Obstacles to vocations.
Natl Cathol. Educ. Ass. Bull., 1960, *57*, 484-488.

> Discussion (no data) from experience with the Diocese of Wilmington's screening program for candidates for the diocesan priesthood. Psychological tests used: Who Am I? SCT, Kuder, Thurstone Primary Abilities. Concludes that obstacles to vocations almost always have their roots in the family.

THOMPSON, J. W.
A comparative study of the religious and socio-economic backgrounds of ordained priests and dropouts from a southern minor seminary.
M.A., Catholic University of America, 1960.

> *Sample:* 152 priests, 55 seminarians, and 244 drop-outs from St. Mary's Seminary in St. Mary's, Kentucky.
> *Procedure:* Questionnaire.
> *Results:* Very few socio-economic differences were found. Among them: amount of education before seminary, age at entrance, relationship between first serious consideration and entrance into high school, attendance at mixed social functions.

TUMBLIN, J. A., JR.
The Southern Baptist missionary: a study in the sociology of the professions.
Ph.D., Duke University, 1956.

> *Sample:* 255 (43% of the 581 active missionaries in November, 1954) replied to a questionnaire.
> *Results:* Analysis produces 6 role stages in the life of a missionary: ideal role (the

call), popular success role (glamour), mission volunteer role (increasing realism during application process), "guild" role (supervised training), professional-to-client role (relationships with natives), furlough role (must act in terms of popular role).

VIDAL, J. R.
A study of the family, cultural, geographical and religious backgrounds of students in five diocesan seminaries.
M.A., Catholic University of America, 1952.

> 438 (78%) of 560 seminarians in 5 archdiocesan or diocesan major seminaries completed the questionnaire.

WILLENBRING, ROSE
The origins and development of vocations to the sisterhoods in North Dakota.
M.A., Catholic University of America, 1954.

> 189 of 249 questionnaires sent to 36 religious institutions in 3 dioceses (80%) were completed. The home and Catholic school are seen as the greatest influences in fostering vocations.

WORDEN, J. W.
The portrayal of the Protestant minister in American motion pictures, 1951-1960, and its implications for the church today.
Ph.D., Boston University, 1962.
Dissert. Abstr., 1962, *23*, 1440.

> *Procedure:* 60 films were content-analyzed.
> *Results:* The ministry is reflected as a poor vocational choice because of its irrelevancy to many areas of life, the minister's personal awkwardness, and conflict between his maleness and the ministry. Lay expectations are also negatively influenced by the film portrayal.

ZERFOSS, K. P.

The background and experience of theological students.

Ph.D., Yale University, 1930.

Sample: 1,776 male theological students in 32 Protestant seminaries (response varying from 8% to 96% in different seminaries).

Procedure: 82-item questionnaire on educational, religious, social, economic, and vocational background and health.

Results: "The average student has spent his life in an economically meagre atmosphere." Pastors and mothers were major influences on decision. Median age for decision was 19.6 years. 36% are married in seminary. 48% described conversion experiences; median age, 14.3 years. Other data tabulated.

FURTHER REFERENCES

For further references on Unique Characteristics: Background, see also: **A1:** Linder; **A1:** Sutter; **B1:** Blizzard 1955b; **B1:** Crawford; **B3:** Dean; **B4:** May; **C:** Kling.

UNIQUE CHARACTERISTICS: PROCEDURES

FROYD, M. C.
A program of recruiting for the Baptist ministry based upon a survey of the pastoral needs of the churches.
Ed.D., Columbia University, Teachers College, 1945.

Sample: 1,207 randomly chosen churches of the Northern Baptist Convention.

Procedure: Questionnaires were sent to pastors, seminarians, pulpit committees, and others.

Results: Social, educational, and religious backgrounds, personnel supply and demand, vocational decision are discussed. Recommendations on recruitment are made to the denomination.

GANSS, G. E.
Prudence and vocations.
Natl Cathol. Educ. Ass. Bull., 1960, *57,* 489-490.

Suggests how the prudent counselor avoids pressure tactics in counseling about vocation.

JAMES, A.
Interviews and vocations.
Natl Cathol. Educ. Ass. Bull., 1960, *57,* 491-492.

Advocates a client-centered approach in counseling about vocations.

KEMP, C. F.
Occupational information for church vocations.

Pastoral Psychol., 1961, *12*(112), 54-58. Similar article on pp. 261-269 in **H:** Oates.

Ministers are expected to be competent vocational counselors to those entering church occupations. Specific sources of information which may be useful in guidance are described.

POAGE, G.
Subconscious factors motivating against a religious vocation.
Natl Cathol. Educ. Ass. Bull., 1961, *58,* 77-83.

Concepts of motivational research are applied to "creating an image" of priests and religious which will encourage new vocations.

SANDUSKY, F. W.
The admission practices and procedures to the Bachelor of Divinity program of studies of the accredited Protestant theological seminaries in the United States.
Ed.D., Duke University, 1964.
Dissert. Abstr., 1964, *25,* 969.

Sample: 79 accredited Protestant seminaries in the United States.

Procedure: Examined catalogues from all and application blanks from 78; 50 admission officers replied to a questionnaire, and 19 were interviewed.

Results: Charcteristics of the admissions officer are described. Applications are most often acted on by an admissions committee, in 19 seminaries by administrative officers, in only 3 seminaries by the entire faculty. In order to qualify for seminary work toward a degree, the applicant must be a college graduate. Liberal arts preparation is stressed. "Medical reports and recommendations from pastors and churches or the normal ecclesiastical endorsements are among the requirements. The applicant is also expected to provide evidence of Christian conduct and character." No mention is made in the abstract of psychological testing.

SHARP, A. R.
A study of Protestant undergraduate pre-theological education in the United States.
Ed.D., Duke University, 1963.
Dissert. Abstr., 1964, *24,* 3613.

    Sample: All accredited colleges, Protestant and church-related, and seminaries in the U.S.
    Procedure: 69% return from a mailed questionnaire.
    Results: Although 87% of the institutions offer a religion major, only 20% of pretheological students take it. The chair-

man of the religion department is usually responsible for the pretheological education program. There is no trend toward larger numbers of pretheological students. 80% of the pretheological students in 61% of the schools go on to graduate school. A strong religion major, built on a broad liberal arts base, is recommended. The seminary program could then be changed to build on the religion major and culminate in an M.A. rather than a B.D.

SOUTHARD, S.
The counseling of candidates for church vocations.
Th.D., Southern Baptist Seminary, 1953.

SOUTHARD, S.
Counseling for church vocations.
Nashville: Broadman, 1957.

    A practical guide for those who counsel candidates for church vocations. Includes discussion of the call, theological relationships, preaching on this subject, and pastoral care of candidates.

FURTHER REFERENCES

For further references on Unique Characteristics: Procedures, see also: **A2:** Fichter 1961; **A2:** May 1934a; **A2:** Nevins.

AGNES, SISTER CECILE
Sisters as graduate students.
Sister Formation Bull., 1960–61, *7*(2), 4-8.

    Summary of **A4**: Forest.

ANDERSON, B. D.
A comparison of the pitch characteristics of selected occupational groups.
Ph.D., Purdue University, 1963.
Dissert. Abstr., 1964, *24*, 5602.

    Sample: 15 speech professors, 15 clergy, 15 Kiwanis Club members.
    Procedure: 2 speech samples were recorded and analyzed—one in a professional environment and one in a conversational setting.
    Results: Speech professors and clergy show a higher and more variable pitch in professional speaking than in conversational speaking. Clergy use significantly larger downward inflections and speech professors use significantly larger upward inflections during professional speaking than during conversational speaking. Speech professors and clergy are significantly more flexible in pitch and extent of inflections than persons from various occupations.

BAIRD, J. A.
Pre-theological training: an empirical study.
J. Bible and Relig., 1959, *27*, 303-310.

    Sample: All students at the College of

Wooster, 1952-56, who declared in their senior year their intention of entering some kind of full-time religious work. 20 of 59 religion majors replied to a questionnaire; 44 of 81 with other majors responded to a different questionnaire.
    Results: The question of redundancy was not seen as important by the students; regardless of major, they felt religion courses in college contributed to their understanding and appreciation of religion courses in seminary. Students desired a broad preparation and many felt that the religion major provided as broad a preparation as any major. Although philosophy, history, and English majors were enthusiastic about their fields as seminary preparation, many students reported that the choice of a major had relatively little importance. There was substantial agreement on courses most helpful as preparation for seminary, both religion and non-religion courses.

BROWN, R. L.
Attitude of ministers and lay leaders of the American Baptist Convention of the state of Washington on selected social issues.
Ph.D., University of Southern California, 1962.
Dissert. Abstr., 1962, *23*, 1102-1103.

    Sample: 67 ministers and 61 deacon chairmen.
    Procedure: Interview, Guttman attitude scales.

74

Results: Ministers were more liberal than the deacon chairmen toward issues of likelihood of war, law enforcement, overseas relief, and Jewish relations. Deacons were more liberal in attitudes toward church-state relations. No difference in attitudes toward liquor traffic and domestic social welfare. Differences in attitudes among ministers were related to age, among deacons to occupational level and education. Democrats tended to be more liberal than Republicans.

BROWN, R. L.

Attitudes among local Baptist church leaders in Washington state.

Sociol. soc. Res., 1963, *47,* 322-331.

Summarizes results of Brown 1962.

CARLIN, J. N.

Grief work and pastoral care practices of Baptist ministers.

Doctoral dissertation, Southern Baptist Theological Seminary, 1963.

CRAWFORD, A. A.

A study of the relative emphasis placed on Christian adult education tasks by ministers and lay workers in Methodist churches of the Indiana Conference.

Ed.D., Indiana University, 1963.

Dissert. Abstr., 1964, *24,* 3215.

Sample: 92 lay workers and 23 ministers in 23 Methodist churches in Indiana.

Procedure: A Q-sort of 56 statements on Christian education tasks sorted according to present and ideal educational emphases.

Results: Ministers are less satisfied than lay workers with the emphases presently being made. Lay workers tend to place primary emphasis upon the climate and evangelistic tasks while the ministers tend to emphasize the social action and the personal growth tasks.

DAVIS, J.

The social action pattern of the Protestant religious leader.

Amer. sociol. Rev., 1936, *1,* 105-114.

Sample: 4,700 religious leaders (97% Protestant) who returned questionnaires sent through the Religion and Labor Foundation to "100,000 religious leaders of 22 major faiths and denominations with a letter signed by 14 religious leaders of the Catholic, Jewish, and Protestant faiths."

Procedure: A 47-item questionnaire on such areas as the following: civil liberties, cooperation with labor leaders, industrial disputes, aid to underprivileged groups, jail service, willingness to organize and participate in social action.

Results: "The intentions of the minister for social justice are higher than the average for his community and this makes for tension between the ideal aims of the minister and his practical and successful functioning in the local community. A minority of the clergy satisfy this tension by radical action which is at variance with the pattern of the herd. A majority seek their outlets and satisfactions in the main in religious work, which does not involve conflict with community standards."

DUNCAN, H. G.

Reactions of ex-ministers toward the ministry.

J. Relig., 1932, *12,* 100-115.

Sample: 200 men who left the active ministry.

Procedure: 124 of them returned a questionnaire.

Results: The author discusses their reactions toward entering the ministry, reactions toward leaving it, and present participation in church activities. The better-trained men withdrew usually because of nonprogressive attitudes of their church group.

EVANS, T. Q.
The Brethren pastor: differential concep-
tions of an emerging role.
Ph.D., Ohio State University, 1960.
Dissert. Abstr., 1960, *21*, 257-258.

Reported in Evans 1963.

EVANS, T. Q.
The Brethren pastor: differential concep-
tions of an emerging role.
J. scientific stud. Relig., 1963, *3*, 43-51.

Sample: 837 lay officeholders in the
Church of the Brethren; 238 pastors. 82%
responded to the mailed questionnaire.
Procedure: A 74-item Likert-type attitude scale (reliability .70-.88; high logical
and empirical validity) was the main fea-
ture of the questionnaire. The scale was
designed to measure professionalism in the
pastoral role.
Results: Hypothesis confirmed that the
pastoral role expectations of lay officeholders differ significantly from those of
pastors. Pastors expected a greater degree
of professionalism in the rationality and
universalism dimensions than did officeholders but a lesser degree in the functional specificity dimension.

There is a discussion of the use of this
schema in studying the needs of local congregations and seminary curricula.

FECHER, C. J.
Mortality and morbidity studies of re-
ligious.
Linacre Quart., 1960, *27*, 157-165.

Previous studies in this area are reviewed. There are lower death rates (1930-
1940-1950) for young sisters than for
white women. The difference is greatest
at age 20 and decreases thereafter. Still,
today's nun lives 3 years longer than her
counterpart in the lay world. Plans for
further studies are discussed.

FECHER, C. J.
Health of religious clergy.
Rev. Relig., 1964, *23*, 316-328.

A review of studies on the mortality of
religious clergy. Some suggestions are
made on promoting better health.

FICHTER, J. H.
The religious professional: part I.
Rev. relig. Res., 1960, *1*, 89-101. (a)

Analysis of some of the literature on
the professional religious functionary, one
who has a vocation or calling from God.
The two concrete signs of such a vocation
are right intention and fitness. Problems of
occupational choice are discussed in a
comparison with the medical profession.
Specific reasons for religious vocational
choice are given, including data from an
unspecified source. The social status of the
religious professional and its determination
by the community with which the person
affiliates is also discussed. The general
high status of the clergy is stressed.

FICHTER, J. H.
The religious professional: part II.
Rev. relig. Res., 1960, *1*, 150-170. (b)

The wide variety of functions the clergy
are required to perform might prevent
those in church vocations from holding
status as "professionals," as specialization
is not frequent. The difficulty of establish-
ing criteria of success and promotion
makes the religious professional himself
the judge of his own success. Changes in
career or leaving the profession are generally more common among Protestants
than Catholics. Problems in such transi-
tions and in the change from active service
to retirement are discussed.

FOREST, CECILE A.
Sisters as graduate students: the integration of the roles of religious, teacher,
student, and scholar.

M.A., Fordham University, 1959.
See also **A4**: Agnes

> *Sample:* 230 sisters, candidates for higher degrees in the arts and sciences.
> *Procedure:* Questionnaire.
> *Results:* Only half have the desire to be productive in the after-degree period by undertaking study and research; the same number find their spiritual lives enriched by their studies. Full-time students feel less role conflict and less pressure than part-time students. More Ph.D. sisters than M.A. sisters have internalized the scholar's role expectations but a lesser number of them have achieved the integration of this secondary role with the primary one of religious.

FULTON, R. L.
The clergyman and the funeral director: a study in role conflict.
Soc. Forces, 1961, *39,* 317-323.

> *Sample:* 633 respondents of 1,802 (35%) clergy of denominations with more than one-half million members. A ratio of 1 clergyman per 95,000 members was used.
> *Procedure:* Open-ended questionnaire on the purpose and functions of the funeral duties of the funeral director and clergy, their conflicts, etc.
> *Results:* Differing views of the funeral were held by Catholics and Protestants: the Catholics emphasized meaning of the ceremony for the deceased, the Protestants for the survivors; the priest saw himself as responsible for the conduct of the service, the Protestant minister saw himself chiefly as counselor and comforter; the Catholics suggested that the funeral director's duties should include those of a social nature, the Protestants that the duties should pertain to the physical, mechanical aspects; considerably fewer Catholics than Protestants reported an overlap of their duties with those of the funeral director and the

Protestants more than Catholics stated that such overlap caused confusion, especially in the matter of final authority for the funeral. Reasons are given for the generally adverse, critical results, and for the Protestant-Catholic differences.

GLOCK, C. Y., & RINGER, B. B.
Church policy and the attitudes of ministers and parishioners on social issues.
Amer. sociol. Rev., 1956, *21,* 148-156.

> *Sample:* Ministers and laymen of 234 congregations of the Protestant Episcopal Church.
> *Procedure:* Questionnaire; content analysis of church social pronouncements.
> *Results:* Ministers' attitudes clearly reflect church policy. Ministers and laymen differ least on issues on which church policy is equivocal and most on issues where church policy is partisan.

HALL, J. O.
Note on relationships between attitudes toward the scientific method and the background of seminarians.
Soc. Forces, 1960, *39,* 49-52.

> *Sample:* 333 students in 11 Protestant seminaries in the Chicago area.
> *Procedure:* Content analysis of essays on scientific method. Additional background data.
> *Results:* "Approximately an even split between attitudes of acceptance and rejection of the scientific method of social research." Those from larger colleges and those with social science courses were found more accepting. There is no significant relation with other variables, such as age, sex, father's occupation, etc.

HIBBARD, D. L., & LEE, J. P.
Presbyterian ministers and their widows in retirement.
J. Gerontology, 1954, *9,* 46-55.

Sample: 920 retired Presbyterian ministers and 1,290 widows of Presbyterian ministers returned questionnaires.

Results: Detailed data are presented on career patterns, present interests, activities, and attitudes. "The majority of both ministers and widows seem to have adjusted adequately to the problems of retirement, report themselves as fairly secure economically, and express their belief in the importance of planning for retirement. Sizable proportions, however, of both the men and women are apparently in genuine need, not only of money, but also of adequate living accommodations, useful activity and of being wanted."

HUNT, R. A.

The semantic space of seminary students.

Unpublished mimeographed report. Fort Worth, Tex.: Author, Texas Christian University, 1964. 14 pp. + 36 supplementary pp. of tables.

Sample: 129 students from 3 Southwestern seminaries.

Procedure: Semantic differential. Subjects rated 18 concepts on 31 dimensions. Index of overachieving and underachieving compiled for 81 students (see **B2:** Hunt 1963).

Results: Clusters of concepts are presented. Interpretations are suggested for differences between underachieving and overachieving groups: e.g., "The underachiever group may seek those aspects of church life which are more structured...."

KLAUSNER, S. Z.

Role adaptation of ministers and psychiatrists in a religio-psychiatric clinic.

New York: Columbia University, Bureau of Applied Social Research, 1957. 64 pp.

Revised as Role adaptation of pastors and psychiatrists. *J. scientific stud. Relig.,* 1964, *4,* 14-39.

Sample: 6 clergymen and 6 psychiatrists at the Religio-Psychiatric Clinic connected with the Marble Collegiate Church in New York.

Procedure: Subjects took part in 15 four-man discussions on prepared questions on the nature of the Religio-Psychiatric Clinic, its ministers and psychiatrists, their roles as related to their professional identification groups, and differences in their approaches.

Results: Content analysis showed the ministers to hold an "ascriptive" concept of their role, since they were "called" to it; their relationships with patients would make the role a diffuse one, based on *integrating* the personality in question. The psychiatrists, on the other hand, saw their roles as "achievement"-oriented, since they had earned them through training. Their relationships with patients were specific and with *instrumental* connotations. The clinic is pointed out to be a joint effort which collects the "deviates" from both professions. Results are interpreted in terms of sociological concepts. A new therapist role for the minister is seen emerging within the clinic, emphasizing the achievement dimension. Results are also summarized in **D:** Klausner 1964a.

KLING, F. R.

Value structures and the minister's purpose.

Pastoral Psychol., 1961, *12*(112), 13-23. Also pp. 51-64 in **H:** Oates.

Sample: 226 ministers from 8 representative denominations (Assembly of God, American Baptist, Southern Baptist, United Lutheran, Lutheran Church-Missouri Synod, Methodist, Presbyterian U.S., and Presbyterian U.S.A.) and a layman and laywoman nominated by each minister as "most informed" about his ministry.

Procedure: 20 "goals of life" were ranked twice by each respondent (1) to represent the value structure underlying the "American way of life," and (2) to represent the minister's "total message."

Results: Minister's message is seen (substantially by ministers, slightly by lay persons) to contradict American way of life. Ministers see themselves as putting less emphasis in their message than do lay people on more traditional values, such as participation in the church and achieving personal immortality, and more emphasis than seen by laymen on more general personal and social values.

MARKERT, D. D.
Opinions about the priesthood in Catholic high school boys and minor seminarians.
Ph.D., Loyola University, 1963.

Sample: 4 groups: high school freshmen, high school seniors, first-year seminarians, fourth-year seminarians.

Procedure: Paper-and-pencil questionnaire using rating method.

Results: Seminarians tend to see other occupations as less similar to the priesthood than do their high school peers. Considerable agreement on the propriety of a priest's engaging in various activities was found. Fourth-year seminarians saw the priest as more understanding than did any other group. High school seniors saw priests as best able to help (e.g., better than counseling psychologist or psychiatrist) less often than other groups. The priest was seen by all groups as best able to help for a large number of problems.

MITCHELL, R. E.
The clergy views the National Council of Churches.
Unpublished mimeographed paper. New York: Columbia University, Bureau of Applied Social Research, 1960.

Sample: 4,031 clergymen from 8 of the 33 denominations belonging to NCC (sample also used in **B1:** Mitchell).

Procedure: Mailed questionnaire (70% return). In addition, 88 clergymen were interviewed.

Results: The sample is examined in terms of socio-economic status, region, and theology, as well as attitudes about ecumenicity, social action, and the NCC and its pronouncements.

MOORE, E. H., & HAMMER, CORRINE
Ministers in retirement.
Sociol. soc. Res., 1948, *32,* 920-927.

Sample: 73 of 90 ministers on pension from 8 Protestant church bodies returned a questionnaire.

Results: 60 were judged to be "satisfied," 11 were termed "uncertain"—"neither especially satisfied or dissatisfied, who were trying to solve their problems and adjust to their new situation"—and 2 judged "dissatisfied." Most and least satisfying experiences of retirement are discussed.

MUELLER, F. F.
The ethical aspects of ministerial practice.
Ph.D., Yale University, 1936.

Summarized as Mueller 1937.

MUELLER, F. F., & HARTSHORNE, H.
Ethical dilemmas of ministers.
New York: Charles Scribner's Sons, 1937.

Report of Mueller 1936.
Sample: 886 (59% return) Protestant clergy in New England, New York, and New Jersey, graduating between 1901 and 1930 from 10 New England seminaries.

Procedure: Questionnaire. Interviews with 100 of the sample.

Results: Summary of practice and attitudes toward such questions as marriage of divorced persons, community social action, membership recruiting practices, relations with predecessors and successors, financial discounts, gifts, fees.

MUNTZ, E. E., JR.
Opinions of divinity and law students on
social class.
J. educ. Sociol., 1961, *34*, 221-229.

Sample: 60 Duke University students:
30 law and 30 divinity.

Procedure: Interview and questionnaire
with scales for rating social classes on
altruism and laziness.

Results: Divinity students had a greater
degree of egalitarian ratings and egalitarian opinions. Law students were almost
wholly lacking in egalitarian ideology.

NEAL, SISTER MARIE A.
Values and interests in the process of
social change.
Ph.D., Harvard University, 1963.

Sample: 25% sample of the clergy in
the Archdiocese of Boston stratified by
age and type of parish.

Procedure: 259 (72%) of 347 responded to a mailed questionnaire.

Results: Of 68 background factors examined, age was most correlated with orientation of interest and value change. Over
two thirds of the value change group were
under 46 years, while less than one third
of the interest nonchange were in this category. Interest change and value nonchange
seem to be historically grounded in the
little community and represent power and
cultural isolation from broader issues of
the larger community or perception of
these broader issues only in terms of what
is already experienced in the ethnic community; thus change is related to a geographical factor. Value choices and interests with regard to social change are
determined by relatively permanent personal characteristics.

O'DONOVAN, T. R., & DEEGAN, A. X.
Some career determinants of church ex-
ecutives.
Sociol. soc. Res., 1963, *48*, 58-68.

Sample: 1,453 of 4,450 questionnaires
(32%) were returned by Catholic pastors
in metropolitan areas of 14 Midwestern
and Western states.

Results: Priests perceived as the basis
of their own selection and present appointment a combination of merit and
previous administrative experience. However, the majority indicated their belief
that seniority alone was the primary basis
for the appointment of their fellow pastors.

OLSON, A. O.
The social attitudes and social action of
some ministers of the New York Conference of the Methodist Church: a
comparative study.
Ph.D., Yale University, 1952.

Sample: 155 (89% return of 184) New
York Methodist ministers; 42 Yale Divinity students in a class in social ethics;
40 Vassar College students in a class in
sociology; 81 suburban New York high
school seniors.

Procedure: Questionnaire assessing attitudes on economics, labor relations,
other domestic and international social issues. Correlation of responses in ministerial sample with amount of education,
type of parish, and age.

Results: Ministers showed highly varying attitudes, except on issues such as al-
cohol, on which official church policy
has been clearest. Generally, ministers appeared conservative, especially in contrast
with divinity students. Ministers in industrial regions were most homogeneous and
most liberal. Ministers reported little social
action.

ROKEACH, M.
The similarity continua for Catholics,
Episcopalians, Presbyterians, Luther-
ans, Methodists, and Baptists.
In M. Rokeach, *The open and closed*

mind. New York: Basic Books, 1960. Pp. 295-299.

Sample: 5 clergy from each of the subject denominations. Also a group of college students from each denomination.

Procedure: Subjects ranked the order in which other denominations are similar to their own.

Results: General consensus on the continua of similarity (in the order given by the title). Clergy and student judgments were correlated (.85) especially among Episcopalians, Catholics, and Baptists.

SHANAS, ETHEL, & HAVIGHURST, R. J.
Retirement in four professions.
J. Gerontology, 1953, *8,* 212-221.

Sample: 4 groups of professional men were studied using a questionnaire: YMCA secretaries (N = 252), schoolteachers (N = 153), Methodist ministers (N = 1,100), and physicians (N = 138).

Results: The average age ranged from 70 for the YMCA secretaries to 75 for the ministers. Overall, 56%, though nominally retired, were still employed; 16% of the ministers were still employed. Continued work after retirement is found to be not necessarily related to either economic necessity or a desire to fill "empty" time. Professional men are found not to retire if they can avoid it.

SMITH, R. J.
An investigation of the counseling done by a group of ministers.
M.A., Northwestern University, 1950.

Sample: 44 (86% reply) full-time Methodist ministers in the Chicago Northern District.

Procedure: Mailed questionnaire.

Results: Ministers preferred counseling choices as follows: probing, evaluative, interpretive (in that order). They showed the following religious attitudes: liberal, moralistic, naturalistic (in that order). No significant correlations between counseling and religious attitudes.

TRABERT, E. A.
When ministers retire.
Lutheran Church Quart., 1945, *18,* 411-416.

Sample: 50 clergy were selected at random from the rolls of the United Lutheran Church in America. 39 (75%) returned a questionnaire.

Results: The average clergyman retired at age 69 after 42 years of service. Data are presented on income, part-time work, and spare time activities.

WAICES, V.
A survey of the attitudes of priests toward training in pastoral psychology.
M.A., Catholic University of America, 1956.

Sample: 233 of 460 questionnaires sent to a random sample (stratified) of American priests were returned (51%).

Results: Respondents favor a course in pastoral psychology in the seminary and institutes for priests already out of seminary. Priests see a need for every diocese to have a priest psychologist or psychiatrist.

WHITE, R. C.
Church leaders attitudes toward aggressive, non-aggressive, and immoral behavior.
Ph.D., University of Kentucky, 1958.
Dissert. Abstr., 1963, *24,* 2371-2372.

Sample: All Directors of Religious Education retained by Disciples of Christ churches in the United States, the ministers and 1 church school teacher from the same churches.

Procedure: 53% return of approximately 900 mailed questionnaires.

Results: In general, church leaders expressed denunciatory attitudes toward immorality, indifference to innocuous behavior, and wide differences in judging aggression and nonaggression. Church school teachers were most in need of orientation to the mental hygiene point of view, ministers next, and DRE's last. Older respondents differed from younger and noncollege-trained differed from college-trained in being more rigidly denunciatory of all behaviors.

WILEY, R. W.

A comparative evaluation of the roles of ministers, school counselors, parents, and others in assisting youth with life-work selection problems.

Ed.D., Pennsylvania State University, 1962.

Dissert. Abstr., 1963, *23,* 4205.

Sample: 4 randomly selected groups of 250 each: ministers who were members of the Pennsylvania Association of Churches, guidance counselors from the Pennsylvania State Department of Public Instruction lists, seniors in Pennsylvania high schools, parents of seniors in Pennsylvania high schools.

Procedure: Respondents read descriptions of hypothetical situations and indicated to whom they would have made the referral in each case: school guidance counselors, high school principal, teachers, family doctor, ministers, close friends of same age, or parents.

Results: Except for situations involving the selection of church work and for "selections made because of their worthwhileness," ministers were assigned less important roles by others than they assigned themselves.

ZEITLIN, J.

Disciples of the wise: the religious and social opinions of American rabbis.

Ph.D., Columbia University, 1945.

Also New York: Teachers College, Columbia University, *Contributions to Education, No. 908,* 1945.

Sample: 218 rabbis—108 reform, 77 conservative, 33 orthodox—completed a questionnaire in 1939.

Results: No theological beliefs were affirmed by the entire group, but individuals were consistently either naturalistic or supernaturalistic. Orthodox and conservative are more naturalistic than reform. The majority are committed to a utilitarian moral philosophy and an increase of social responsibility. Their preaching emphasizes the philosophy of Jewish life, theology, and the social functions of religion.

FURTHER REFERENCES

For further references on Unique Characteristics: Miscellaneous, see also: **A2:** Harte 1957; **A2:** Schmelling; **B1:** Blizzard 1955b; **B1:** Blizzard 1956b; **B1:** Hartman; **B1:** Kling; **B1:** Schnitzer; **B1:** Wood; **B4:** Herr 1962.

EFFECTIVENESS: DEFINITION

BAMBERGER, B. J.
The American rabbi—his changing role.
Judaism, 1954, *3,* 488-497.

An analysis of multiple, sometimes conflicting, demands on a rabbi, regardless of denomination, from tradition and from contemporary American culture. Attention to multiple functions of preaching, personal ministry, and community enterprise, and especially to the rabbi's desires to honor the scholarly traditions. Varying attitudes towards rabbis by laymen are cited. "Perhaps the era of confusion about rabbinical functions is now at its peak, and the process of clarification will soon begin."

BIGMAN, S. K.
Evaluating the effectiveness of religious programs.
Rev. relig. Res., 1961, 2, 97-121.

"Evaluation of the Effectiveness of the Ministry" (pp. 119-120) deals with the problem of objectives and criteria. The author recognizes that the various objectives of the roles of the minister need to be distinguished. An example is cited of the evaluation of the minister as a preacher, teacher, or communicator of norms of behavior. Depending on the objective of such preaching, a rating by the congregation, an attitude measure, or a projective test could be used to ascertain whether the specific goals have been reached.

BLIZZARD, S. W.
Changing roles of the Protestant parish minister.
CCAR Journal (Central Conference of American Rabbis), June, 1955. (a)
General introduction to study reported in subsequent publications, dealing especially with clergy role ambiguity.

BLIZZARD, S. W.
The roles of the rural parish minister, the Protestant seminaries, and the sciences of social behavior.
Relig. Educ., 1955, *50,* 383-392. (b)
Sample: 344 (65% return of initial 516) rural Protestant ministers representing a national distribution of 20 denominations, trained at 80 different seminaries.
Procedure: Questionnaire on background, rating of 6 roles according to importance, enjoyment, effectiveness (see Blizzard 1956a), rating of adequacy of pretheological studies and of seminary training.
Results: Questionnaire results are summarized, giving data on age, church size and staff, educational background, etc. Roles were ranked similarly to larger sample (see Blizzard 1956a), except that rural ministers rated organizational work higher and preaching work lower on enjoyment and effectiveness. Extensive summary of rural ministers' recommendations on education.

BLIZZARD, S. W.
The minister's dilemma.

Christian Century, 1956, *73¹,* 508-509. (a)

Sample: 690 clergymen representative of the theologically trained American Protestant parish ministry.

Procedure: 6 practitioner roles of the parish ministry—administrator, organizer, pastor, preacher, priest, teacher—were ranked 3 times according to importance, effectiveness, and enjoyment. Ministers also reported the number of hours spent each day on the above activities and their felt adequacy of preparation for each role.

Results: The rank orders within each orientation were reported as follows:

Importance: preacher, pastor, priest, teacher, organizer, administrator.

Effectiveness: preacher, pastor, teacher, priest, administrator, organizer.

Enjoyment: pastor, preacher, teacher, priest, organizer, administrator.

Time: administrator (2/5 of the day), pastor (1/4), preacher and priest (1/5), organizer (1/10), teacher (1/20).

The traditional roles of preacher, teacher, and priest were those in which the ministers felt most comfortable, while the need for more training was indicated for the neotraditional or contemporary roles of pastor, organizer, and administrator—those roles involving the necessity for personal relationships with no patterns of behavior expected or universally sanctioned.

BLIZZARD, S. W.

The parish minister evaluates his work.

Report of the 4th biennial meeting of the Association of Seminary Professors in the Practical Fields, 1956. Pp. 14-17. (b)

Progress report of research findings in the following areas: professional self-image, image of practitioner roles, churches served, community image, evaluation of education.

BLIZZARD, S. W.

The training of the parish minister.

Union Seminary Quart. Rev., 1956, *11*(2), 45-50. (c)

Seminaries should attempt to understand the "bench marks" which those in the pastoral ministry deem important: desire for self-understanding, a working doctrine of the ministry, the importance of the practitioner orientation, the need for a theology of the nontraditional offices of the ministry and behavior patterns to fulfill them, a clarification of success and effectiveness goals, and the functional use of substantive training in the content disciplines.

BLIZZARD, S. W.

The Protestant parish minister's integrating roles.

Relig. Educ., 1958, *53,* 374-380. (a)

Also pp. 143-155 in **H:** Oates.

Sample: 1,111 college- and seminary-trained clergymen in local parishes, representing 22 Protestant denominations.

Procedure: Content analysis of ministers' statements.

Results: For almost two thirds of ministers studied, one of 4 "people-oriented" role patterns is primary; they are father-shepherd, interpersonal relations specialist, parish promoter, communication problem solver. More than one sixth held two primary "idea-oriented" patterns: believer-saint and evangelist.

BLIZZARD, S. W.

The parish minister's self-image of his master role.

Pastoral Psychol., 1958, *9*(89), 25-32. (b)

Also pp. 111-122 in **H:** Oates.

Sample: 1,111 college- and seminary-trained clergy in local parishes, representing 22 Protestant denominations.

Procedure: Content analysis of ministers' statements. Informants were asked to: (1) describe the picture they give of a minister when they explain their work to others; (2) name the personality characteristics of a minister which seem to lead to effective ministry; (3) describe aspects of a minister's conduct which seem to assure success.

Results: 2 dimensions emerged as elements of the master role: the ideological or theological dimension (the minister articulates the ideology of the church, he *is* religion, his job is that of mediator, servant of God), and the functional dimension (the minister is service-oriented, filling the needs of his people). Lutheran, Presbyterian, and Protestant Episcopal clergy were most strong in expressing the theoretical or ideological aspects, while Methodist clergy tended to see their role from the operational, functional point of view. Contradictions in answers to 2 and 3 above (effectiveness and success) gave evidence of the conflict of ministers. The 3 most-mentioned criteria in each classification were as follows: (1) effectiveness: character, outgoing personality, skill as a pastor-counselor; (2) success: general ability in practitioner roles, cooperation in denominational programs, outgoing personality.

BLIZZARD, S. W.

The layman's understanding of the ministry.

Pp. 50-65 in **H:** Southard. (a)

A summary of the sources of attitudes towards clergymen which laymen receive from the general culture, including novels and news accounts, through local community activities, and through church participation.

BLIZZARD, S. W.

The parish minister's self-image and variability in community culture.

Pastoral Psychol., 1959, *10*(97), 27-36. (b)

Granting the differences in community structure and culture, there exists an implication that there is a basic orientation that every minister needs, whatever the uniqueness of the demands and expectations he may encounter in a particular community.

BLIZZARD, S. W.

The clergyman views himself.

Christian Advocate, 1960, *4*(25), 10-11.

Condensation of Blizzard 1958a.

CLIPPINGER, J. A.

The pastoral role of the minister.

Ph.D., Yale University, 1950.

Also see **B4:** Clippinger.

Sample: 61 ministers in northeastern United States nominated as successful by local or regional church officials, or by others, such as professors or physicians.

Procedure: Structured interviews with ministers.

Results: A report of the ministers' pastoral activities and methods and conceptions of their pastoral work (Chap. 5). Compilation of ministers' perceptions of influences which contributed to their success as pastors and with extended quotes and summaries of interviews. Empirical study is in the context of historical and theological discussion of the pastoral role and the author's recommendations concerning the pastoral role and pastoral training.

CORR, MIRIAM H.

The relationship of "ego-strength" to adjustment in religious life.

M.A., Catholic University of America, 1963.

CRAWFORD, E. E., JR.
The leadership role of the urban Negro minister.
Ph.D., Boston University, 1957.

>   *Sample:* 161 Negro Baptist ministers in the urban Chicago area.
>   *Procedure:* Interview.
>   *Results:* The ministers' leadership is a "crescive type with a predominance of crisis roles." 81% are from the South; 72% have no academic degree. The ministers' role expectations revolve around the crisis of urbanization.

DONOVAN, J. D.
The Catholic priest: a study in the sociology of the professions.
Ph.D., Harvard University, 1951.

>   Analysis is made of 30 interviews and questionnaires from 139 seminarians. The ecclesiastical life history of the diocesan priest is described in terms of the different temporal status positions he holds and the separate patterns and problems of each. The priesthood is analyzed in terms of the structural imperatives functionally and dysfunctionally present to its definition as an office in the bureaucratic organization of the church.

FAIRCHILD, R. W., & WYNN, J. C.
Families in the church: a Protestant survey.
New York: Association Press, 1961.

>   Chap. 7: "The Church's ministry to families," pp. 202-257.
>   *Sample:* 2,645 Presbyterian ministers (75% return from 3,541). Data from random sample of 1,000 returned questionnaires were analyzed.
>   *Procedure:* 120-item mailed questionnaire covering attitudes towards family

life and problems and understandings of the relation of the church and pastor to family life.

>   *Results:* Summarized, including 9 tables. Individual counseling and referral is emphasized as an effective form of ministry to families. 9 reported problems in the pastors' own family life are discussed.

FICHTER, J. H.
Social relations in the urban parish.
Chicago: University of Chicago Press, 1954.

>   Chap. 10, "Social roles of the parish priest," pp. 123-137. "The present dynamic situation in the urban American parish seems to require not so much the emphasis of one role more than another as a simultaneous co-ordination of multiple roles." The traditional basic functions of the priest as mediator and father have become subdivided into the following roles: communal, administrative, businessman, civic, recreational, ameliorative, educational, socio-spiritual, and liturgical.

FLEMING, D. S.
The university parish pastor: a national study of the functions of the preaching pastor at a college or university Methodist church as they relate to student life in the U.S.
Th.D., Pacific School of Religion, 1961.
Dissert. Abstr., 1963, *23,* 3244-3245.

>   The "ideal" university parish pastor, described from the author's experience and reading, is compared with the "typical" university parish pastor, described from a 53% return (N = 224) of a questionnaire to Methodist college ministers.

FURTH, H. G.
The psychology of John Cassian.
M.A., University of Ottawa, 1953.

>   An examination of the "ideal" monk

from an analysis of the fourth-century writings of Cassian.

GLOCK, C. Y., & ROOS, P.
Parishioners' views of how ministers spend their time.
Rev. relig. Res., 1961, *2,* 170-175.

Sample: Members of 12 urban Lutheran congregations in the East and Midwest.
Procedure: Descriptive questionnaire survey.
Results: The pastoral (including evangelistic) and preaching functions are seen by parishioners as most time-consuming and they prefer that the minister focus on these tasks. Comparisons are made with Blizzard's results. (**B1:** Blizzard 1956a.)

GOLDSTEIN, S. E.
The roles of an American rabbi.
Sociol. soc. Res., 1953, *38,* 32-37.

A brief description of each of the multiple functions of an American rabbi: teacher and scholar, educator, preacher, prayer leader, pastor, organizer, administrator, and an ambassador of good will to the non-Jewish world. Rabbis must make decisions as to relative priorities among these. Their decisions of relative priorities are not always the same as their congregations'; this is often because the laymen are not so familiar with Jewish traditions and base their preferences on personal opinions.

GOODLING, R. A., & WEBB, S. C.
An analysis of faculty ratings of theology students.
Relig. Educ., 1959, *54,* 228-233.

Sample: 144 students at Candler School of Theology (Emory), 56 of whom took field work.
Procedure: Faculty rating scales, SVIB, academic averages, GZTS, field work ratings, OSUPE, Cooperative English.

Results: Faculty ratings for intelligence, interest, personality, and total effectiveness showed high intercorrelations significant at .01 level. Associative, not causative, relationship of predictor variables and faculty ratings are discussed. The study is presented as exploratory.

HARTMAN, C. Y.
Social casework and pastoral counseling: a study of perceived similarities and differences of the goals and methods of two helping professions.
D.S.W., Washington University, 1962.
Dissert. Abstr., 1963, *24,* 1739.

Sample: 50 Protestant ministers and 50 social caseworkers.
Procedure: Recorded interviews.
Results: Differences in philosophical orientation were apparent: ministers aimed at realizing a harmonious relationship between man and God while caseworkers aimed at helping man achieve stable relationships with man and society. However, in general, similar problems were treated by both and similar techniques were used. Problems related to religion were not encountered frequently but were dealt with in different ways by the two groups. There was agreement that clients chose a minister or caseworker more often because of the nature of the counseling relationship than because of the differences in philosophical orientation or perceptions of the competence of the practitioner. A need was found to clarify the professional counseling roles of both groups, especially with regard to religious problems.

HILTNER, S., & COLSTON, L. G.
The context of pastoral counseling.
New York: Abingdon Press, 1961.

Sample: 9 pairs of counselees, matched by age, sex, and type of problem.

Procedure: The same person counseled with half the subjects in the role of a minister within a church, and with half the subjects in the role of a psychologist in a counseling center. 3 tests were administered before and after counseling and again, to half the subjects, several months after counseling: TAT, "Adjustment-through-self-concept" Q-sort by Butler and Haigh, and 3 social attitude scales from "The Authoritarian Personality": Ethnocentrism, Religious Conventionalism, and Traditional Family Ideology.

Results: Nonsignificant tendency on some data for church-counseled persons to have improved more. The report descriptively summarizes some of the differences in role perception in the 2 contexts.

INSLEO, W. R.

A study of women directors of Christian education in the parishes of the Episcopal Church in the continental United States.

Ed.D., Duke University, 1960.

A descriptive study of 169 women Christian education directors in the Episcopal Church (66 of the 257 originally contacted); 56 were also interviewed. 75% are full-time, 54% hold a B.A., 34% hold graduate degrees. Results are discussed in terms of responsibilities, satisfactions, dissatisfactions.

JACKSON, D. E.

Reliability of ratings in terms of effectiveness within the ministerial profession.

M.A., Northwestern University, 1946.

Ministers were assigned to "effective" and "ineffective" categories on the basis of peer ratings. A significant relationship was found between effectiveness and various "statistical items" (salary, number of members, etc.) and among the statistical

items themselves. These ratings were apparently used in **B3**: Jackson.

JAMMES, JEAN M.

The Catholic people and their priests: expectations—criticisms—mistakes.

Ph.D., University of Chicago, 1954.

Sample: 389 adult Catholic laymen and nuns, recruited on various occasions by author, a priest. Regarded by author as representative of Catholics in Chicago.

Procedure: Questionnaire of 17 open-ended items, chiefly concerning attitudes towards "mistakes" by priests.

Results: Priest is regarded "familially" as an intimate member of the group he serves, not as a remote religious specialist. He is expected more to participate in the life of his people than to assume special functions or powers delegated by them. His mistakes are regarded "tenderly," as his personal human failings and not attributed to his role or institution, to be discussed frankly with him and with other Catholics but to be disguised from non-Catholics. Laymen regard themselves more as a "partner" than a "client" of pastor. Biggest possible mistake would be to "become professional."

JAQUEZ, O.

Personality integrated on the Franciscan ideal.

B.A., Duns Scotus College (Detroit, Michigan), 1956.

Examines the "ideal" Franciscan in terms of an Allport personality theory. Special emphasis is placed on integration of traits around a personal ideal.

JOHNSON, J. G.

An analysis and description of role expectations for ministers of the Southern California district of the Lutheran Church-Missouri Synod.

Ph.D., University of Southern California, 1961.

Dissert. Abstr., 1962, *22,* 4431-4432.

> *Sample:* Ministers, teachers, laymen, etc. N not reported in abstract.
>
> *Procedure:* Questionnaire.
>
> *Results:* With increasing size of congregation, the minister is expected to handle a smaller number of tasks. There is a stereotype about the type of obligation the minister has to engage in specific activities.

KLING, F. R.

Roles of the parish minister.

Princeton, N. J.: Educational Testing Service, 1959. 5 pp.

> *Sample:* 226 ministers from 8 representative denominations (Assembly of God, American Baptist, Southern Baptist, United Lutheran, Lutheran Church-Missouri Synod, Methodist, Presbyterian U.S., and Presbyterian U.S.A.) and a layman and laywoman nominated by each minister as "most informed" about his ministry.
>
> *Procedure:* Ministers and laymen each ranked the 30 activities twice (1) to describe the minister's activities and (2) to indicate their expectations of the ideal minister's performance. Rankings were factor-analyzed.
>
> *Results:* 7 identifiable factors appear to confirm common distinctions of practitioner roles. Laymen perceived minister as doing less visiting in homes, less counseling and working with adults, and more private prayer and study, than ministers perceived themselves. Laymen expected more work with children and young people, more peace-making in the church and promoting of church activities, and less personal study and devotions, than ministers expected. Many more rankings, however, showed congruence than differences.

KLINK, T. W.

The career of preparation for the ministry.

J. pastoral Care, 1964, *19,* 200-207.

> "The career of theological education is the passage of a young *layman* through the various stages of *student* and *proto-minister* to established clergyman." While there is some success in estimating narrow-range success and adjustment (in seminary) and long-range or ultimate success (in the ministry), we lack intermediate process criteria for evaluating progress in professional preparation. The study of persons involved in clinical pastoral training at various points in the "career" of preparation for the ministry is recommended. Generalizations are listed which define intermediate processes in that "career."

KOLARIK, J. M.

A study of the critical requirements of the Lutheran ministry.

Ph.D., University of Pittsburgh, 1954.

Dissert. Abstr., 1954, *14,* 2395-2396.

> *Sample:* 472 laymen and 127 ministers from the Lutheran Church-Missouri Synod.
>
> *Procedure:* Questionnaire booklet asking for critical requirements for the ministry.
>
> *Results:* The 1,152 behaviors contained in the responses provided a listing of 13 major areas of activity. The list can be used for a minister's own self-evaluation and in field work training.

LAZURE, J. M.

The definition of the priest-teacher's role: role theory applied to an empirical survey.

Ph.D., Harvard University, 1963.

> *Sample:* 225 priest-teachers from 15 of

the 58 classical colleges of Quebec. 214 were interviewed.

Procedure: An interview schedule was derived from a 4-part role theory: motivations, goals, norms, and external activities.

Results: A great deal of variability in the definition of the priest-teacher's role was found together with a role differentiation process along the time dimension and an inner source of tension and conflict within the role definition itself. The priest role (pastoral) plays a greater part in the definition of the composite role than does the teacher (academic) role. The strength and extension of the pastoral conception of the priest-teacher's role depends upon the goals pursued by the classical colleges where they teach, while that of the academic conception of the role depends upon his degree of academic specialization.

LEIFFER, M. H.
The layman looks at the minister.
New York: Abingdon-Cokesbury, 1947.

Sample: All district and associate district lay leaders in the Methodist Church. In order to avoid homogeneity within the sample, a supplemental sample of a "representative group" of women and two groups of young people under 25 years of age were included. An estimated 1,500 individuals were represented in the total response.

Procedure: 71-item questionnaire with the format, "How acceptable will a minister be in your church if . . . ?" Responses were given on a 5-point scale ranging from "We very much desire this . . ." to "This would disqualify."

Results: Generally, Methodists were socially liberal, with a high ideal for the ministry. The respondents ranked as undesirable the pessimistic minister who takes no initiative on "Christian issues,"

who takes a part-time job or whose wife works, whose theological views disagree with those of the congregation, who makes few pastoral calls or is unable to counsel, who refuses to try and correct "unwholesome community conditions," who is of a different race than the majority of the congregation, who is untidy in personal appearance, or who does not get along with his wife. Ranked as desirable was the man who spends the major portion of his time with the young people's program, who stresses loyalty to the denomination and its organization, who cooperates in community, interchurch services, and who stresses equal opportunity for all races. Responses to other items are included in the sections on the minister as preacher, pastor and administrator; the minister and community responsibilities and social issues; the minister as a man; and the minister the laymen want.

MADDEN, MARY L.
Role definitions of Catholic sister educators and expectations of students, their parents and teaching sisters in selected areas of the U.S.
Ph.D., Catholic University of America, 1960.
Abstract published by Catholic University of America Press: *Stud. Sociol. Abstr. Series,* 1960, *14.*

Sample: 2,597 persons associated with 15 Catholic high schools: 38% parents, 57% students, 5% sisters.

Procedure: Questionnaire.

Results: There is clear support for the hypothesis that "religious educators teaching in secondary schools differ among themselves in the definition of their role and that expectations of that role expressed by sophomore and senior girls and the parents of these students vary significantly both on an intragroup and intergroup basis."

MARIAN, DOLORES
Creative personality in religious life.
New York: Sheed and Ward, 1963.

Perfection and maturity on the natural level should serve as supplements to a life of grace; mental health should make the religious more receptive to the movements of grace. Elementary psychological information for the religious is provided in such areas as personality theory, defense mechanisms, adjustment, interpersonal relationships, counseling, and creativity. Illustrations consistently involve the religious. "The measure of religious maturity is the measure of progress toward a Christ-o-centric spirituality and a severance from an egocentric mentality."

McCANN, R. V.
The churches and mental health.
New York: Basic Books, 1962.

A compiled description of direct and indirect mental health activities engaged in by clergy and religious institutions. Data from 4 original studies are summarized:

Chap. 8: "The mental hospital patient looks at the chaplain."
Sample: 100 patients at each of 2 state hospitals.
Procedure: Interview on relations with chaplains and other clergy and their relative helpfulness.
Results: Half the patients received and wanted help from the chaplain, half did not. They desired his role to be that of a religious pastor, not an adjunctive therapist.

Chap. 9: "Religion and mental health in two communities."
Sample: 160 laymen in 2 communities.
Procedure: 1-hour interview on attitudes towards clergy and psychiatrists.
Results: Qualitative summary of interviews suggests a strong tendency for persons to deal with problems themselves and to resist professional help of either clergy or psychiatrists. Clergymen seem far more accessible than psychiatrists but whether or not anyone actually approaches the clergymen is seen to depend on personality characteristics of both.

Chap. 10: "Self-observation of the clergy in mental health endeavor."
Sample: 166 Protestant ministers, 45 Roman Catholic priests, 80 rabbis. A relatively random national sample.
Procedure: Mailed questionnaire asking broad questions on relation of ministry to mental health.
Results: "A picture emerges . . . of men in a dilemma: considerable ambivalence about the efficacy of religious resources, and at the same time reservations and anxiety about referring parishioners to psychiatrists and other professional resources. Serious barriers to communication, to understanding, to perception seem to exist between clergyman and psychiatrist, between clergyman and parishioner, and often between clergyman and clergyman."

Chap. 11: "Psychiatrists view the clergy."
Sample: 24 psychiatrists in private practice, a random selection of psychiatrists in one city.
Procedure: Interview up to 1 hour asking general questions on attitudes towards religion and the clergy.
Results: "On the whole there seems to be an uninhibited recognition of the importance of the clergyman's role in mental health combined with criticism directed at the way this role has been played in the past and a lesser degree of criticism directed at the way it is still being played. None is opposed to religion. . . ." Psychiatrists emphasize prospective counseling role of clergyman, rather than other activities of the clergyman or the congregation.

McCARTHY, T. N.
Characteristics of the psychologically
   healthy brother.
Unpublished paper. Philadelphia: Author,
   LaSalle College, 1963. (a)

   The following characteristics of a
healthy brother are discussed with reference to psychological theory and research:
is aware of himself as an individual, lives
by a unifying philosophy, has attainable
goals to which he is deeply committed,
has a finely developed sense of right and
wrong, an objective view of people, and
charity for others.

McCARTHY, T. N.
Signs of psychological trouble.
Unpublished paper. Philadelphia: Author,
   LaSalle College, 1963. (b)

   Anxiety is often indicated in brothers
by behavior such as withdrawal, alcoholism, compulsive behavior, and excessive
intellectualization. Hostility may lead to
passive resistance and even suicide.
Healthy, positive ways of expressing the
sex impulse should be explored.

McCARTNEY, J. L.
Eliminating unstable personalities in can-
   didates for the mission field.
Med. J. & Rec., 1930, *131,* 627-630.
Psychol. Abstr., 1930, *4,* 3459.

   A detailed account of the numerous
types of failure in missionary work with
a recommendation for the psychiatric
analysis of candidates for such work, in
order to save the large expense, time, and
trouble now entailed by invaliding the unstable workers home.

MEYER, R.
Responses of seminarians and laymen to
   the Religious Apperception Test.
M.A., Loyola University (Chicago), 1960.

Sample: 50 seminarians from several
religious orders.
   Procedure: The RAT is a 10-picture
projective test patterned after the TAT.
Each picture shows a priest in some situation.
   Results: Only 4 of the cards elicited
explicit themes concerning mental health
principles. Similar themes in stories seem
to have been prompted by a specific object around which the story was built. 5
of the cards produced more of a description than an ego-involved story.

MITCHELL, R. E.
Minister-parishioner relations.
New York: Columbia University, Bureau
   of Applied Social Research, Report
   #263, 1962.

   Sample: 3,928 parish ministers from 8
Protestant denominations (also used in
A4: Mitchell).
   Procedure: Questionnaire on facts and
attitudes.
   Results: The occupation is examined
sociologically in terms of what ministers
do and why they do it, as well as the
sources and functions of intellectual, social, and personal obstacles separating
ministers from their parishioners.

MURPHY, G. L.
The social role of the prison chaplain.
Ph.D., University of Pittsburgh, 1956.
Dissert. Abstr., 1957, *17,* 1142.

   Sample: 200 prison wardens and superintendents and 385 chaplains at the same
institutions.
   Procedure: 125 warden and superintendent and 136 chaplain questionnaires
were analyzed. Inmates from one institution contributed critical incidents of
chaplain behavior.
   Results: In general, wardens and chaplains agree on the definition of the chaplain's role. In only a few activities were

differences based on religious affiliation found. 43% of chaplains exhibit role conflict. Protestants are somewhat better satisfied with prison work than Catholic or Jewish chaplains.

PLYLER, H. E.
Variation of ministerial roles by size and location of church.
Ph.D., University of Missouri, 1961.
Dissert. Abstr., 1962, *22,* 2904-2905.

> *Sample:* 63 Methodist ministers, the bishop, and 12 district superintendents of the Missouri area.
> *Procedure:* Interviews.
> *Results:* Discusses the activities of ministers in relation to single or multiple church charges and size of membership.

ROUSSET, SUZY
Woman's psychological maturity.
In *Obedience.* Westminster, Md.: Newman, 1953. Pp. 154-166. (Religious Life Series, III.)

> Psychological maturity can perhaps be described as that of a woman who has a hold over herself. Problems encountered on the way to maturity include attachment to mother, sexual attitudes, relationship to the superior.

RUSCH, W. G.
Critical requirements for directors and ministers of Christian education in the Presbyterian Church in the U.S.A.
Ph.D., University of Pittsburgh, 1957.

SANTOPOLO, F. A.
The priest: a projective analysis of role.
Ph.D., Fordham University, 1956.

> *Sample:* A pilot study with no attempt at a representative sample or statistical analysis. Uses lay and ordained subjects.
> *Procedure:* Priest Role Apperception

Test, 10 drawings of priest-laity relations, in conventional and nontraditional relations, about which stories are written.

> *Results:* Males are less committed than females in classifying interactions as either antagonistic or harmonious. More males than females accept priests' conventional actions. Religious, more than seminarians or lay collegians, view interaction as harmonious. Religious more than seminarians or laity are consistently inclined to reject lay persons' actions.

SCHNITZER, J.
Rabbis and counseling: report on a project.
Jewish Soc. Stud., 1958, *20,* 131-152.

> *Sample:* 682 questionnaires were analyzed (576 of 2,000 mailed to rabbis plus 106 rabbis who were attending a conference) and interviews were completed with 106 conference attendees. The research was done in 1950.
> *Results:* Most rabbis agreed on the importance of the pastoral and counseling roles but showed little acceptance of the fact that counseling has already developed as an organized field of practice. Many felt that their education, which included no specialized training in counseling, was adequate. Such training usually emphasized the role of good preacher who is logical and persuasive.

SCHROEDER, W. W.
Lay expectations of the ministerial role: an exploration of Protestant-Catholic differentials.
J. scientific stud. Relig., 1963, *2,* 217-227.

> *Sample:* 800 church members, stratified sample, in 2 Midwest towns.
> *Procedure:* 2 questions included in interview concerning (1) qualities most valued in a religious professional, and (2) the degree to which a religious profes-

sional should conduct himself differently from other persons.

Results: Protestants and Catholics agreed in preferring "emotive" (e.g., "be able to get along with people") qualities as compared with "religious" or "instrumental." Protestants, and Catholics in a Protestant-dominated town, did not expect a difference between lay and clergy behavior. Catholics in a Catholic-dominated town did.

SEGER, IMOGEN

Responsibility for the community.

Ph.D., Columbia University, 1961.

Totowa, N. J.: Bedminster Press.

Sample: Pastors and laymen of 7 Lutheran churches in the downtown areas of U.S. cities.

Procedure: Analysis of information already obtained by National Lutheran Council questionnaires and clergy interviews.

Results: Part of the analysis divides the congregations into satisfied (3) and dissatisfied (4). Role of the pastor is then examined in terms of community activity, sermons, etc.

SIZER, L. M.

Role conception, role discrepancy, and institutional context: a study of the Protestant ministry.

Ph.D., State University of Iowa, 1954.

Dissert. Abstr., 1954, *14,* 2428.

Sample: Ministers and lay leaders in (1) student minister churches, (2) non-student minister churches in Bangor, Maine, and (3) Boston area churches.

Procedure: Questionnaire items on the tasks of a minister.

Results: No significant differences found in role discrepancy (minister and lay) according to type of church (denomination, size, theology, location, etc.).

SOMMERFELD, R. E.

Role conceptions of Lutheran ministers in the St. Louis area.

Ph.D., Washington University, 1957.

Dissert. Abstr., 1957, *17,* 915.

Sample: 65 ministers of the Lutheran Church-Missouri Synod.

Procedure: Open-ended interview.

Results: Lutheran ministers have a sharply conceived preaching role but are confused about their role as liturgist. They counsel within a supernatural and spiritual framework. There is little cooperative effort and mutual exchange of thoughts and ideas between congregations.

SOUTHARD, S.

Criteria for evaluating supervisors-in-training.

J. pastoral Care, 1963, *17,* 193-202.

The training of supervisors in clinical pastoral education through a graduate training seminar has supported the following criteria: competence as a counselor of patients, communication of pastoral attitudes to students, and identity as a theological teacher. They will be more useful as criteria when used from the beginning of supervision to determine the effectiveness of instructors in clinical pastoral education.

SPOERL, H. D.

The social psychology of pastorship.

The New Christianity, 1945, *11*(1), 11-21.

Traditional pastoral psychology may be said to suffer from its own emphasis on the "specialist attitude" and from its almost exclusive preoccupation with individual problems. The prime essential of the pastoral relationship is that it be cooperative. The minister is primarily a pastor and secondarily a priest or preacher. The pastor is one who adjusts religious insights to shared experience.

STERN, G. G.
Assessing theological student personality structure.
J. pastoral Care, 1954, *8,* 76-83.
Also see Chapter 4 in **A1:** Stern 1956.

Report of a study which attempted early prediction of the student's success or failure as a minister. From discussions with the faculty a model of the ideal student was determined. With that model in mind the assessment team evaluated 6 students (3 ideal, 3 poor) selected by the faculty. In each case the student was identified correctly as ideal or poor. The study is presented as successful exploratory work in identifying successful students (not necessarily successful ministers).

STOGDILL, R. M., GOODE, O. S., & DAY, D. R.
New leader behavior description subscales.
J. Psychol., 1962, *54,* 259-269.

Sample: 150 ministers: Protestant, Roman Catholic, Jews; 150 community leaders.

Procedure: 103 ministers returned 2 questionnaires in which members of their congregations described their leadership. 579 descriptions of other community leaders were also returned.

Results: Factor analysis produced 10 factors. Most clearly identified: initiation of structure, facilitation of group action, prediction accuracy, representative of member interest, motivation of congregation, persuasive role enactment. Demand reconciliation was associated with low role enactment for community leaders but with low consideration for ministers.

VALLEJO-NAGERA, A.
Influencia de la psicología normal y anormal en la vida religiosa.
In *Conducta religiosa y salud mental.*
Madrid: VII Congreso Catolica Inter-

nacional de Psicoterapía ya Psicología Clinica, 1959. Pp. 235-241.
Also in *Rev. Espir.,* 1957, *16,* 475-483.

The principal aim of Catholic life is the direction of our psychic life and psychological reactions to God's service. Psychic tendencies which draw us away from following God's moral code must be curbed. Abnormality does not hinder salvation, nor is it incompatible with religious life. Testing procedures for selection of candidates to religious life are discussed. (Abstract by Meissner.)

VIVONA, A. F.
Some attitudes and practices of the clergy on marriage counseling.
M.A., Catholic University of America, 1960.

Sample: 151 (39%) of the priests of the Dioceses of Brooklyn and Rockville Centre, New York.

Procedure: Questionnaire, some interviews.

Results: A typical priest averages 2.7 marriage cases a month and considers 3 or less interviews per person or couple adequate. He avoids outside lay assistance but sometimes makes referrals to an M.D. or psychiatrist. The counselor's theoretical approach is eclectic.

WEBB, N. J.
Measurement of attitude and information changes in mental health concepts among seminarians.
Ph.D., Loyola University (Chicago), 1959.
See also **B4:** Webb.

Describes development and validation on a seminary population of the Loyola NIMH Attitude to Psychiatry Scale and the NIMH Achievement Test to be used to measure changes produced by new curriculum materials. Both instruments showed adequate reliability, validity, and sensitivity to changes if they do occur.

WEBB, S. C.

A factor analytic study of the roles of the minister.

Unpublished paper. Emory University, Ga.: Author, Emory University, undated.

Sample: 310 male students entering 13 Protestant seminaries in 1961.

Procedure: 300-item "inventory of religious activities and interests," constructed to represent 30 (10 items each) intended roles. Factor analysis.

Results: Author interprets the factor analysis as confirming the intended 30 roles. 17 higher-order roles emerge from the correlation among the original 30.

WHIPPLE, C. E.

The teaching ministry of the priest in the Episcopal church.

Ed.D., New York University, 1959.

Dissert. Abstr., 1960, *20,* 3412.

Procedure: Literature defining the teaching ministry of the Episcopal priest was surveyed. A questionnaire was sent to each parochial priest (N not given in abstract).

Results: There seems to be no discrepancy between the theoretical and actual teaching ministry of the priest in the Episcopal Church. The average priest spends over 50% of his time in education, half of this in connection with the church school. Other regular duties include Confirmation instruction, Baptism, and Matrimony.

WOOD, C. L.

Functions of the parish priest in the Episcopal diocese of New Jersey.

Ed.D., Rutgers University, 1964.

Dissert. Abstr., 1964, *25,* 2870.

Sample: 81 (50%) of the active clergy of the diocese made valid replies. Clergy recruited the lay sample of 622 valid returns, from 46 parishes.

Procedure: A 3-page questionnaire containing 66 paired comparison items of 12 clergy activities: community activity, member visitation, ministry to the sick, parish administration, parish meetings, personal counseling, private prayer, study, teaching, visiting nonmembers, worship services, and youth activity. Subjects were asked to check the item in each pair which they thought was more important in the daily work of the parish priest in the Episcopal Church, or which they thought the priest should do if he had a choice between the 2 items.

Results: No significant differences between over-all selections of clergy and over-all selections of lay people; both gave high priority to public worship, ministry to the sick, and pastoral counseling, and low priority to community activity and visiting of nonmembers. Despite over-all agreement, there were significant differences between lay and clergy groups on specific activities, including youth activity, which ranked third in total number of lay choices and eighth in total number of clergy choices, and private prayer, fifth in total number of clergy choices and tenth in total lay choices.

FURTHER REFERENCES

For further references on Effectiveness: Definition, see also: **A1:** Judy; **A2:** Fichter 1961; **A2:** May 1934b; **A2:** Rotz; **A4:** Crawford; **A4:** Kling; **A4:** Smith; **A4:** Wiley; **B2:** Ashbrook 1964; **B2:** Douglas; **B2:** Hamilton 1956; **B2:** Parrot; **B4:** May; **C:** Kanter; **C:** Maurer; **C:** Oden; **D:** Blizzard; **D:** Chamberlain; **D:** Kendall; **D:** Scherer 1964 and 1965.

EFFECTIVENESS: PERSONALITY

ANDERSON, G. C.
Emotional health of the clergy.
Christian Century, 1953, *70²*, 1260-1261.
Also pp. 33-39 in **H:** Oates.
Reprinted by Academy for Religion and
Mental Health, 16 E. 34th St., New
York 16, N. Y. 8 pp.

A popular article discussing several
neurotic needs which serve as barriers to
maturity in ministers.

ARBAUGH, G. B.
Guiding men out of the ministry—and in.
Lutheran Church Quart., 1943, *16,*
227-248.

Concludes that the chief mark of un-
fitness for the ministry is a poor personality. "Personalized guidance for broad
growth" is suggested as a new technique
for guiding men into the ministry and
within it. The SVIB and Bell are mentioned.

ARNOLD, MAGDA B.
The self-image through self-projection.
Cathol. Counsel., 1962, 7, 17-23. (a)

Preliminary report on Arnold 1962b.

ARNOLD, MAGDA B.
A screening test for candidates for re-
ligious life.
Pp. 1-63 in Arnold *et al.* 1962. (b)

A special scoring system for the TAT,
the "story sequence analysis," was developed, based on abstracting the theme
repeated in a series of responses to selected TAT cards. Illustrations are offered
of how these schemes are abstracted and
interpreted. A simple 4-point scale is suggested for quantitatively assessing "positive" or "negative" attitudes. Definition
of positive or negative is left to the clini-
cian's judgments of the requirements of
the particular situation, such as of a religious vocation. Three validating studies
are cited, **B2:** Burkard, **B2:** Quinn, and
a study finding high positive correlation
(.84) between college grades and positive
attitudes inferred from this TAT method.

ARNOLD, MAGDA B., HISPANICUS, P.,
WEISGERBER, C. A., & D'ARCY, P. F.
*Screening candidates for the priesthood
and religious life.*
Chicago: Loyola University Press, 1962.

Report of 4 studies growing out of the
Catholic part of the NIMH Religion and
Mental Health Project. See entry for each
author.

ASHBROOK, J. B.
Evaluating seminary students as potential
ministers.
M.A., Ohio State University, 1962.

Sample: Colgate Rochester Divinity
School students: 28 second-year, 30 third-
year.
Procedure: Criterion variables: ranking
as potentially scholarly pastors by faculty,
peers, and self; seminary grade point
average; field work ratings. Tests used:

97

MAT, GRE, Cooperative English 1, MMPI.

Results: Highly significant correlations among faculty ratings, peer ratings, and grades. Very high self-rating related with low ranking on other criteria.

ASHBROOK, J. B.

Protestant ministerial attributes and their implications for church organization.

Ph.D., Ohio State University, 1964.

Sample: 117 ministers (65% of the population) from 6 denominations in the Rochester, New York, area (Episcopal, Presbyterian, National Association of Evangelicals, Baptist, Methodist, and Lutheran). 534 (91%) of 585 lay people nominated by these pastors (5 each) also participated; these tended to be men, married, educated, attenders of worship, and generally representative of church leadership.

Procedure: Clergy sample: T-F and J-P scales of Myers-Briggs Type Indicator; self-ratings of satisfaction in nine career tasks and of effectiveness. Lay sample: Leader Behavior Description Questionnaire; ratings of effectiveness, church's religious training, church success. Data on church size and budget.

Results: Correlation among criteria: Lay ratings, except of church success, not correlated with church size or budget. Clergy ratings of effectiveness not correlated with any other criteria. Characteristics of clergy: score high on F (more aware of people than of ideas) and on J (prefer planning life than adapting to it flexibly); scores validated by self and lay descriptions. Correlation with criteria: Myers-Briggs scores not correlated with church size; T and P scores correlated with lower lay ratings. Self-ratings of satisfaction correlated with criteria in patterns suggesting moderate satisfaction optimal. On LBDQ, toleration of member freedom,

task skill, initiation of structure correlated with criteria generally.

ASHBROOK, J. B., & GUTHRIE, H.

When ministers face themselves: a candid study of the personal life of the minister.

The Pulpit, 1960, *31,* 168-172.

A report on the personal life of the minister resulting from experience with a year's group therapy. Areas discussed: guilt, uncertainty, insecurity, competition, criticism. It is essential for a minister to be as "whole" a person as possible. He needs to be so integrated that his outer life and his inner life complement each other rather than compete with each other.

ATWATER, C. R.

A study of personnel services in Protestant theological schools.

Ed.D., Boston University, 1961.

A questionnaire study of 65 seminaries and of middler students at 25 of them. Surveys such areas as psychological testing, faculty advising, professional counseling service.

AYD, F. J.

Types suited or unsuited for religious vocation.

In *Proc. 8th annu. Convocation of the Voc. Inst.* Notre Dame, Ind.: Notre Dame Press, 1955. Pp. 36-42.

BARNES, C. W.

Some aspects of guilt as related to the preaching of Protestant ministers in Massachusetts.

Th.D., Boston University School of Theology, 1962.

Dissert. Abstr., 1962, *23,* 1805.

Sample: 92 ministers, a 5% sample of ministers of the churches affiliated with the Massachusetts Council of Churches.

Procedure: Motivational Analysis Test, Sentence Completions Test, content analysis of sermons, interview.

Results: Preaching represents and symbolizes the dynamic relationship of personality factors. The unrealized self-image and vocational-image of the minister contribute to his sense of guilt and carry consequences for his preaching activity and his pastoral effectiveness.

BECKER, A. J.
A study of the personality traits of successful religious women of teaching orders.
In M. Katz (Ed.), *The twentieth yearbook of the National Council on Measurement in Education*, 1963, *20*, 124-125.

Sample: 18 teachers who had been in religious life at least 10 years and been judged successful teachers by their superiors.

Procedure: MMPI, Thurstone Temperament Schedule, Loyola Language Study, Q-sort Rate Yourself Test.

Results: MMPI: All subjects were in the normal range on every scale. Significant differences on depression, psychasthenia, social introversion, and schizophrenia were found in a comparison with 27 "unsuccessful" nuns in another study. TTS: Nuns scored above average in all areas except impulsiveness and sociability. LLS: Subjects appeared well balanced emotionally and free from schizophrenic tendencies. QRYT: Used as a measure of empathy with highly variable results. Intercorrelations of various scales are examined with suggestions for further research.

BEIRNAERT, L.
The psychoanalytical investigation of the candidates.
Suppl. Vie Spir., 1960, *13*, 179-186.

BEIRNAERT, L.
Criteria of vocation—psychological approach.
In **B4:** Ple.

The importance of mental health is stressed. Doubtful candidates for religious life, but not all candidates, should be given psychological examinations.

BENKO, A.
Examen de la motivation.
Suppl. Vie Spir., 1954, *7*(29), 152-159.

The underlying motives of an attraction to the religious or priestly life can only be adequately evaluated by the techniques of modern psychology and psychiatry. Neurotic motivation is discussed and contrasted with the true motives for a vocation, which must be ultimately spiritual. (Abstract by Meissner.)

BENTON, J. A., JR.
Perceptual characteristics of Episcopal pastors.
Ed.D., University of Florida, 1964.
Dissert. Abstr., 1965, *25*, 3963.

Sample: 17 Episcopal priests who were rated by their bishops as effective and 15 as ineffective in respect to their pastoral counseling.

Procedure: The Pastoral Problem Response Blank, consisting of 10 bits of conversation setting forth pastoral problems, a picture story using card 13 of the TAT, and 3 incidents which the subject reported as his own effective pastoral counseling. Judges rated responses on 9-point scales for each of 5 dimensions.

Results: Effective pastors, as compared with ineffective pastors, (1) see themselves as more identified with people; (2) see other people as more able; (3) tend to relate to others more as persons; (4) see their role more as being involved with people; (5) perceive the purpose of their

pastoral task more as freeing their counselees.

BIER, W. C.

A comparative study of a seminary group
and four other groups on the MMPI.

Ph.D., Catholic University of America,
1948.

*Stud. Psychol. Psychiat. Cathol. Univer.
Amer.,* 1948, 7(11). 107 pp.

   Sample: The MMPI was administered
to 924 subjects divided into 5 matched
groups of college students: medical (N
= 208), law (N = 55), dental (N =
121), students (N = 369), Catholic
seminary (N = 171).

   Results: All groups in this study gave
evidence of less satisfactory adjustment,
on the basis of MMPI scales, than does
the population at large. The seminary
group proved to be the most deviant portion of an already deviant population. An
item analysis was undertaken and a comparative study was made of the extremes
of the sample (top and bottom 27% of
each group). The well-adjusted seminarian differed far more from the poorly
adjusted seminarian than he did from the
well-adjusted members of the 4 comparative groups. Recommendations are made
for changes in the MMPI which would
make it more suitable for use with seminarians.

BIER, W. C.

A comparative study of five Catholic
college groups on the MMPI.

In G. S. Welsh & W. G. Dahlstrom
(Eds.), *Basic readings on the MMPI in
psychology and medicine.* Minneapolis: University of Minnesota Press,
1956. Pp. 586-609.

   A slightly abridged revision of Bier
1948.

BIER, W. C. (Chm.), BOOTH, G.,
DOUGLAS, W., HARROWER, MOLLY,
TORRE, M. P., REITH, H. R., AND
OTHERS.

Selection of personnel for the clergy.

In W. C. Bier, S. Z. Klausner, & H. C.
Meserve (Eds.), *Research in religion
and health, proceedings of the 5th
Academy symposium,* 1961, Academy
of Religion and Mental Health. New
York: Fordham University, 1963.

   Edited transcript of symposium. Booth
suggests a comprehensive study of the
clergy who have functioned successfully
and the use of psychological instruments
to provide information which could not
be gathered in other ways. Douglas discusses historical aspects of the call and
selection procedures. Harrower presents
results of a study of Unitarian-Universalist seminarians as reported in **H:** Benson
and **B2:** Harrower 1963. Torre discusses
his work in UN projects. Reith describes
a study of candidates at Notre Dame University. Other discussion is summarized.

BILLINSKY, J. M.

An inquiry into procedures of admissions
of students in theological schools.

Ed.D., Harvard University, 1952.

   The author used mail questionnaires
and visited 40 seminaries, interviewing
70 faculty members. He contends that
theological education's chief difficulty is
the lack of proper methods of selection.
Problems in the areas of personality, intelligence, and finance are held responsible for failures among students. Also
discussed are reasons for entering the
ministry and criteria of ministerial success. Suggestions for the improvement of
selection procedures are made.

   Of psychological testing, the author
says that progress is very slow and almost
nothing is done in cooperation. Lists of

tests in use and the uses to which they are put are presented. A detailed description of the 19-year-old Andover-Newton Theological Seminary testing program is included. A copy of the author's original Theological Seminary Entrance Test is appended.

BOOTH, G.
The psychological examination of candidates for the ministry.
In H. Hofmann (Ed.), *The ministry and mental health*. New York: Association Press, 1960. Pp. 101-124.

Sample: 163 of the 350 candidates examined by the author, most of them first-year students at General Theological Seminary in New York (Episcopal).

Procedure: Szondi, Rorschach, drawing tests (Koch, Machover), written self-evaluation, interview. Most of the article is given to the author's method of interpreting the tests, especially the Rorschach. Personalities were described on the basis of the tests, but no advanced predictions of adaptation to seminary life were attempted.

Results: The 24 candidates who subsequently dropped out of school for psychological reasons (including academic failure) were found to be insecure but ambitious, or emotionally frustrated, often with overt or latent homosexuality. But these traits were also found among those who did not drop out. Since the tests used cannot distinguish, they are not useful as predictors.

BOWES, N. T.
Professional evaluation of religious aspirants.
Derby, N.Y.: St. Paul Publications, 1963.

Sample: N is not stated in the text but information about the author includes "consultant to 39 Religious Congregations, Orders, and Dioceses over an 18-

year period, during which 7,000 aspirants have been examined, and many religious treated in psychotherapy."

Procedure: Rorschach, SCT, TAT.

Results: Most frequent problems which constitute incompatibility with healthy adjustment in a religious setting occurred in the following order: (1) psychosexual development; (2) interpersonal relationships; (3) scrupulosity; (4) dependency; (5) obsessive-compulsive (perfectionist); (6) depression; (7) affect-laden.

Criteria for determining danger points are discussed. The following recommendations are made: (1) Some opportunities for association with the opposite sex should be provided during seminary training. (2) The best time for the second novitiate is between the tenth and fifteenth postordination years. (3) Provision comparable to the second novitiate should be made for the secular clergy. (4) Aged priests should not be housed in a training house or novitiate. (5) Vocation directors and spiritual directors in houses of training should be more selectively chosen.

BREIMEIER, K. H.
Leadership traits as reflected in psychological tests.
Unpublished study. Dayton, O. (1810 Harvard Blvd.): Ministry Studies Board, undated. 14 pp.

Sample: 156 men in the fourth year at Concordia Seminary, St. Louis (Lutheran).

Procedure: The class designated 20 leaders by ballot. Every eighth member up to 20 was chosen as a control. Groups were compared on the ACE, Ohio, Bell, CTP, Kuder, and grades.

Results: ACE and Ohio scores are consistently higher in the leader group but the difference is not significant. The Bell and the CTP results suggest that leaders are better adjusted socially and personally.

Kuder suggests that leaders have higher interest in "social" activities while controls showed more introversion (not significant). Leaders have significantly higher grade point average.

BREIMEIER, K. H.
The prediction of academic success at a theological seminary.
M.A., Washington University, 1948.

> *Sample:* 107 first-year theological students at Concordia Seminary, St. Louis.
> *Procedure:* ACE, SVIB, Kuder, Bernreuter, Bell; grades in Hebrew, Greek, homiletics.
> *Results:* The following correlated significantly with grades. ACE: total .31, linguistic .24, quantitative .27. SVIB: CPA scale .34, president of manufacturing concern .19, minister .11 (not significant). Kuder: Musical .19. Concluded that the use of tests, other than the ACE, to predict academic achievement is little justified.

BURKARD, SISTER M. INNOCENTIA
Characteristic differences determined by TAT sequential analysis, between teachers rated by their pupils at the extremes of teaching efficiency.
Ph.D., Loyola University (Chicago), 1958.
Summarized in **B2:** Arnold 1962b. Pp. 47-51.

> *Sample:* 300 teaching sisters, half in elementary grades, half in high school.
> *Procedure:* Teachers were rated by pupils. 50 of the best-rated teachers were paired with 50 of the lowest-rated on age and intelligence. 20 pairs were used to discover discriminating themes using the TAT sequence analysis (**B2:** Arnold 1962b).
> *Results:* Blind scoring of the remaining 60 TAT protocols showed perfect correlation with the criterion.

BURKE, H. R.
Personality traits of successful minor seminarians.
Ph.D., Catholic University of America, 1947.
Washington, D.C.: Catholic University of America Press, 1947.
Abstract published by Catholic University of America Press: *Final examinations for the degree of doctor of philosophy,* July, 1945–June, 1947.

> *Sample:* 191 first-year high school and 91 fourth-year high school minor diocesan seminarians.
> *Procedure:* Faculty rating scale, home environment measure, SVIB, Cleeton Vocational Interest Inventory.
> *Results:* A super-G factor called "general moral fitness to go on for the priesthood" is identified. Concludes that the vocational inventories and personality tests with the scoring methods then available seem to have no positive value for selecting minor seminarians of promise. This first-year group probably does not differ much from other college preparatory groups at that level on academic achievement, intelligence, adjustment, and socio-economic status.

CASH, W. L.
Relation of personality traits to scholastic aptitude and academic achievement of students in a liberal Protestant seminary.
Ph.D., University of Michigan, 1954.
Dissert. Abstr., 1954, *14,* 630-631.

> *Sample:* 134 students registered at the Oberlin Graduate School of Theology, 1949-50, 1951-52.
> *Procedure:* Bernreuter, OSUPE, and sociological data. Criteria: grade point ratios, completion of seminary.
> *Results:* The most significant relationships found were between: (1) self-suffi-

ciency and length of seminary attendance, grades in New Testament courses, and unskilled parental occupation; (2) neurotic tendency and scholastic aptitude; (3) scholastic aptitude and grades in theoretical and practical courses, and courses in New Testament; (4) grades and social class status; (5) grades in practical courses and parental socio-economic status characterized by "service" occupations.

CASH, W. L.
Relationship of personality traits and scholastic aptitude to academic achievement in theological studies.
J. psychol. Studies, 1962, *13,* 105-110.

Based on Cash 1954.

CÉSAR VACA, P.
Apuntes para un profesiograma del oficio de confesor (Items for a job analysis of the functions of confessor).
Psicotecnia, 1941, *2,* 231-252.

Besides the customary profile chart (of which a sample is given for this profession) it is desirable to employ a questionnaire designed to bring out special aptitudes and the candidate's subjective orientation in relation to objective and social qualifications. A tentative form of the questionnaire is presented and discussed. (Abstract by Meissner.)

CHOISY, M.
Motivations fausses et vocation vraie.
Psyché, 1954, *93-94,* 463-479.

The author examines the effects of psychoanalysis on student priests, outlining the case of a seminarist when neurotic motivations did not prevent the development of a genuine religious vocation. She concludes that psychoanalysis would certainly weed out a large number of "false" vocations, but that priests undergoing it

successfully would be of exceptional worth. (Abstract by Meissner.)

COCKRUM, L. V.
Predicting success in training for the ministry.
Relig. Educ., 1952, *47,* 198-202.

Sample: Not reported clearly but perhaps the same as **A1: Cockrum.**
Procedure: MAT (N = 43), Cooperative Reading Comprehension Test (N = 79), college grade average (N = 79), seminary grade average (N = 43).
Results: Seminary grades correlated significantly (p < .01) with: college average .51, reading .41, MAT .50.

CORCORAN, C. J. D.
"Types" suited or unsuited for religious vocation.
In *Proc. 8th annu. Convocation of the Voc. Inst.* Notre Dame, Ind.: Notre Dame Press, 1955. Pp. 28-36.

COVILLE, W. J.
Personality assessment of candidates to seminaries: a study of clinical and psychometric methods and their effectiveness as predictors of success in minor and major seminaries.
In S. W. Cook (Ed.), *Research plans.* New York (545 W. 111th St.): Religious Education Association, 1962. Pp. 175-188.

This is a proposal for a study of clinical and psychometric methods and their effectiveness as predictors of success in minor and major seminaries. Reports will follow over a 3-year period.
Sample: 80 women and 283 men in 2 seminaries and 1 religious community in 1961.
Procedure: College Qualification Test, MMPI, SCT, DAP, biographical inventory, personality inventory for seminar-

ians, clinical interview. Criterion measures will be faculty ratings, drop-out rate,
and grades.

DEL ARROYO, T.
An experiment in the discernment of
vocations.
Suppl. Vie Spir., 1959, *12*, 183-202.

DIGNA, MARY
Practical application of psychometrics to
religious life.
Rev. Relig., 1950, *9*, 131-139.

Describes 7 cases from a study of applicants for the religious life. Predictions
made on the basis of MPS, and in some
cases the SVIB and ACE, are compared
with the background of the candidates.
The study is presented as exploratory,

DITTES, J. E.
TSI scores in relation to personal back-
ground, performance in seminary, and
post-seminary vocational choice.
TSI Research Bull. #3. Dayton, O. (1810
Harvard Blvd.): Ministry Studies
Board, 1963. 20 pp.

Sample: 497 theological students (7
seminaries) tested on entering in 1959;
204 of them tested as seniors again in
1962.

Procedure: Product-moment correlations were calculated for both samples on
TSI scale scores, several indices of seminary experience including grades, faculty
and field work ratings, records of immediate postseminary career, items in sections
I and III of the TSI.

Results: Correlations which bear on
validity generally support suggested interpretation of the TSI and are discussed in
the TSI manual (**A1:** Dittes 1964).

DOUGLAS, W. G. T.
Predicting ministerial effectiveness.
Ph.D., Harvard University, 1957.

Sample: 45 clergymen accepted and ordained in the Diocese of Massachusetts
since 1949.

Procedure: Rorschach, SVIB, A-V
Study of Values, Cooperative Botany administered in seminary; clergy and lay
ratings of parish performance; extended
interview.

Results: Prediction and selection are
limited more by the criterion problem than
by the test. Ratings indicate that the effective minister must be both good and
able, both a task specialist and a social-
emotional specialist. Tests may aid in selecting the able but something else is
needed to get at the good.

Lay raters indicate that effective ministers have (1) a genuine love of people,
(2) definite convictions, (3) ability to
sacrifice immediate impulse satisfaction to
long-range goals, (4) flexibility of temperament, (5) concern for institutional
and organizational life of the local church.

Recommendations to the diocese and
for further research are included.

EVANS, B.
A personality inventory.
D.R.E., New Orleans Baptist Theological
Seminary, 1960.

Sample: 105 Southern Baptist church
workers, including 39 pastors, 17 teachers, 13 musicians, and 36 men and women
directors of religious education. 25 theological students, 9 college students, 14
active laymen; data not reported for latter group of laymen.

Procedure: A 100-item forced-choice
personality inventory was devised to measure characteristics thought important in
religious workers: sense of superiority and
a need to direct versus lack of self-confidence; socio-emotional dependence and
reliance on personal support; exhibition-
ism versus inhibition; need to control life
versus freedom; and Christian maturity,

defined as ability to love creatively.

Results: Pastors tended to show greater sense of personal superiority and need to control, greater personal dependence and less Christian maturity than other workers, especially pastors of larger churches, workers nominated as "leaders," and students with lower grades. Teachers tended to show least superiority and least personal dependence. Musicians showed the greatest freedom and Christian maturity.

EVOY, J. J., & CHRISTOPH, V. F.
Personality development in the religious life.
New York: Sheed and Ward, 1963.

Lectures given to religious women on "understanding human nature." The original dialogue form is retained in the printed version. A developmental approach is followed; the personality theory orientation is that of Ausubel. Constant reference is made to the religious by way of illustration.

FAIRBANKS, R. J., BARTELME, PHYLLIS F., & CAMBRIA, SOPHIE T.
A study of admission of women for church work.
New York (815 Second Ave.): Unit of Christian Vocation, Protestant Episcopal Church, 1961. 50 pp.

Sample: 48 women who had applied (34 accepted, 14 rejected) to two schools for training professional women church workers 5 to 10 years previous to the study. Sample decreased for several reasons from the original group of 135.

Development of Criterion: 100 descriptions of personal characteristics, e.g., enjoy living and being with people, were Q-sorted twice (subject sort and ideal church worker sort) by each subject, her rector, and a lay person who knew her work. 30 pairs of ratings (10 from each group of raters) were factor-analyzed,

yielding 6 factors, 4 of which were identifiable by the authors: high-church view, low-church view, feminine view, and lay person's view. For each subject, a "hidden consensus rating" was derived by averaging the correlations between the descriptive Q-sorts made for her by rector and layman and each of the 4 identifiable factors.

Results: Correlations between this hidden consensus rating and whether or not the woman had been accepted for training were .35 and .90, respectively, for the two training houses. That only the house with the lower correlation had used psychological tests is taken to "provide no support for the continued use of psychological test reports." There was a correlation (not specified) between the criterion and the ENF groups of the Myers-Briggs Type Indicator, the type in which a large portion of the sample was concentrated. No relation was found between more direct ratings of a woman's performance and likelihood of admission. No data are systematically reported from personal interviews held with each of the subjects.

FUCHS, O.
Character traits of candidates for the priesthood.
M.A., Catholic University of America, 1946.

Sample: 413 male Catholic high school students in 6 schools in Atlantic seaboard states.

Procedure: Criterion ratings by judges on suitability for priesthood. Terman-McNemar, Bell.

Results: Ratings correlated highly with the Bell. Intelligence had a significant but low correlation with the criterion.

GRATTON, H.
Incompatibilités psychiques avec l'état sacerdotal.

Suppl. Vie Spir., 1959, *49,* 154-182.

The life of perfect chastity and the other obligations of the priest's office require psychological maturity and balance. The psychic disabilities which would make a candidate unfit are discussed in light of the Church's legislation on the admission of candidates to the priesthood. Select bibliography. (Abstract by Meissner.)

GRIMBERT, C.
Psychopathologie et vocation religieuse.
La Pensée Catholique, 1960, *66,* 10-22.

HAM, H. M.
Personality correlates of ministerial success.
Iliff Rev., 1960, *17,* 3-9.

Sample: 350 ministers in main line Protestant denominations followed over a 10-year period.
Procedure: WAIS, Rorschach, laymen's descriptions of ministers, evaluations by former seminary professors. 84 were judged "successes," 35 "failures," the rest "moderate" by change in salary, size of church, etc.
Results: Correlation (.01 level) was found between "success" and (1) verbal score on WAIS; (2) emotional distance from people; (3) flexibility of personality structure; (4) moderate allocentric tendencies; (5) superior marital adjustment; (6) relatively weak ego strength.

HAMILTON, H. L.
The causes of failure among recently ordained ministers.
Unpublished mimeographed paper. Columbus, O.: Presbyterian Church U.S.A., Office of Personnel Relations, Undated.

Several field work supervisors in the Presbyterian Church speculate on the subject. No statistical analysis. A call for careful research is included.

HAMILTON, H. L.
Proposal for a research study designed to discover and define the professional skills needed for an adequate ministry.
Report of the 4th biennial meeting of the Association of Seminary Professors in the Practical Fields, 1956. Pp. 38-43.

The Presbyterian Church U.S.A. proposes a case study and psychological test research project to determine what skills (communication, organization, research, etc.) are possessed by successful ministers.

HARROWER, MOLLY
The use of psychological tests in the Unitarian-Universalist ministry: a service and research program.
In **H:** Benson.
Similar report in *J. Relig. Hlth,* 1963, *2,* 129-142: Psychological tests in the Unitarian-Universalist ministry.
Also reported in **B2:** Bier 1963.

Sample: 31 Unitarian-Universalist seminary students entering in 1955.
Procedure: Performance on psychodiagnostic battery while student is compared with ratings of effectiveness 7 years later. Ratings made for each minister by 2 laymen and 2 denominational officials. Drop-outs noted.
Results: Diagnostic battery relatively predictive of those lowest on criterion. Data are discussed in terms of the author's "scales of personality endowment derived from similarity of performance on 8 projective techniques." Results are plotted graphically; no statistical analysis is reported.
Expanded in **B2:** Harrower 1964.

HARROWER, MOLLY
Mental-health potential and success in the ministry.
J. Relig. Hlth, 1964, *4,* 30-58.

Expansion of **B2:** Harrower 1962.

Sample: 135 entering Unitarian-Universalist seminary students, 1955-1958.

Procedure: Tests given at seminary entrance: Rorschach, Szondi, verbal Wechsler-Bellevue, Miale-Holsopple Sentence Completion, several drawing tests, and TAT. Scores on Harrower's Scales of Mental Health Potential are derived from results of the tests. 4 judges—2 laymen, 2 denominational officials—provided evaluations of ministers still in the parish ministry 6 to 7 years later (N = 79).

Results: Reported in tables and by individual case summaries. Generally a correlation is found between test interpretation and later evaluation, to the degree that the test battery discriminates those scoring lowest on criterion. Of 20 ministers rated as unsatisfactory on criterion, 75% were in the "impoverished" or "disorganized" quadrants of the test-based rating, compared with 14% of ministers rated successful, basically successful, or questionable on criterion, and compared with 23% of the students who had dropped out of the ministry or were still in school. The tests failed to distinguish among the groups rated successful, basically successful, or questionable on the criterion.

HISPANICUS, P.

Selecting seminarians.

Pp. 65-105 in **B2:** Arnold *et al.* 1962.

Sample: 50 seminarians in one seminary. 10 dropped out during course of study.

Procedure: MMPI, SCAT; 3 faculty ratings for each subject on likelihood of remaining in seminary and of becoming successful priests. Faculty ratings intercorrelated in .70's.

Results: Faculty ratings slightly correlated with SCAT. Significant negative correlation between faculty ratings and Pa scale, near significant with Pd and Pt; near significant positive correlation with Mf. Pd, Pt, and Sc scores discriminated dropouts significantly.

HODGE, M. B.

Vocational satisfaction of ministers: an introductory experimental study of younger Presbyterian ministers.

Ph.D., University of Southern California, 1960.

Dissert. Abstr., 1960, *21,* 251.

Sample: 58 Presbyterian ministers from the Los Angeles Presbytery (all but 2 of the men who had been ordained there 6-14 years prior to the study).

Procedure: Modified Brayfield-Rothe Job Satisfaction Scale, Attitude Inventory, Q-sort for ideal minister and self, Wonderlic Personnel Test, taped interview.

Results: Vocational satisfaction was correlated significantly with only 2 of the personality variables studied: feelings of fellowship with others and acceptance by others, and the tendency to perceive optimistically the attitudes and practices of others. Satisfaction was not related to feelings of vocational and financial security, feelings of personal growth and fulfillment, mental ability, college major, religious activity of parents.

HUBBARD, J. F.

A study of occupational pattern of the Presbyterian ministry of the synod of North Carolina.

M.A., University of Richmond, 1965.

Sample: Presbyterian ministers (N not given) from North Carolina, drawn in proportion to size of church served, so that all success levels would be included.

Procedure: Kuder, A-V Study of Values, SRA Verbal Mental Ability, Watson-Glaser, GZTS, Michigan Vocabulary Profile Test in human relations, commerce, government, and fine arts, and self-evaluation form including 19 tasks of the Presbyterian ministry with rating as to personal success from 1 to 5.

Results: Means and standard deviations are given for each of the factors of the above instruments, with the exception of the last, and distributions and/or comparisons with the results of an adult male group are also made in some cases. Coefficients are given for the following variables: Guilford-Zimmerman A scale, Kuder working with ideas, Kuder avoiding conflict, A-V religious scale, Guilford-Zimmerman T scale, A-V aesthetic scale, Kuder activity in groups, Guilford-Zimmerman masculine scale, Michigan Vocabulary human relations area. By multiplying a raw score by the specified coefficient, a prediction of success level can be derived. Some variables differentiating ministers from other occupational groups also tend to predict success level; e.g., high scorers on the A-V aesthetic scale tend to exhibit low ministerial success.

HUDSON, R. L.
The emotions of the minister.
Pastoral Psychol., 1951, *2*(14), 32-37.

The minister cannot know his people unless he knows himself and recognizes how much of his thinking is colored by his emotions, especially his handling of his own sexual and hostile impulses. Seminaries should provide expert counselors who can screen candidates and aid them in self-understanding.

HUNT, R. A.
An exploratory study of some relationships between personality variables and achievement in seminary.
Unpublished mimeographed paper. Fort Worth, Tex.: Author, Texas Christian University, 1963. 47 pp.

Summarized in *Ministry Studies Board Newsletter,* 1964, *3,* 2-3.

Sample: 45 students from Brite Divinity School; 36 students from Perkins School of Theology.

Procedure: Seminary grade point averages, faculty ratings of achievement and of future effectiveness, Otis (Brite only), MAT (Perkins only), Self-activity Inventory (Worchel), semantic differential rating 18 concepts on 31 dimensions, Pensacola Z survey, MAS, K and L scales of MMPI, Philosophy of Human Nature Survey (Wrightsman), Theological School Inventory.

Results: Faculty ratings correlate .70 with each other and with grade point average. Tests of academic ability and grades correlate in the .30's. Successful students score higher on R and lower on A and L scales of TSI, are more flexible, less authoritarian, and less dependent. Interpretations are suggested for correlations between TSI scores and personality measures.

INGRAM, O. K.
Student recruitment.
Duke Divinity School Bull., 1963, *28,* 188-198.

Sample: Students of the Duke Divinity School, 1957-1961 (N not given).

Procedure: Otis, MMPI; grouping of students according to (1) geographic location; (2) type of undergraduate institution, major, and degree; (3) socio-economic status (father's occupation); (4) marital status; and (5) type of field work.

Results: (1) A 10-point average difference on the Otis was found between students earning a "B" or a "D" average their first year in seminary, with the "B" group higher, and a "C" group falling somewhere between. (2) The Pd scale of the MMPI correlated negatively with successful academic performance in seminary.

(3) In terms of regional groups, those from the Southeast, outside of North Carolina, produced the highest grade average the first year in seminary. Differences between geographic groups were also found in English mechanics and effectiveness of expression. (4) Graduates of public colleges were higher in intelligence than those from Methodist or other denominational schools. Grade average in college, but not major or curriculum of study, is predictive of seminary academic success. Type of degree (B.S. or B.A.) is not a significant factor in success. (5) No correlation between social status and academic performance. (6) Married students, except those whose wives worked, showed lower grade averages and lower intelligence than single students. (7) Students with no field work were higher in intelligence than those serving as student pastors or engaged in summer or winter field work. However, those engaged in field work produced higher grade averages. Student pastors are lowest in both intelligence and grade average.

Other factors to be considered in recruitment are discussed.

JEANNE D'ARC, SISTER
Pour les différentes étapes de l'entrée dans la vie religieuse.
Suppl. Vie Spir., 1959, *12*(48), 64-94.

A series of questionnaires is provided to evaluate the religious vocation of young women at several stages of their religious formation: first contact with the girl seeking admittance, before postulancy, before admission to the novitiate, before admission to first profession, and during the temporary profession. (Abstract by Meissner.)

KELLEY, P.
Rorschach measures of affect-adjustment in candidates to the religious life.

M.A., Catholic University of America, 1951.

Sample: 38 candidates: 19 in high school, 19 in college.
Procedure: Rorschach, Bernreuter, faculty ratings. The affect-adjustment checklist was designed to quantify Rorschach responses denoting interpersonal relations.
Results: The checklist correlated significantly with some faculty ratings of the high school students but not of the college students. For both groups the checklist correlated slightly with 2 Bernreuter scores: positive with sociability and negative with self-sufficiency.

KILDAHL, J. P.
The hazards of high callings.
Pastoral Psychol., 1961, *12*(112), 41-46.
Also pp. 201-208 in **H: Oates.**

The minister must have sufficient satisfaction and security in his nonprofessional life so that he does not use his parishioners for the attaining of those emotional needs.

KNOWLES, R. H.
Differential characteristics of successful and unsuccessful seminary students.
Ph.D., University of Nebraska, 1958.
Dissert. Abstr., 1959, *19,* 1655-1656.

Sample: 256 men from 4 classes of one seminary. Unsuccessful: those on scholastic probation; successful: honor students.
Procedure: SVIB, reading comprehension and speed, Wrenn Study Habits Inventory, Otis, MMPI, Bernreuter, etc.
Results: Clearest differentiation of the 2 groups was provided by vocabulary proficiency, reading competence, study habits, professional interest, general mental ability.

KOHLS, SISTER THOMAS A.
The relation between personal adjustment and spirituality in religious sisters.

M.A., Fordham University, 1959.

Sample: 82 members of 5 congregations in the Midwest engaged in apostolic and teaching activity.

Procedure: GZTS and a specially constructed Spirituality Scale (split-half reliability of .86).

Results: Significant differences (.05 level) were found between the high and low adjustment groups. Spirituality correlated with personal relations and emotional stability (.05) and with friendliness and objectivity (.01). Those aspects of the Spirituality Scale which are directed toward God and neighbor and away from self are related to favorable personality adjustment.

Long, L. L.

The American Board's experience with psychometric testing of candidates for overseas work.

Boston (14 Beacon St.): Personnel Secretary of the American Board of Commissioners for Foreign Missions, 1958.

Sample: 375 persons, of whom 23 were experienced missionaries and 352 were new candidates.

Procedure: OSUPE, SVIB, and Bernreuter scores were correlated with ratings by field secretaries.

Results: No statistically significant differences in test results between rated groups was found, nor can predictions be based on such variables as age, vocation, regular or term appointment. In December, 1957, the Board discontinued the use of all tests except the OSUPE.

Lucassen, Mary R.

Appraisal of potential leadership qualities among young women religious.

Ph.D., Loyola University (Chicago), 1963.

Sample: 20 professed religious at the end of third or fourth year of college work.

Procedure: 12 TAT pictures were projected for the group. Story sequence analysis was used in the scoring. A leadership score was derived from a test in which sisters were ranked according to 12 criteria; factor analysis revealed 16 different leadership variables.

Results: TAT scores were able to discriminate potential leaders according to two variables: initiative, and capability for insight and expression. With one subject eliminated correlation of TAT scores with the entire leadership test or with the two variables alone was significant at the .01 level.

Maehr, M. L., & Stake, R. E.

The value patterns of men who voluntarily quit seminary training.

Personnel Guid. J., 1962, *40,* 537-540.

Sample: 100 persisting seminary students at Concordia Seminary, St. Louis; 71 at the same seminary who failed to complete the program (nonpersisters).

Procedure: ACE and A-V Study of Values completed at entrance.

Results: No difference in academic ability. Persisters were higher than nonpersisters on economic and lower on aesthetic scales; there was no significant difference on religion scale. Compared with college men in general, the seminarians were more religiously and socially oriented and less theoretically, economically, and politically oriented.

Marcozzi, V.

Problemi psicologici nella formazione.

Roma: Tipografia poliglotta Pont. Univ. Gregoriana, 1957.

Addresses to spiritual directors of seminaries delivered in Rome, September, 1956. The first part discusses psychic maturity, the factors which affect it, and the need for it in the priest of today. The second part treats of several categories of psychic abnormality. Causes, symptoms, therapy, attitudes of spiritual directors, and the obstacles which these abnormalities place to acceptance in the priesthood are discussed. (Abstract by Meissner.)

McCabe, S. P.
Perception of self as related to personal adjustment.
M.A., Catholic University of America, 1956.

Sample: 75 theological students from a diocesan major seminary.
Procedure: 100 statement Q-sort (rated self and ideal seminarian); "objective sort" derived from sorts of several judges; SVIB, MMPI.
Results: Relationship between self-ideal congruence and self-objective congruence is quite high. Congruence between self and ideal was significantly related to adjustment.

McCarthy, T. N.
Evaluation scientifique des aptitudes psychologiques à la vocation religieuse.
Suppl. Vie Spir., 1958, 11(45), 188-196.

Summary of psychological studies on selection procedures and personality traits of religious.

McCarthy, T. N.
Characteristics of the promising candidate.
Unpublished paper. Philadelphia: Author, LaSalle College, 1961.

Suggestions to counselors on the most desirable characteristics of normal candidates. Intellectual ability should be compared with college norms. Interests should be evaluated with scales constructed specifically for that purpose, such as the Priest Scale of the Kuder. College norms are appropriate for evaluating personality traits.

Miller, R. W.
Emotional tension in ministerial students as shown by the use of the Counseling Aid Form.
M.A., Northwestern University, 1949.

Leiffer's CAF was standardized on 632 ministerial students. Illustrative cases are described for high scorers on each of the form's factors. It is concluded that the form has high validity.

Nabais, J. A.
La vocazione alla luce della psicologia moderna.
Roma: Edizioni Paoline, 1955.

The teaching of the Catholic Church on the nature of the vocation to the priesthood is discussed in detail. After treating the history and nature of a vocation, the author develops the role of psychological factors in determining a vocation. Desirable and undesirable factors in a priest are discussed in terms of the selection of candidates. (Abstract by Meissner.)

Nabais, J. A.
Le vocation sacerdotale à la lumière de la théologie et de la psychologie.
Rev. Univer. Ottawa, 1956, 26, 350-388; 451-490.

The first part of this article is concerned with the theological aspects of vocation. The second part is more directly concerned with psychological aspects, such as the personality requirements and their development, positive and negative signs of a vocation, necessity for adequate selection techniques, and the need to apply psychological methods to this problem. (Abstract by Meissner.)

Parrot, P., & Romain, R. P.
Maturité affective et vocation sacerdotale.
Suppl. Vie Spir., 1958, 11(46), 307-322.

Psychic maturity is characterized by personal autonomy, dominance of reason, sociability, sexual integration, and balance. The qualities are related to the priestly vocation. (Abstract by Meissner.)

PERTEJO, J.
Rorschach, sublimación y vocación religiosa.
Rev. Espir., 1958, *17*, 90-93.

The use of the Rorschach in selection of candidates for the religious life is discussed. Evidence from protocols taken on seminarians seems to indicate that a high capacity for sublimation and efficient reality contact are the best indicators of ability to resist neurotic tendencies and possible traumata. (Abstract by Meissner.)

PHILIP, MARY
Intellectual qualifications in prospective candidates.
Natl Cathol. Educ. Ass. Bull., 1958, *55*, 354-355.

Communities should set up admission norms relative to intellectual qualifications. Roles of school records, ACE, and SCAT are briefly mentioned.

QUINN, T. L.
Differences in motivational patterns of college student brothers as revealed in the TAT, the ratings of their peers, and the ratings of their superiors: a comparison.
Ph.D., Loyola University (Chicago), 1962.
Summarized in **B2:** Arnold 1962b. Pp. 51-60.

Sample: 45 student brothers.
Procedure: Measured agreement between TAT scores (using Arnold's sequential story analysis; **B2:** Arnold *et al.* 1962) and ranking as to promise for the

brotherhood by three groups of judges: peers, superiors, and 10 high scorers on the TAT.
Results: Rankings among judges were in substantial agreement for candidates at the extremes of the range of promise but in less agreement for those whose rank fell in the middle range. TAT scores correlated .59 with peer ratings, .61 with superiors' ratings, and .57 with high scorers' ratings. Limitations of the study are discussed in some detail.

RÉTIF, L.
La maturité en termes de pastorale.
Suppl. Vie Spir., 1958, *11*(46), 328-335.

The relation between the psychic maturity of the priest and the effectiveness of his pastoral work is discussed. (Abstract by Meissner.)

RICHARDS, J. M., JR.
Psychological tests as predictors of academic achievement in theological seminary.
Unpublished study. Decatur, Ga.: Author, Columbia Theological Seminary, 1957.

Sample: First-year class (N not given) at Columbia Theological Seminary, Decatur, Georgia.
Procedure: First-year seminary grade point averages were correlated with OSUPE, ACE, Cooperative English, Cooperative General Culture, and college grades.
Results: Best prediction of academic performance is obtained by considering OSUPE, college grades, and total English score in that order for those who are college graduates and the OSUPE and total English in that order for those not college grads. No significant improvement results from using subtest scores. Preliminary results suggested that the substitution of ACE for OSUPE produces a substantial drop in accuracy of prediction. OSUPE

alone is the best predictor of success in both Hebrew and Greek.

ROUSSET, SUZY
Health and nervous equilibrium in the novitiates of women's congregations.
In *A manual for novice mistresses*. London: Blackfriars, 1958. Pp. 74-90. (Religious Life Series, IX.)

There are false vocations which do not spring from a true self-dedication, but from an unconscious counterfeit of it. But there are also physical defects and serious psychological difficulties of adaptation which must be overcome. Various physical and psychological problems are discussed specifically from data given by Dominican novice mistresses attending a conference.

SHIMADA, K.
Social role and role conflicts of the Protestant parish minister: focused on S. W. Blizzard's study.
Jap. Sociol. Rev., 1960, *10*(2), March, 29-50.
Sociol. Abstr., 1963, *11*(6), A6838, 573.

The major points of Blizzard's **(B1)** thesis are developed. A study of the relationship of role conflict and authority revealed that (1) the minister who has an authoritarian personality structure tends to have less conflict at the level of awareness in a given situation, and (2) the authoritarian minister tends to identify himself with or adhere to the traditional and nonoccupational roles. Further research is suggested.

SKLARE, M.
The Conservative rabbi.
In M. Sklare, *Conservative Judaism: an American religious movement*. Glencoe, Ill.: The Free Press, 1955. Pp. 159-198 (Chap. 6).

Based on Conservative Judaism: a sociological analysis.
Ph.D., Columbia University, 1953.

Describes the formation of the Jewish Theological Seminary in America and the seminary program. Discusses role conflict, especially between emotional and "scholar-saint" roles. Difficulty of achieving clear conviction on religious ideology is seen to lead to 4 compensating devices: "objectivism," "scholarship," "eclecticism," and "compartmentalism." Undue deference by "practitioner"-oriented students towards scholastic-oriented faculty is seen to produce intra- and interpersonal conflicts.

SMITH, A. H.
The development and validation of an attitude scale for ministers.
Ph.D., University of Missouri, 1961.
Dissert. Abstr., 1962, *22*, 2892-2893.

Sample: Initial (N = 83) and cross-validating (N = 87) groups of Presbyterian ministers.
Procedure: A 104-item attitude scale was developed. Means and variances were significantly different for upper and lower validation groups.
Results: The scale differentiated between ministers nominated as more or less effective in interpersonal relations in a gross fashion except in the low range of scores. Further validation studies are recommended.

SOUTHARD, S.
Motivation and mental health.
Pp. 97-108 in **H:** Oates.

A serial summary of interpretations and hypotheses concerning actual and desirable patterns of motivation, growing out of a conference. See **H:** Southard.

SOUTHARD, S.
The personal life of the frontier minister: 1760-1860.

Unpublished mimeographed paper. Louisville, Ky.: Author, Southern Baptist Seminary, 1964.

Presented at the annual meeting of the Society for the Scientific Study of Religion, Washington, D.C., Oct. 31, 1964.

Sample: Several dozen Baptist, Methodist, and Disciples ministers in North Carolina, Virginia, Tennessee, and Kentucky.

Procedure: Study of autobiographies, diaries, and other historical materials.

Conclusion: "The fatigue and loneliness of long journeys to preach was a depressing factor in the lives of some frontier ministers. But personality also played a part. Ambitious, competitive, restless or compulsive men drove themselves until they dropped with 'the religious blues,' exhaustion or consumption. More settled personalities stayed at home, preached in the neighborhood, and taught in the schools and academies. The former group of ministers formed the frontier denominations, but at the price of family deprivation. The latter group left a more lasting impression in one community, and were more satisfied and satisfying in their own homes."

SOUTHARD, S.
The spiritual development of successful students.
J. Relig. Hlth, 1965, *4,* 154-163.

Relations between 3 students and their professor are examined over a period of 3 courses at Southern Baptist Theological Seminary. The students were initially highly "successful," inwardly pushed by desire for approval and perfectionism, intellectualizing, repressive of affect. They learned to channel their anxieties of personal development from academic and church activity to increased personal involvement with peers, authorities, family,

or church members. The students felt they had moved "from a childhood state of religious feeling to a college inhibition of feeling and now to a return of faith during their seminary career." Their development occurred through small class sessions rather than through personal counseling.

TAGESON, C. F.
Relationship of self-perceptions to realism of vocational choice.
Ph.D., Catholic University of America, 1960.
Washington, D.C.: Catholic University of America Press, 1960.

Sample: 120 minor seminarians rated by faculty members for realism of their initial vocational choice and by a randomly selected peer group of fellow students.

Procedure: A Q-sort defined self-concept and ideal self.

Results: There is a positive relationship between both faculty and peer group ratings for realism of vocational choice and (1) congruence of an individual's ideal self with his personal concept of the ideal seminarian, and (2) congruence of his self-concept with his personal concept of the average seminarian. There is a positive relationship between faculty ratings of an individual student for realism of vocational choice and the congruence of his ideal self with the faculty concept of the ideal seminarian.

THAYER, C. R.
The relationship of certain psychological test scores to subsequent ratings of missionary field success.
Ph.D., University of Pittsburgh, 1951.
Abstracted in *University of Pittsburgh Bull.,* 1952, *10,* 1-6.

Sample: 69 foreign missionaries.

Procedure: Compared the results of tests given in 1931-33 to missionary appointees of various denominations with subsequent measures of field success on the Prefurlough questionnaire (Presbyterian U.S.A.) or letters from associates or superiors.

Results: Candidate secretary's ratings were not valid predictors, although tests of vocational and religious interests were. Tests of intelligence and social attitudes were most effective in the selection of women. Tests of neurotic tendency were valuable in reverse in the selection of men. The battery of tests correlated about .50 with field success.

THAYER, C. R.
The neurotic minister: a type study.
Church management, 1953, 29(10), 17; 18; 54-63; 75-76.

The minister who is most likely to become a casualty to nervous difficulties suffers from some or all of these "seven deadly sins": lack of adequate self-expression, self-pity, social detachment, over-ambition, perfectionism, inhibitions and compulsions, lack of self-confidence.

THOMPSON, J. S.
A study of the relationships between certain measured psychological variables and achievement in the first year of theological seminary work.
Ph.D., University of Minnesota, 1956.
Dissert. Abstr., 1956, *16,* 1846-1847.

Sample: 113 first-year students from a Lutheran seminary in Minneapolis-St. Paul area.
Procedure: 10-trait faculty rating scale and honor point ratio were criteria compared with SVIB, MMPI, OSUPE.
Results: These seminarians appear to be similar to other graduate students in academic aptitude and personality structure but homogeneous as a group with interests in human relations occupations. Men with the interests of ministers were given higher ratings and earned higher grades.

Men with deviate MMPI profiles achieve less well. Therefore, these instruments seem to measure dimensions which are related to seminary achievement.

TROISFONTAINES, R.
À propos de la vocation sacerdotale: indications et contre-indications.
Nouv. Rev. Théol., 1954, *76,* 716-721.

A listing of the positive and negative indications, including psychological, for encouraging a vocation. The minimal age for ordination should be set at 28, especially if candidates have led sheltered lives.

WAUCK, L. A.
An investigation of the use of psychological tests as an aid in the selection of candidates for the diocesan priesthood.
Ph.D., Loyola University (Chicago), 1956.
Summarized in *Amer. Cathol. Psychol. Newsletter,* 1958, Suppl. No. 35.

Sample: 206 major seminarians.
Procedure: OSUPE, Kuder, MMPI, group Rorschach against a criterion of ratings by 7 prefects.
Results: Scores on the various tests yielded a multiple correlation of .38, significant at .05. The highest of any one score with the criterion was .26 for the group Rorschach; others were very low or negative. When the top 29 and the bottom 33 cases of the rating scale score distribution were isolated, several variables proved able to discriminate the 2 groups. Both groups were within the normal range of MMPI scores.

WEBB, S. C., & GOODLING, R. A.
Test validity in a Methodist theology school.
Educ. psychol. Measmt., 1958, *18,* 859-866. (a)

Sample: 220 students in sixth or lower quarter; 136 entering students.

Procedure: OSUPE, Cooperative English, Cooperative General Culture Test, MMPI, GZTS, SVIB. Criteria are average grades, selected grades, ratings of written work.

Results: (1) There were significant correlations of academic average with dominance on MMPI, 5 scales of SVIB, OSUPE, Cooperative English, and Cooperative General Culture Test. (2) Significant correlation of selected grades with OSUPE. (3) Significant correlations of scores on written work with scores on Cooperative English Test.

WEBB, S. C., GOODLING, R. A., & SHEPHERD, IRMA L.
The prediction of field work ratings in a theological school.
Relig. Educ., 1958, *53,* 534-538. (b)

Sample: 277 theological students at Emory.

Results: Scores on the GZTS and MMPI did not possess validity of sufficient magnitude to be of any practical value for predicting the field work ratings made by the students' field work supervisors.

WHITCOMB, J. C.
The determination of the relationship between personality characteristics and the nature and persistence of problems in the Protestant ministry.
Ph.D., University of Michigan, 1954.
Dissert. Abstr. 1954, *14,* 1182-1183.

Reported in Whitcomb 1957.

WHITCOMB, J. C.
The relationship of personality characteristics to the problems of ministers.
Relig. Educ., 1957, *52,* 371-374.

Sample: 156 seminarians (69% return) and 96 seminary graduates of 5 years (67% return).

Procedure: GZTS and a specially constructed paired comparisons instrument on the problems of ministers.

Results: The problems of seminarians were generally the same as those of seasoned ministers. A student who thinks things will be different after graduation is likely to be wrong.

WRIGHT, H. W.
Memorandum for the chief of chaplains: predicting the success of army chaplains.
Unpublished report. Minneapolis: Author, University of Minnesota Counseling Bureau, 1951. 11 pp.

Sample: 309 army chaplains (basis of selection not described).

Procedure: The following were administered at the time of the study (not at the time of selection): AGCT, MMPI, Kuder, West Point Self Analysis Test, biographical information.

Criterion: Nominations of failure by any 3 of a panel of 12 senior supervising chaplains; 15% of the group were so designated.

Results: A failure group was significantly distinguished from others by lower scores on the AGCT; higher scores on Hs, D, Pd, Mf, Pa, Sc, L, F, and by lower score on Si; lower Kuder literary skill.

FURTHER REFERENCES

For further references on Effectiveness: Personality, see also: **A1:** Godfrey; **A4:** Hunt; **B1:** Mitchell; **B3:** Cavanagh; **D:** Falk 1963; **D:** Nodet; **I:** Brown; **I:** Digna.

EFFECTIVENESS: BACKGROUND

ABRAMS, R. H.
The clergy and their honorary degrees.
Crozer Quart., 1934, *11*, 190-204.

A study of the 1932-33 volume of *Who's Who in America* reveals 2,015 clergymen who hold honorary degrees (76.3% of all clergy in *Who's Who*). Data are presented on the denominations of these men and on the degree-granting institutions.

ALLEN, P. J.
Childhood backgrounds of success in a profession.
Amer. sociol. Rev., 1955, *20*, 186-190.
Excerpt in M. L. Haimowitz & Natalie Haimowitz (Eds.), *Human development: selected readings.* New York: Crowell, 1960. Pp. 736-742.

Sample: 316 usable replies from population of 44 white bishops plus 564 men in Methodist ministry 20-26 years.

Procedure: Questionnaire on life history. Salary data from church records equalized for regional variation.

Results: More successful (higher salary) came from larger towns and schools, better-educated and higher-status parents, and smaller families; most likely to be only child and to have parents who were only children and to report other evidence of closeness to parents; to have majored in social science or philosophy but not religion.

BIOT, R., & GALIMARD, P.
Guide médical des vocations sacerdotales et religieuses.

Paris: Spes, 1952.
Medical guide to vocations.
Westminster, Md.: Newman, 1955.

Psychophysiological aspects of vocation to the priesthood and to the religious life are discussed. The influence of physiological conditions on vocational choice and the factors to be taken into consideration in the entrance examination are considered. They include heredity, temperament, past experience, and physical, mental, and psychological aptitudes. The psychopathic difficulties which can arise in the years of formation and in connection with the life of the vows of religion are also discussed.

CAMPBELL, E. Q., & PETTIGREW, T. F.
Christians in racial crisis: a study of Little Rock's ministers.
Washington, D.C.: Public Affairs Press, 1959.

Research Account: Racial and moral crisis: the role of Little Rock ministers. *Amer. J. Sociol.,* 1959, *64*, 509-516. Reprinted in W. W. Charters & N. L. Gage (Eds.), *Readings in the social psychology of education.* Boston: Allyn & Bacon, 1963. Pp. 51-57.

Brief popular accounts: Men of God in racial crisis. *Christian Century,* 1958, *75*[1], 663-665. Vignettes from Little Rock. *Christianity and Crisis,* 1958, *18*, 128-136.

Sample: 42 ministers and rabbis in Little Rock.

Procedure: Observations and repeated interviews from October, 1957, through

December, 1958, during the school desegregation crisis.

Results: The Protestant ministry is potentially the most effective agent of social change in the South in the decade ahead, but it has not provided the united and forceful leadership expected. Reasons include the influence of sects, lack of status for progressive young clergymen, and need to maintain a smoothly functioning parish. Public support of desegregation is greater among younger ministers, newer in their churches, in local neighborhood churches, in less popular denominations, in churches not engaged in membership or fund-raising campaigns.

CAMPBELL, T. C.
A study in the relation of theology and sociology: the method of correlation applied to minister's conceptions of the relation between church and culture.
Ph.D., University of Chicago, 1963.

Sample: 115 ministers of the Congregational Christian Church were divided into 4 groups: (a) "high potential," those attending a workshop for suburban mission ministers (N = 36), (b) upper-middle and upper class (N = 31), (c) middle class (N = 23), (d) lower middle to low class (N = 25). (b), (c), and (d) were determined from 1960 census data.
Procedure: Questionnaire and interview.
Results: The correlation between social class and the following is discussed: minister's roles (significantly correlated), conflict with parishioners (sig.), general satisfaction with role (not sig.), specific satisfactions (not sig.), number of persons counseled (sig.), minister's theology (not sig.), role in the community (sig.), reading habits (not sig.), feelings of relevancy to culture (sig.), challenge by laymen (sig.). These categories are also examined in relation to age and occupa-

tion of father. In general, a professional and organizational (but antiadministrational) orientation of the ministry is found, with particular emphasis on privatized and personal concerns. Orientation on social concerns tends to follow the expectations of the social-class group to which the clergyman ministers. They feel the church should carry out its role as an extension of the way they feel they should carry out their roles. The dissertation also contains an extended discussion of the relation between sociology and theology.

CAVANAGH, J. R.
Fundamental pastoral counseling: technic and psychology.
Milwaukee: Bruce, 1962.

A textbook on counseling with sections on personality development and mental illness. Chap. 20 (pp. 272-291), "Selection of candidates for the religious life," discusses the factors of heredity, environment, and motivation.

COLLINS, C.
Admission and placing of veterans and belated vocations in minor seminaries.
Natl Cathol. Educ. Ass. Bull., 1949, *46,* 118-121.

Description of experience with 31 veterans in the seminary. In general, the experience has been highly satisfactory.

DEAN, D. G.
Collegiate sources of ministerial recruits.
M.A., Northwestern University, 1947.

A survey of background characteristics of students in Methodist seminaries from about 1900 to 1945. Among other findings: ministers who were ranked as "effective" by their associates participated to a greater degree in college activities than those who were ranked as "ineffective" in their pastoral work by their associates.

DEEGAN, A. X.
Study of career and administrative patterns of pastors.
M.B.A., University of Detroit, 1963.

Some results of this research are reported in Deegan 1964.

DEEGAN, A. X.
Significant factors in the choice of pastors.
Amer. eccl. Rev., 1964, *61*, 97-111.
Reports part of thesis research, Deegan 1963.

Sample: 4,450 pastors, of all parishes in the metropolitan dioceses of 14 Midwestern and far Western states, were sent questionnaires. 36% were returned.
Results: ". . . The following hypothesis has been proven true: there is a tendency to choose parish administrators (pastors) on the basis of seniority, and not on the basis of previous administrative experience, advanced studies, or any other measurable merit or talent."

DUKEHART, C. J.
Screening boys for the minor seminary.
Priest, 1957, *13*, 185-190.

Use of IQ tests is discussed. No boy should be accepted who comes from a broken home or from a home where religion is not taken seriously, or whose parents oppose his entering seminary.

GOUGH, G. A.
An exploratory study of counseling responsibilities of Nazarene pastors with implications for professional training.
Ph.D., Michigan State University, 1963.
Dissert. Abstr., 1963, *24*, 2561.

Sample: Of a stratified random sample of 250 pastors, 5% of the Nazarene pas-

tors in the U.S., 168 were used in the final tabulation.
Procedure: Mailed questionnaire.
Results: Significant relationships were found in amount of time spent in counseling and (1) size of community, and (2) size of church membership; between perceived adequacy of training and (1) regional distribution of pastors, and (2) age of pastors. Courses helpful for the pastor's training are recommended.

GUSTAFSON, J. M.
The clergy in the U.S.
Daedalus, 1963, *92*, 722-744.

The multiple activities of the clergy may be analyzed in terms of three conditions: the voluntaristic character of U.S. religion; the loss of a sense of independent authority in the clergy; the need for relevance to changing socio-cultural patterns.

JACKSON, D. E.
Factors differentiating between effective and ineffective Methodist ministers.
Ph.D., Northwestern University, 1955.
Dissert. Abstr., 1955, *15*, 2320-2321.

Sample: 159 ministers nominated as effective by peers (three fourths provided data), 86 nominated as ineffective (one third provided data). Effectives were told they had been nominated as such. Validity of ratings had been assessed in **B1:** Jackson.
Results: Effectives were less likely to have stepsiblings; less likely to be born in rural areas; fathers more likely to be ministers, proprietors, or managers; less likely to be farmers, skilled, or semiskilled laborers; mother attended church frequently; both parents leaders in the church; more family worship; more reported leadership in church and college, especially college. Effective ministers scored higher on these scales of the Coun-

seling Aid Form: domination, professional habits, effectiveness ratings, early leadership. On CAF, effectives were more likely to describe motivation in terms of a Christian solution to social and political problems, less likely to describe their motivation, "I felt a distinct and divine call."

JAMISON, W. G.
Factors related to the academic achievement of theological seminary students.
Unpublished mimeographed paper. Dubuque, Iowa: Author, Theological Seminary of the University of Dubuque, 1961.

> *Sample:* 207 students who earned a B.D. from this seminary from 1950-59.
> *Procedure:* Correlations were made between seminary grades and college grades, IQ test scores, seminary language grades, college language grades, marital status, age.
> *Results:* College grades gave the most significant relation but exceptions were too numerous to use them for individual prediction. Other factors had little if any relationship. Recommendations to the seminary are reported.

JAMISON, W. G.
Predicting academic achievement of seminary students.
Rev. relig. Res., 1965, *6,* 90-96.

> Report of Jamison 1961.

JOHNSTONE, R. L.
Militant and conservative community leadership among Negro clergymen.
Ph.D., University of Michigan, 1963.
Dissert. Abstr., 1964, *25,* 2099.

> *Sample:* Interviews with (1) a random sample of 59 Negro clergy in Detroit, (2) 10 Negro clergy designated as leaders by the 59, (3) 20 outside "experts," (4) members of the Detroit Board of Educa-

tion and the Detroit Common Council.
> *Procedure:* Clergy designated, on the basis of organizational affiliation, into militants (N = 12), moderates (N = 16), and conservatives (N = 31).
> *Results:* "In summary it can be said that whereas the militant is an aggressive activist, of independent mind, critical of surrounding institutions, organizationally involved, community oriented, young, highly educated, and of relatively high status background, the conservative is unaggressive, inactive beyond his own congregation, verbally uncritical, over 45 years old, poorly educated, and of low status background. Moderates, in general, are in an intermediate position, in which they express social concern and often express militant attitudes, but are careful to avoid alienating the surrounding community." Militants were seen to have a community contact and impact disproportionate to their numbers. While community and political activity are increasing, these Negro clergy have not become a pressure group.

LAWSON, L. B.
The Protestant minister in Chicago: a sociological study of work.
Ph.D., University of Chicago, 1955.

> *Sample:* 50 ministers: 7 Methodist, 8 Presbyterian, 7 Baptist, 7 Lutheran, 7 Congregational, 7 Episcopalian, 7 Disciples.
> *Results:* Factors which lead to or prevent advancement in the ministry are discussed. Advancement is usually determined in the age period 36-49. "Sponsorship" of a man by a denomination promotes the institution's stability. The minister's relationship to his church is more important for advancement than his relationship to his denomination. Suppression of personal opinion is often necessary for advancement.

MOXCEY, MARY E.

Some qualities associated with success in the Christian ministry.

New York: Teachers College, Columbia University, *Contributions to Education, No. 122*, 1922.

(1) A study of the members of the New York and the New York East Conferences of the Methodist-Episcopal Church regarding ratings by fellow ministers, salary, and ability. Concludes that the achievements recorded in annual reports are not those by which "success" should be judged.

(2) A study of graduates from Boston University School of Theology, Drew, and Garrett *re* the relationship of grades to ability and income. Associated with success are high general intelligence and general ability to handle human problems and relationships.

(3) A study of estimated values of curriculum subjects in college and theological training.

MURPHY, G. M.

Our experience with delayed vocations.
Natl Cathol. Educ. Ass. Bull., 1950, *47*, 133-139.

Article by the director of a school for delayed vocations. Matters of stability, letters of recommendation, ability, poor risks of teen-agers, etc., are discussed.

POEHLER, W. A.

The appraisal of the outcomes of two kinds of pre-ministerial training of the Lutheran Church-Missouri Synod.

Ph.D., University of Minnesota, 1954.

Sample: Students at Springfield Seminary (from a wide variety of public and private schools) were compared with those at St. Louis Seminary (from a single

system of private church high schools and junior colleges).

Procedure: ACE scores. A "ministerial aptitude test" was developed to measure spiritual maturity, Bible knowledge, doctrinal knowledge, and adult Christian behavior.

Results: (1) Differences in intellectual ability, as measured by ACE, favor the St. Louis students. (2) Effectiveness of a preministerial program does not seem to be reduced with respect to spiritual maturity when part or all of a student's high school work is in a public school. (3) The aptitude test appears to measure factors other than intelligence and may be useful in predicting success in ministerial training.

QUIGLEY, J. A. M.

Family background in the candidate for the priesthood.
Natl Cathol. Educ. Ass. Bull., 1949, *46*, 122-126.

The following criteria should be adhered to in "almost every case": legitimate birth, Catholic parents, Christian home, personal as well as family good name, and good family stock.

ROSSMAN, P.

The morale of the campus pastor.
Relig. Educ., 1962, *57*, 110-113.

Sample: 127 of 250 Protestant ministers assigned to work at state universities replied to a mailed questionnaire.

Results: 103 indicated that they "wouldn't trade their present job for any other," although some said that they were subject to fluctuations in their optimism. "Lack of support and encouragement from the churches" was the problem most frequently checked. "Ecumenical" campus ministers (employed by a number of denominations) stay for a shorter time but report higher morale than those employed by a single denomination. Morale is higher among those who feel they were "sent" than among those on the campus "by their own decision."

FURTHER REFERENCES

For further references on Effectiveness: Background, see also: **A2:** Mateo; **B1:** Clippinger; **B2:** Burke; Ingram; **B4:** Shissler.

EFFECTIVENESS: PROCEDURES

ALLPORT, G. W., & FAIRBANKS, R. J.
*An evaluation of present methods for se-
lecting postulants in the Episcopal Diocese of Massachusetts.*
Boston (1 Joy St.): The Diocese of Massachusetts, 1953. 28 pp.

The following methods are briefly discussed and evaluated: application blanks,
letters from sponsors, vocational interviews, psychological examinations. A
small ($N = 25$) validation study is reviewed. Continued research is recommended.

ATWOOD, BARBARA M.
Personal change in clinical pastoral train-
ing.
Ph.D., Columbia University, 1958.
Dissert. Abstr., 1958, *19*, 169.

Sample: 54 white male B.D. students
enrolled at 13 centers of the Council for
Clinical Training.
Procedure: Data were collected by
supervisors using the Cornell Index, diary,
questionnaire.
Results: Individuals changed in varying
degrees during the training, but no specific
element of personality and life situation
other than the student's view of himself
and of his relations with others was significantly associated with change.

BONACKER, R. D.
Clinical training for the pastoral ministry:
purposes and methods.
J. pastoral Care, 1960, *14*, 1-12.

Three purposes are listed: spiritual
health, intellectual insight, and pastoral
skill. These purposes are discussed in
terms of the training groups and the chaplaincy program.

BRUDER, E. E., & BARB, MARIAN L.
A summary of ten years of clinical pastoral training at Saint Elizabeth's Hospital.
J. pastoral Care, 1956, *10*, 86-94.

Sample: 122 (88% of the population)
people who had received clinical pastoral
training at Saint Elizabeth's.
Procedure: Mailed questionnaires on
the subjects' development and work as it
related to clinical training.
Results: Highly favorable attitudes to
the training were found, indicating that
clinical training has significant contributions in regard to vocational decisions and
personality development and insight.

CLIPPINGER, J. A.
Attitudes toward pastoral training of
sixty-one outstanding pastors.
Relig. Educ., 1953, *48*, 113-116.

A report of material from **B1:** Clippinger on actual and desired academic
training, especially in pastoral areas.

DURY, G.
An investigation of a means of developing group leadership in religious candidates.

M.A., Catholic University of America, 1949.

> *Sample:* 22 high school sophomores.
>
> *Procedure:* A special leadership training course, featuring discussion, self-analysis, and projects, was evaluated using behavioral observations, student questionnaire, and peer ratings.
>
> *Results:* All students, not just natural leaders, seemed to profit from the training.

FAIRBANKS, R. J.
One seminary looks at clinical training.
J. pastoral Care, 1964, *18*, 208-212.

> *Sample:* 33 students at Episcopal Theological School (Cambridge, Mass.).
>
> *Procedure:* Questionnaires, personal conferences, clinical training reports.
>
> *Results:* Students rated supervisor as of primary importance to their training; next came the program and then the center. They felt the program gave most emphasis to understanding, next to service to others, and least to skills. Consensus was that the training was helpful and should be required and that the supervision was good. Similar results were obtained from the faculty (N not reported) except that faculty rated skills over service.

GYNTHER, M. D., & KEMPSON, J. O.
Personal and interpersonal changes in clinical pastoral training.
J. pastoral Care, 1958, *12*, 210-219.

> *Sample:* Chaplain supervisor and 4 ordained ministers at South Carolina State Hospital for a 3-month summer program.
>
> *Procedure:* MMPI and Interpersonal Checklist, given before and after training, were scored according to Leary's system.
>
> *Results:* Personality structure, as measured, tended to remain relatively constant. Self-descriptions also remained unaltered. The group seemed to be in the preliminary stages of development even after 3 months.

GYNTHER, M. D., & KEMPSON, J. O.
Seminarians and clinical pastoral training: a follow-up study.
J. soc. Psychol., 1962, *56*, 9-14.

> Replication on seminarians of Gynther 1958.
>
> *Sample:* 6 seminary students and a supervisor in a 3-month program at South Carolina State Hospital.
>
> *Procedure:* MMPI and Interpersonal Checklist.
>
> *Results:* Practically no significant changes of public or underlying personality or of self-perception occurred, although seminarians perceived changes in each other.

HERR, V. V.
The Loyola NIMH project: a progress report.
Amer. Cathol. sociol. Rev., 1960, *21*, 331-336.

> Early report on the development of the Loyola (Chicago) NIMH Attitude Scale, curricular materials, and a casebook.

HERR, V. V.
Mental health training in Catholic seminaries.
J. Relig. Hlth, 1962, *1*, 127-152.

> Report of the Religion and Mental Health Project at Loyola (Chicago) under NIMH. Summary also made of **A4:** Markert; **B1:** Meyer; **B2:** Arnold 1962b; **B4:** Keller; and **B4:** Webb.
>
> *Sample:* 980 seminarians from 21 schools.
>
> *Procedure:* NIMH Attitude Scale assessing attitude psychiatry. 12 Chicago priests and 24 Ohio priests were interviewed. 50 seminarians were interviewed and given a battery of clinical tests. Factor analysis (Abraham Rittenhouse).
>
> *Results:* Seminary curricular materials were prepared in the light of assessed

attitudes. A revised curriculum of study is proposed, including practicum training.

HOPKA, E. P.
An investigation of the nature of physical science education for pre-theological students at Lutheran colleges.
Ed.D., University of Colorado, 1956.

Concludes that "science courses for pre-theological students should be taught by instructors who have acquired the ability to apprehend and expound the implications of science for the religious, social, and economic institutions of society."

IRWIN, P. B.
A study of the student personnel program of the School of Religion, University of Southern California, and recommendations for its improvement.
Ed.D., Columbia University, Teachers College, 1955.

A descriptive survey of the student (N = 140) and faculty-administrative staff of the School of Religion. A general discussion and survey of student personnel work with a review of relevant literature is included.

KELLER, J. W.
Comparison between priests with pastoral counseling training and priests without it as measured by the Religious Apperception Test.
Ph.D., Loyola University (Chicago), 1961.

Sample: 2 groups of 29 priests each in matched pairs, differing only in presence (Group I) or absence (Group II) of counseling training; another group of 12 who had just enrolled in a counseling training course (Group III).
Procedure: The Religious Apperception Test (RAT) was designed for the study. It is derived from the TAT and consists of 15 pictures. Stories are scored from 1 to 5 on the following dimensions: self-insight, sensitivity, affect, defensiveness, and adequacy. Interjudge reliability was satisfactory.
Results: Groups II and III were not significantly different on the 5 dimensions. Groups I and II differed significantly on all dimensions. Greatest difference was in self-insight followed by adequacy, affect, sensitivity, and freedom from defensiveness in that order. Improvements in the RAT and further research are discussed.

KENNEDY, E. C.
Differentiated discipline in the seminary.
Unpublished paper. Chicago: Author, Loyola University, 1964.
Delivered at National Catholic Education Association, 1964.

Conditions in seminaries, convents, rectories, and other houses of training and religious life should be made as normal (healthy) as possible. Sometimes seminaries merely reinforce what the seminarian is already good at (self-control) by insisting on practices which further inhibit the very kind of social development he most needs. Teachers must be mature enough to be real with students, and students, too, will be healthy, normal, and mature.

KIM, L. E.
A critical study of selected changes in Protestant theological students with clinical pastoral education.
Ph.D., University of Southern California, 1960.
Dissert. Abstr., 1960, *21*, 1646-1647.

Sample: 17 students with one quarter of clinical education under the Council for Clinical Training; control group of theological students without clinical training. Matched pairs.

Procedure: TAP Social Attitude Battery, Interpersonal Checklist, Religious Attitude Inventory, Security-Insecurity Inventory.

Results: Experimental group showed less authoritarian attitude, no change in self-acceptance, more conservative religious attitudes, and significant increase in insecure feelings.

MAY, M. A.

The education of American ministers. Volume II. The profession of the ministry: its status and problems.

New York: Institute of Social and Religious Research, 1934.

Results are summarized in **A2:** Brown. Detailed data are reported in **A2:** May 1934b.

Sample: Varying samples, totaling about 1,000 for most data.

Procedure: Questionnaires and interviews with clergy and laymen, sample sermons, newspaper files, etc.; census and yearbook data.

Criteria of "success": Size of church, salary, accomplishments (increase in number of members, expenditures, etc.), efficiency of church (derived from proportions of members under 30, volunteer workers, attenders; average contribution; percentage of contribution given to benevolences, etc.), participation by the minister in local and church activities, ratings of social insight and effectiveness. Criteria were generally intercorrelated about .30, except for efficiency index, which had low reliability and was not correlated with other criteria.

Results: Case studies and statistics summarize the work of rural and urban ministers, especially as distributed among priestly, homiletical, pastoral, administrative, educational, civic, and mechanical duties. Ranking of relative importance and difficulty of duties by various subsamples.

Generally, the study finds "lack of a clear definition of the functions of the pastor that can be widely accepted." Success was found generally correlated with amount of training but not with other educational variables such as type of school or major field of study. Seminary grades were found correlated with size of church and efficiency of church. Summary of ministers' questionnaire appraisals of their training. Summary of census statistics on number and social characteristics of clergymen.

MEISSNER, W. W.

Psychiatric training for theology students: a report.

Psychiat. Quart., 1961, *35*, 720-725.

Procedure: 26 priests participated in lectures, demonstrations, discussions, and patient contact on the wards at St. Elizabeth's Hospital over 9 separate days during a 5-month period. The Loyola Test of Religious Attitudes was administered before and after the program.

Results: The program was found to produce more favorable attitudes toward psychiatry in general, but the change was not significant. Various significant changes in particular attitudes were found.

MOSES, J. D.

The intercultural knowledge and attitudes of Episcopal seminary students and the implications for Episcopal seminary education.

Ph.D., University of Southern California, 1955.

Sample: 116 senior Episcopal seminary students in 4 Episcopal seminaries in 1954-55.

Procedure: 100-item index of intercultural knowledge and opinions, opinionnaire (measuring feelings toward Roman Catholics, Chinese, Mexicans, Jews, Negroes, Japanese).

Results: Subjects are said to have inadequate intercultural knowledge, but have "relatively favorable" intercultural attitudes. They are least favorable toward Mexicans. There was more knowledge about the Jews than about Roman Catholics. Students who had completed courses in anthropology, educational or general psychology, international relations and sociology (N = 94) had greater intercultural knowledge but identical intercultural attitudes compared with those who had not had such courses (N = 22).

O'KEEFE, SISTER MAUREEN
Mental health education for religious women.
Ed.D., Loyola University (Chicago), 1962.

An evaluation of programmatic facilities. Integrated religious living is not an automatic process; provision for special learning is necessary. Practical directives for a functional philosophy of life are given.

OLIVER, G. L.
The Millsaps College education of students who expect to enter professional church work.
Ed.D., Columbia University, Teachers College, 1951.

Sample: Present and former ministerial students at Millsaps College (Jackson, Miss.), laymen and district superintendents of the Methodist Church (total N = 95).

Procedure: A questionnaire evaluation of the college curriculum for professional church workers.

Results: Evaluations were generally favorable. Greatest criticism concerned the limited provision for direct experience.

PERRY, J. B.
A study of late vocations in three houses of the Divine Word Missionaries.

M.A., Catholic University of America, 1961.

Sample: 150 late vocations in the 3 houses maintained for them in the United States, Wales, and Germany.

Procedure: 100% return of a questionnaire.

Results: "The present study indicates the need for professional priest counselors in the three houses for students with late vocations."

PLÉ, A. (Ed.)
The priest and vocations.
Westminster, Md.: Newman, 1962. (Religious Life Series, XI.)

A collection of articles on the nature of the call and the role of religious on awakening and encouraging vocations. "Clerical prejudices concerning nuns" (pp. 3-17) and "Criteria of vocation—psychological approach" (see **B2:** Beirnaert 1962) include psychological content, but no data.

RAMSDEN, W. E.
The processes and effects of a training group in clinical pastoral education.
Ph.D., Boston University, 1960.

Sample: 1 group (no control) of 8 members meeting at Boston State Hospital through 35 one-and-a-half-hour sessions.

Procedure: Data was gathered using Leary's Interpersonal Checklist and categorized in terms of inclusion, individuation, and responsibility-taking. Both individual and group changes were plotted. 90 days later, sociometric questionnaires and an interview were used.

Results: Self-understanding and interpersonal effectiveness increased. Leary's system showed little value as a measure. The theory of inclusion, individuation, and responsibility-taking was useful in interpreting the group and is suggested as a fruitful framework.

SCHOLEFIELD, H. B.
Psychoanalysis and the parish ministry.
J. Relig. Hlth, 1963, 2, 112-128.
Similar article in **H:** Oates, pp. 318-329.

This graduate of the Philadelphia Psychoanalytic Institute describes how his educative analysis relates to his own parish ministry. Preaching and pastoral counseling are discussed in some detail.

SHISSLER, H. H.
An experiment in attitudinal outcomes resulting from seminary courses in "the church and community"
Ph.D., Pennsylvania State University, 1956.

Sample: 450 male seminarians in 8 Methodist graduate schools of theology taking "church and community" or, for the controls, courses in church history, Bible, or church administration.

Procedure: Constructed a Thurstone-type attitude scale with 100 items (reliability .71 alternative forms, and .73 split-half). 9 weeks after the first administration, 326 took the scale again.

Results: Community-centeredness was related to location in the North rather than the South, high grades in college, city background, length of time in seminary, graduate of nonchurch college, social science major in college. Upon retesting there was a significant gain (.05) in the retest scores of 210 seminarians of the experimental group over their original scores. Scores of the control group were slightly less in the retest than in the original test.

STRUNK, O., JR., & REED, K. E.
The learning of empathy: a pilot study.
J. pastoral Care, 1960, 14, 44-48.

Sample: 18 male theological students and parish clergymen.

Procedure: The empathy test was given at the beginning and at the end of a 12-week clinical pastoral training course.

Results: Before and after scores correlated .545. Near-significant trend for increase in empathetic ability. Some of the meanings of empathetic ability are discussed and related to the role of the minister.

SWANSON, P. R.
Some effects of clinical pastoral education on a group of theological students and pastors.
Ph.D., Boston University, 1962.
Dissert. Abstr., 1962, 23, 1812-1813.

Sample: 13 theological students in the 12-week Institute of Pastoral Care program at Massachusetts General Hospital.

Procedure: Personality tests and behavior rating scales were administered: Cattell 16 Factor, EPPS, A-V Study of Values, DAT: Verbal Reasoning, self-concept test, peer perception rating. Criterion for the effectiveness of the student's pastoral calls was the student's and supervisor's perception of the patient's reactions to the calls followed by later interviews by the chaplain-supervisors.

Results: Significant change during the 12 weeks on (1) EPPS need for achievement, order, dominance, aggression; (2) decrease on social on A-V Study of Values; (3) increase in discrepancy between self and social self; (4) progressive increase in peer rejection; (5) increase in supervisor's ratings of usefulness of student's visits. Other results showed that students underevaluated their pastoral impact on patients, and that there was no change in personal insight or insight into past performance.

TAGGART, M.

A study of attitude change in a group of theological students.

Ph.D., Northwestern University, 1962.

Dissert. Abstr., 1962, *23*, 2236.

Sample: 83 seminarians enrolled in a basic course in pastoral counseling: 41 experimental, 42 controls.

Procedure: ESDS, MMPI, TSI, OSUPE, and a specially constructed Pastoral Psychology Attitude Survey (split-half reliability .90; test-retest reliability .81). The experimental group was tested before and after the course; the controls only after.

Results: No relationship between attitude change and MMPI or TSI. A significant relationship was found between attitude change and OSUPE. Less change in students who had taken or were taking courses in theology.

Other relationships suggest that students who conceive the "call to the ministry" as a supernatural singling-out are less likely to conform to the attitude of the instructor than students conceiving the call in another way. Those students who had taken or were taking courses in theology were less likely to end up with attitudes similar to those of the instructor, than were those who had taken no theology at all.

THOMPSON, SISTER MARY

Modifications in identity: a study of the socialization process during a sister formation program.

Ph.D., University of Chicago, 1963.

Abstracted in *Relig. Educ.*, 1965, *60*, 77.

Sample: 226 young sisters (including entire list of third-, fifth-, and eighth-year classes) in a training program of a congregation of teaching sisters.

Procedure: Personal Data Questionnaire, Cattell 16 Personality Factor Test, Digna Identity Scale, Paired Direct-Projective Sentence Completion Series.

Results: The program seemed to aim at increasing the "accuracy of the young sister's self-concept and to inculcate in her those Christian ideals to which the religious life commits a young woman." The novitiate (3rd year) was a "period of change and a period of conformity"; the scholastic (5th year) was a time during which ideals became more realistic and self-identification increased.

URSCHALITZ, M. ODELIA

Selected areas of personal adjustment as related to length of community membership and vocation values among religious women educators.

Ph.D., Fordham University, 1959.

Sample: 5 groups of 100 Catholic women: 3 groups represent a gradient in length of community membership, education, teaching experience, and age; 2 groups of Catholic college students.

Procedure: All took the GZTS. The religious groups also took the investigator's Insight Scale for Sister Teachers and a checklist of religious interests.

Results: 6 personality trait scores were significantly related with length of community membership: general activity and masculinity increase, and ascendance, sociability, objectivity, and personal relations decrease.

WAGNER, M.

Seminarians' attitudes in personal counseling and their relation to selected personality traits.

B.A., Duns Scotus College (Detroit, Mich.), 1957.

Sample: 65 Franciscan clerics.

Procedure: GZTS and Porter Counseling Procedures Pretest.

Results: The "understanding" trait appears only when training is added to favorable personality traits. Traits were found to correlate with the different counseling methods when the group was divided into psychologically trained and untrained groups.

WEBB, N. J., & KOBLER, F. J.
Clinical-empirical techniques for assessing the attitudes of religious toward psychiatry.
J. soc. Psychol., 1961, *55*, 245-251.

Data from the following battery given to 55 seminarians were analyzed: interview, Loyola Balloon Drawing Test, Loyola SCT, Religious Apperception Test. From these data a 35-statement attitude scale was constructed combining Likert and Thurstone methods. Cross-validation was done on 296 seminarians. Reliability: split-half .95, test-retest (2 weeks) .93. Validity: difference (.001) between the group taking a course expected to produce an attitude change and a matched control.

WISE, C. A.
Teaching so that the student becomes alive.
Report of the 2nd biennial meeting of the Association of Seminary Professors in the Practical Fields, 1952. Pp. 7-15.

Varieties of theological students are described in order to examine problems which arise in the seminary. Issues discussed include curriculum, teaching methods, student selection, and clinical training.

WUERFFEL, L. C.
A study of changes in a theological student's concept of the ministry during the year of internship.
Ed.D., Washington University, 1961.
Dissert. Abstr., 1962, *22*, 4279.

Sample: 46 students at Concordia Seminary, St. Louis.

Procedure: Both before and after the intern year, subjects took an instrument especially designed for this study, consisting of 7 open-ended questions. Expert opinion, faculty and student, on change resulting from the internship experience was gathered.

Results: Essentially negative. This may mean that the cognitive understanding of the student does not undergo a substantial change during the year of internship.

FURTHER REFERENCES

For further references on Effectiveness: Procedures, see also: **A1:** Wagoner; **A2:** Brown; **A2:** Higdon; **A2:** May 1934b; **B1:** Clippinger; **B1:** Webb; **B2:** Atwater; **B2:** Southard; **E:** Howe; **E:** Lyon 1964.

C

DIFFERENCES AMONG CLERGYMEN

ALBERTS, W. E.
Measuring ministers' attitudes toward juvenile delinquency.
Ph.D., Boston University, 1961.
Dissert. Abstr., 1961, *22*, 1262.

Sample: From population of 92 Protestant ministers in the Boston area with which juvenile offenders brought to court in 1957 and 1958 had been actively or nominally associated, 74 completed a questionnaire and 40 were interviewed.

Procedure: Authoritarianism (F) Scale, Traditional Family Ideology Scale, and original Juvenile Delinquency Attitude Scale, assessing the authoritarian or supportive attitude toward delinquents. Content analysis of recorded interviews with 20 highest and 20 lowest scorers on JDA.

Results: 3 scales intercorrelated between .77 and .83. Interview data elaborated the coercive and punitive or supportive and rehabilitative attitudes toward delinquents. Theological beliefs, determined from interview data, were not correlated with attitude toward delinquents. "It is concluded that a minister's deeply-lying emotional dispositions, more than his abstract theological beliefs, generally determine the nature, extent, and effectiveness of his approach to juvenile delinquency."

ALBERTS, W. E.
Ministers' attitudes toward juvenile delinquency.
Washington, D.C.: Division of Temper-

ance and Welfare, The Methodist Church, 1962. 84 pp.
Personality and attitudes toward juvenile delinquency: a study of Protestant ministers.
J. soc. Psychol., 1963, *60*, 71-83.

Summaries of Alberts 1961.

ALLEN, J. E.
Family planning attitudes of Methodist seminary husbands and wives.
Ph.D., Boston University, 1964.
Dissert. Abstr., 1964, *25*, 3132.

Sample: Married couples in 10 Methodist and 13 non-Methodist seminaries.

Procedure: 1,780 questionnaires with 72 items were returned (92.4%).

Results: Responses reported include number of children desired, use of contraceptives, perception of denominational policy, sources of information, counseling received.

BALDWIN, P. A.
Vocational values of 100 Unitarian ministers.
Ph.D., Boston University, 1964.
Dissert. Abstr., 1964, *25*, 3133.

Sample: 100 Unitarian ministers were divided into 2 subgroups with median ages distinguished from one another by 17 years. About 25% were trained in non-Unitarian seminaries.

Procedure: Essays on current concepts of the liberal ministry and church were content-analyzed using a 2 dimensional-3 level classification, with 138 categories in all, derived from Maslow's theory.

Results: The ministers demonstrated predominant interest in a pastoral ministry to members helping each creatively to realize his potential. Their next general area of concern related to the professional qualifications of ministers and the norms of the liberal church as an institution and movement. About half were concerned with gaining an understanding of life and with discovering personal meaning, faith, hope. Differences were found between two groups aged in their 30's and 40's.

BILLINSKY, J. M.
Roles of clergymen and their effect upon his pastoral counseling.
In *Connecticut Conference on Pastoral Counseling, The Partnership of Clergymen and Psychiatrists.* West Hartford, Conn.: Holy Family Monastery, 1960. Pp. 20-38.

Priestly roles of the pastoral counselor include the wise old man, dispenser of God's grace, intermediary between God and man, protector, and healer; of the professional role: knower, doer, intermediary, and defender; of the personal role: individual, family man, and weakness as a human being. These roles are considered in relation to counseling situations. Audience questions and answers are included.

CARLIN, J. E., & MENDLOVITZ, S. H.
The rabbi: a sociological study of a religious specialist.
M.A., University of Chicago, 1951.

Sample: 34 rabbis, representing a random sample of Chicago rabbis, stratified by denomination (8 Reformed, 8 Conservative, and 18 Orthodox).
Procedure: Structured interview, mostly wire recorded.

Results: 3 types of roles determined: (1) Traditional, orthodox rabbi, attempting to preserve the authority and role of "scholar-saint" of traditional Eastern European rabbi. "Little or no influence in a rapidly diminishing congregation." (2) Intellectual reform rabbi, reacting against scholar-saint role, and claiming authority by intellectual skills and activities. (3) Between these 2 extreme roles, a newly evolving role represented in all 3 denominations, but especially characteristic of the Conservative: organizing and administrating work, to retain the institution; multiple functions of preaching, counseling, teaching, etc., imitating Protestant pastor's role; aspirations towards scholar-saint role.

CARLIN, J. E., & MENDLOVITZ, S. H.
The American rabbi: a religious specialist responds to loss of authority.
In M. Sklare (Ed.), *The Jews: social patterns of an American group.* Glencoe, Ill.: The Free Press, 1958. Pp. 377-414.
Summary of **C**: Carlin 1951.

CUMMING, ELAINE, & HARRINGTON, C.
Clergyman as counselor.
Amer. J. Sociol., 1963, 69, 234-243.

Sample: 1 clergyman from each of 59 churches in Syracuse, N.Y., representative of the counseling activities of the city's churches (Protestant, Catholic, Orthodox, Jewish).
Procedure: Interview.
Results: Data on three variables are presented: characteristics of the clergyman and his congregation, nature of the problems counseled, articulation of the clergyman's counseling role with the remainder of the system. This articulation was indicated by a "boundary activity score": "a clergyman who participates in a system of divided labor with others can be thought of as having a high level of

activity across the boundary of his counseling role." The highest such score (3),
earned by 26 clergymen, indicates an active rather than passive form of referral.
This score was related to size and social
class of congregation but not to its denomination. "Strains" to which the counseling role is subject are discussed.

DITTES, J. E.
Impulsive closure as reaction to failure-
induced threat.
J. abnorm. soc. Psychol., 1961, *63*, 562-
569.

Sample: 57 Yale Divinity School students.
Procedure: "Failure" or "success" on
an intellectual task (the Space Relations
Test) was induced at random by fictitious
keys and norms. Closure was assessed by
written tasks measuring the tendency (1)
to find a positive meaning in an essentially
incoherent prose passage rather than to
acknowledge its incoherence, and (2) to
base an impression of another person exclusively on more prominent traits and to
ignore inconsistent traits.
Results: Subjects experiencing failure
subsequently showed significantly more
impulsive closure.

FOSTER, BARBARA R.
Some interrelationships between religious
values, leadership concepts, and perception of group process of professional
church workers.
Ph.D., University of Michigan, 1958.
Dissert. Abstr., 1958, *19*, 1282-1283.

Sample: 70 professional church workers
attending a training conference.
Procedure: Subjects listed and ranked
the importance of separate characteristics
of their beliefs. Sensitivity to group processes was measured by written reactions
to two role-playing situations.

Results: Hypothesis confirmed that religious beliefs and concepts of leadership
are related and that these two cognitive
structures affect the perception of group
process. For example, those who were
high affect-oriented in their concept of the
"role of man" were also high affect (process)-oriented to leadership; those who
were high task-oriented in their concept
of the "role of man" were also high task
(content)-oriented in their leadership
concepts. Those with a highly differentiated religious belief system were low affect-
oriented, high task-oriented, and creedal.
Noncreedal persons had a highly complex
religious structure.

GOLD, R. L.
The role of clergymen in community
mental health.
Final progress report of a small grant
study (M-3128 A) to National Institute of Mental Health.
Missoula, Mont.: Author, Montana State
University, undated (about 1962).
15 pp.

Sample: 148 of the 167 clergymen in
western Montana.
Procedure: Interviews; no quantitative
data reported.
Results: Fundamentalists emphasize
spiritual over mental problems and solu-
tions; they also emphasize the role of
preaching. Liberalists do not distinguish
spiritual and mental and are more self-
conscious about assuming a confident pastoral role. Other discussion is offered of
the role problems of a pastoral counselor,
including relations with parishioners, and
other professionals.

GUSTAFSON, J. M.
Theological students: varieties of types
and experience.
In H. R. Niebuhr, D. D. Williams, & J.

M. Gustafson, *The advancement of theological education*. New York: Harper, 1957. Pp. 145-173.

A discussion of data from interviews in many seminaries, intensive interviews at 7 seminaries. 10 "kinds of men who come to our seminaries" are listed. There is also a discussion of the types of experiences which men have while at seminary.

JOHNSON, C. D.
Priest, prophet, and professional man: a study of religious leadership in a small community.
Ph.D., University of Minnesota, 1961.
Dissert. Abstr., 1963, *23*, 346.

Sample: 107 parishioners and 12 clergy in a small Minnesota town.
Procedure: Interview; analysis of preaching and worship services. The hypothesis, based on Weber's typology of authority and Parsons' analysis of the professions, was that priestly authority is found in sacramental churches, prophetic authority in sectarian churches, and professional authority in churches neither sacramental nor sectarian in nature. A typology embodying this hypothesis was established on the basis of 25 clergy interviews.
Results: 75% of the clergy responses and somewhat fewer lay responses supported the hypothesis in the direction predicted.

JOHNSON, S. D.
Issue perception and decision-making among religious leaders.
Ph.D., University of Washington, 1961.
Dissert. Abstr., 1962, *22*, 4109-4110.

Sample: 27 ministers affiliated with a council of churches; 27 associated with an association of Evangelical churches.
Procedure: Interviews yielding ratings on issues and a schema of action categories.
Results: Decision-makers varying with respect to the issues in which they become involved according to their social characteristics and theological position. Similar relationships exist with respect to how issues are perceived.

KANTER, LOUISE M.
Modes of orientation among Protestant clergymen: authoritarianism and humanism.
Ph.D., University of Nebraska, 1955.
Dissert. Abstr., 1955, *15*, 1664-1665.

Sample: 40 Protestant ministers selected at random.
Procedure: F scale, content analysis of sermons, an "open-mindedness" questionnaire, including projective questions.
Results: Protestant clergymen could be distinguished on the basis of authoritarianism and humanism, as formulated by Fromm. The author discusses the more salient lines of differentiation. The humanist is concerned with helping people, while the authoritarian is concerned only with getting people right with God.

KLING, F., PIERSON, E., & DITTES, J. E.
Relation of TSI scores and selected items of biographical information.
TSI Research Bull. #1. Dayton, O. (1810 Harvard Blvd.): Ministry Studies Board, 1963. 5 pp.

Sample: 220 students entering 23 theological schools in fall of 1959.
Procedure: TSI scores were correlated with 32 items of biographical information, concerning family, church experience, and history of vocational decision.
Results: Results are taken as generally supporting interpretation of scales offered by the test's manual, especially of D, NL, A, and L. Correlations with I, R, and P

suggest these scales reflect mild rebellious-
ness. High F score is found characteristic
of men making a late decision.

LESLIE, R. C.
The background and intentions of theo-
logical students.
Report of the 5th biennial meeting of the
Association of Seminary Professors in
the Practical Fields, 1958. Pp. 65-75.

Sample: An entering class at Pacific
School of Religion (N = 40).
Procedure: Students classified according to Gustafson's 10 types of theological
students (see **C:** Gustafson) using autobiographies, psychological tests, application
blanks, letters of reference.
Results: The criticism of theological
students by Whyte in *The Organization
Man* as tending toward conformity, conservatism, and collaboration is discussed
in light of the data.

MAURER, BERYL B.
A study of selected factors associated with
the professional behavior-image of
Protestant parish ministers.
Ph.D., Pennsylvania State University,
1959.
Dissert. Abstr., 1959, *20*, 788.

Sample: 581 Protestant parish ministers
in 22 denominations from all parts of the
country. (See **B1:** Blizzard.)
Procedure: Mailed questionnaire.
Results: Significant differences in the
professional behavior-image of ministers
were related with rural-urban, metropoli-
tan-nonmetropolitan, and region; organizational complexity; age and occupational
mobility. No significant difference was
found between the degree of variation in
the minister's behavior-image related with
the urban-rural factor, and that related
with organizational complexity.

MEISSNER, W. W.
Affective response to psychoanalytic death
symbols.
J. abnorm. soc. Psychol., 1958, *56*, 295-
299.

Sample: 40 Catholic seminarians.
Procedure: 20 death-symbol words
(e.g., bird, black) mixed with 30 control
words were presented to subjects individually, relaxed on a couch, as a word
association test. GSR response was recorded. Subjects were subsequently asked
to group the 20 words into those with common associations.
Results: Death-symbol words showed
significantly greater average amplitude of
GSR response, and tended, in written test,
to be grouped with association of death.

MILLER, R. L.
An exploratory analysis of the preferences
of first year theological students designated as liberal and conservative
toward directive and non-directive responses in the pastor-parishioner counseling relationship.
Ph.D., Michigan State University, 1963.
Dissert. Abstr., 1964, *25*, 1011.

Sample: First-year students in 14 "representative" theological seminaries in the
United States.
Procedure: Religious Beliefs Inventory
to designate students as liberal or conservative; interview sets to indicate preference for directive or nondirective responses in each of the following problem
areas: emotional, spiritual, ethical, marital; information questionnaire.
Results: Significantly more liberals than
conservatives chose nondirective responses. The differences were not significant in the emotional and ethical areas.
Both liberals and conservatives preferred
more nondirective than directive responses.

MILLS, E. W.
The minister's decision to leave the parish.
Unpublished paper. Cambridge, Mass.:
   Author, Harvard University, 1965.
Presented to the Eastern Regional Meet-
   ing of the Religious Research Associ-
   ation, New York City, January 29,
   1965.

Sample: 60 Presbyterian ministers who
had recently moved from a pastorate, 15
into secular employment, 15 into graduate study, 15 into church executive service,
15 into another United Presbyterian pastorate.

Procedure: Extended interview on bases
for vocational decision. Content analysis
of reasons for moving.

Results: Men tended to move into secular work because of serious conflicts,
marital crises, and a sense of helplessness
in the parish. Dominant themes for re-
suming study were previous plans to do
so and serious conflicts in the church. Men
tended to move into executive service for
the attractiveness of the position and into
new pastorates because of restlessness for
a new challenge.

NAMECHE, E. F.
The minister and his counselee.
In H. Hofmann, *The ministry and mental
   health.* New York: Association Press,
   1960. Pp. 221-251.

Sample: 100 Protestant ministers in
Boston area, 50 in San Francisco area,
random, stratified by denomination. Members of these ministers' churches: 50 counselees and 25 noncounselees in Boston, 25
counselees and 15 noncounselees in San
Francisco.

Procedure: Structured interview.

Results: Ministers ranked counseling
high in importance, low in time spent, and
administrative work low in importance
and high in time spent. Median amount

of counseling was 4 hours per week.
Amount of counseling correlated slightly
with low social class, with liberal theological position, and with amount of counseling training, not with size of church or
staff. Summary of types of problems counseled, ministers' opinions on need for more
training, and a report of relations with
mental health agencies. Summary of attitudes toward counseling and minister by
interviewed laymen. Some differences between 2 cities were attributed to greater
conservatism in San Francisco.

NORTHWOOD, L. K.
Ecological and attitudinal factors in
   church desegregation.
Soc. Probl., 1958, *6,* 150-163.

Sample: 78 Protestant clergymen in Des
Moines, Iowa.

Procedure: Questionnaire assessing attitudes and practices in relation to segre-
gation-integration.

ODEN, W. B.
Preaching and personality: a functional
   typology related to perceptions of selected pastors.
Th.D., Boston University School of Theology, 1964.

Sample: 59 pastors in Oklahoma (of an
initial group of 100).

Procedure: Bernreuter and a preaching
inventory. Karen Horney's personality
typology was used to analyze personality
data.

Results: The following hypotheses were
confirmed: (1) A preacher with a personality oriented toward people tends to
preach people-oriented sermons (.05).
(2) A preacher with a personality oriented away from people tends to preach
concept-oriented sermons (.01). (3) A
preacher with a personality oriented

against people tends to preach verdict-oriented sermons (.025).

OSSORIO, ELIZABETH D.
Clergymen and community resources.
Ph.D., Washington University, 1963.
Dissert. Abstr., 1964, *24*, 4851.

Sample: 12 clergy from each of Evangelical and Reformed, Missouri Synod Lutheran, Roman Catholic, and Jewish, in the St. Louis area.
Procedure: Interview.
Results: Formal and informal training in mental health problems has little effect on resource use. Marriage problems are most frequent of those brought to the minister and are seldom referred. Little use is made of child guidance clinics. Prolonged service to the same congregations, particularly in interdenominational or secular organizations, and sponsorship of mental health agencies is related to a high rate of referrals.

PAHNKE, W. N.
Drugs and mysticism: an analysis of the relationship between psychedelic drugs and the mystical consciousness.
Ph.D., Harvard University, 1964.

Sample: 20 volunteer theological students.
Procedure: Administration of psilocybin to half the sample preceding a Good Friday worship service in a small chapel. Subjects attended services or remained in nearby rooms individually or in groups. Data included content analysis of subjects' and observers' accounts during and after a session, questionnaires, and interviews, including a 6-month follow-up study. Data were coded as to degree of correspondence with 9 categories of mystical experience, such as "transcendence of time and space," "deeply felt positive mood."
Results: Subjects receiving psilocybin showed significantly greater similarity to mystical experience on each of the 9 categories.

PORTER, H. T.
Ideas of God reflected in published sermons of 25 American Protestant preachers selected as "most influential" in 1924.
Ph.D., University of Pittsburgh, 1956.
Dissert. Abstr., 1957, *17*, 179.

Sample: 25 ministers selected in a national *Christian Century* poll in 1924 as "most influential."
Procedure: Content analysis of published sermons.
Results: Varieties of theological opinion are reflected only to a limited extent. The major observed difference is on the transcendent-immanent argument as this affects the view concerning revelation. These preachers were influenced by and sensitive to the "world situation." The main type of sermon aims at solving the life situations of actual people by leading the discussion to doctrinal and biblical sources.

PROCTOR, R. A.
A study of attitude changes in theological students during one year of seminary training.
Ed.D., Temple University, 1961.
Dissert. Abstr., 1961, *22*, 343.

Sample: 130 seminary students.
Procedure: A-V Study of Values, GPP, and the Theological Opinionnaire, a specially constructed 68-item Thurstone-type scale for measuring theological position (test-retest reliability .85; validity significant at .05).
Results: A shift of opinion toward a less conservative theological position was significant at the .01 level. The emotionally stable person probably feels freer to

change his opinion than does the less stable individual.

RANCK, J. G.
Some personality correlates of religious attitude and belief.
Ph.D., Columbia University, Teachers College, 1955.

Sample: 800 Protestant male theological students drawn selectively from 28 schools which represent the theological continuum from extreme conservatism to extreme liberalism.

Procedure: Anonymous questionnaire and personality tests including MMPI, Bernreuter, Authoritarianism, Wallen Food Aversion, Levinson-Lichenberg & McLean Scales of Religious Attitude and Belief.

Results: Theological conservatism was substantially correlated with authoritarianism, significantly but less correlated with submissiveness. Liberalism showed significant but small correlation with over-productivity, impulsivity, and feminine interests. Pathology was not related to ideology.

RANCK, J. G.
Some personality correlates of theological conservatism and liberalism.
The Drew Gateway, 1957, *27,* 59-70.
Summary of Ranck 1955.

RANCK, J. G.
Religious conservatism-liberalism and mental health.
Pastoral Psychol., 1961, *12*(112), 34-40.
Pp. 65-75 in **H:** Oates.
Abridgment of Ranck 1957.

RODEHAVER, M. W., & SMITH, L. M.
Migration and occupational structure: the clergy.

Soc. Forces, 1951, *29,* 416-421.

Data: Reasons for moving of 196 Universalist clergymen in 1947. A statistical study of the length of pastorates in the Roman Catholic, Episcopal, and Universalist denominations in 79 localities in New York and New England for the years 1924-1949.

Results: The job-seeking clergyman, who acted in a free market, had as his subjective goal "success," rather than merely utilitarian goals of some sort of traditional security. The objective result of such migration was very frequently the *achievement* of greater "success" symbols, rather than the *loss* of these symbols. Frequency of migration increased with an increase in the free market structuring of the occupation, and decreased as bureaucratic structuring increased.

SAMSON, A.
Church pastors in four agricultural settings in Montana.
Bozeman, Mont.: Agricultural Experiment Station Bulletin #539, April, 1958.

Sample: Interviews were completed with 53 pastors serving the 62 occupied pulpits of 76 churches in agricultural Montana in 1955.

Results: More resident pastors were found at the most rural and most densely populated extremes. In general, the more rural the community, the higher the percentage of churches served by resident pastors. 60% of open-country church pastors were also employed in nonreligious work. Over 90% were born outside Montana and over two thirds were born in rural communities. Nearly half had 4 years of college and 3 of seminary. Generally, the more rural the church, the less was its pastor's formal preparation. There was a decline in membership as the participation of the pastor in community organizations increased.

SCHORR, M. M.

Conformity strength and its relationship to personality characteristics of ministerial candidates.

Ph.D., University of Denver, 1960.

Sample: 150 male students at Iliff.

Procedure: MAT, Gustafson Scale of Religious Beliefs, Rorschach, and TAT were administered in a group situation. Faculty ratings were obtained.

Results: Highest 30 and lowest 30 were selected on basis of Rorschach Conformity Strength Index (based on cliché responses, popular responses, animal responses, pure form responses, usual detail responses). Conformity associated with the following responses on Rorschach: greater productivity, animal %, W %, usual detail, warm-blooded animal, small detail, experience balance (productivity on last 3 cards). High conformity group gave more responses on TAT. No difference on MAT, Gustafson, or teacher ratings of interior vs. instutionalized religion.

SCHULTZ, K. V.

The psychologically healthy person: a study in identification and prediction.

J. clin. Psychol., 1958, *14*, 112-117.

Sample: 40 male graduate students at the School of Religion, University of Southern California, homogeneous with respect to age, social background, and social acquaintance.

Procedure: Subjects were sociometrically matched with paragraph personality descriptions by fellow subjects, yielding a score of "self-actualization" or health, according to the degree with which each subject had been matched with the "self-actualizing" paragraph and not others. Subjects then took 2 tests: (1) an adaptation of Guilford's Social Institutions Test, on which subjects were scored for their creative written reactions to social prob-

lems, (2) a written appraisal of characteristic personal conflicts, on which subjects were scored for their sensitive creative responses.

Results: Subjects' self-actualization could be designated by fellow subjects reliably different from chance. The self-actualization index was correlated (about .40) with test performances.

SHAND, J. D.

A factor-analytic study of Chicago Protestant ministers' conceptions of what it means to be "religious."

Ph.D., University of Chicago, 1953.

Sample: 54 Protestant clergymen selected to represent (at least 2 each) every major Protestant viewpoint in Chicago, as judged by a panel of church leaders.

Procedure: A pool of 2,400 items defining "religious" was collected from extended interviews with 142 Roman Catholic, Jewish, and Protestant clergymen. These were sorted, by 5 judges, into 180 groups of similar items. (All items, sorted into groups, are recorded in appendix.) A representative item from each group comprised the 180 items Q-sorted (forced distribution, 11 piles) by subject. Correlations among subjects factor analyzed.

Results: No general factor. 4 clearly identifiable factors:

"Righteous-formalistic fundamentalist," emphasizing conversion, scriptures, creeds, ritual, morality, stability, and courageousness. (Associated especially with National Baptist, Missouri Lutheran, Evangelical Lutheran, United Lutheran, and conservative representatives of American Baptists, Disciples, and Presbyterians.)

"Practical fundamentalist" emphasizing conversion, scriptures, and moral courage, proper comportment, and other trait characteristics, rather than traditional forms of religion.

"Theistic-brotherliness, nonfundamentalist" emphasizing trait characteristics of

brotherliness, ethics, truth, honesty; emphasizing belief in God but not in Christ.
"Theistic-Christian, nonfundamentalist"
emphasizing some trait characteristics as
other nonfundamentalist factor, and also
belief in both God and Christ. (Represented especially by Congregational Christian, high Episcopalian, and liberal
representatives of American Baptists,
Disciples, and Presbyterians.)

Some suggestions of a fifth factor, "Fel-
lowship-formalistic fundamentalist."

STANLEY, G.
Personality and attitude characteristics of
  fundamentalist theological students.
Australian J. Psychol., 1963, *15*, 121-
  123.

Sample: 347 theological students from 8
different denominations.
Procedure: Maudsley Personality Inventory, Melvin Inventory, Dogmatism Scale,
MMPI, and various religious belief measures. Belief items defined a fundamentalist (N = 130) and a nonfundamentalist
group (N = 217).
Results: The fundamentalist group was
higher on the lie scale, more conservative,
more certain and more dogmatic than the
nonfundamentalist. Fundamentalism represents the religious manifestation of the
"closed mind."

THOMAS, J. S.
A study of the social role of the Negro
  rural pastor in four selected southern
  areas.
Ph.D., Cornell University, 1954.

Sample: 107 rural Negro pastors in
Georgia, South Carolina, Virginia, and
Arkansas were interviewed.
Results: Subjects considered preaching
their most important duty; most came from
homes of farmers or preachers and were
40 years old or more. "Otherworldly" calls
were frequent but decreased with rising

education. Further data on education, income, and role behavior are given.

VAUGHAN, R. P.
A study of personality differences between
  contemplative and active religious
  women.
Ph.D., Fordham University, 1956.

Sample: 150 contemplative cloistered
women were individually matched with
150 active teaching and nursing religious.
Procedure: MMPI, Sacks SCT, Draw-a-
Person, all self-administered.
Results: As a group, the contemplative
and active were higher on the MMPI than
a normative sample. The two groups differed significantly (.05) on 7 of 10 MMPI
scales but not on the SCT or DAP. Differences between the groups increased with
time in religion.

VOOR, J. M.
The relation between the religious attitude
  and the conservative-radical attitude
  among seminarians.
M.A., Catholic University of America,
  1953.

Sample: 251 students in 2 Midwestern
seminaries.
Procedure: Kerr's General Attitudinal
Values Profile.
Results: The conservatism-radicalism
attitude may not be considered a unitary
trait; greater religious conservatism does
not seem to indicate any greater conservatism in the political, social, economic, and
aesthetic fields. Students who are longer
in residence at the seminary are significantly more conservative.

WHITESEL, J. A.
Parental relationships of theological students in reference to dominance-sub-
  mission.
Ph.D., Boston University, 1952.

Sample: 40 male theological students selected at random from the first-year class at Boston University School of Theology.

Procedure: A-S Reaction Study, GAMIN, TAT, SCT, situations questionnaire for parent-child relationships, religion questionnaire, autobiographical statement, structured interview.

Results: (1) Dominant students varied and submissive students were unvaried in ratios of descriptions and types of relationships described for each parent. (2) Dominants experienced more acceptance. (3) Mothers of both groups were accepting, but dominants reported more rejecting situations. (4) Fathers of submissives were characterized as rejecting.

WITHROW, C. Q.
A study of the possible correlation between theological orientations and certain variables of personality.
Ph.D., University of Southern California, 1960.
Dissert. Abstr., 1960, *21*, 1651-1652.

Sample: 98 first-year male students from 4 theological seminaries.

Procedure: Subjects were differentiated into conservative-liberal groups using Gustafson Scale of Religious Beliefs. Groups were then compared on the EPPS.

Results: The two theological orientations are basically different in mood and concept. There were significant differences between groups on heterosexuality, order, deference, intraception, abasement. There is a definite relationship between the theological orientation and the direction of the differences.

WOODS, D. C.
The personality adjustment and social, economic, and political attitudes of liberal and conservative ministerial students.
Ph.D., University of Chicago, 1956.

Sample: 51 students from a "conservative" seminary; 18 students from a "liberal" seminary.

Procedure: Biographical data, A-V Study of Values, Authoritarianism, Ethnocentrism, Politico-economic Conservatism scales (Adorno); lie scale (MMPI), TAT, SCT, Projective questions (Adorno), arithmetic problems (Rokeach).

Results: Correlations from .69 to .82 were found between personality adjustment and religion, social and politico-economic and ethnocentric attitudes. In most cases these were higher than those in Adorno's study, in that both groups expressed significantly less prejudice than average and the high group was middle-of-the-road in ethnocentrism. Their arithmetic scores are average rather than extreme as one might expect. Successful cross-validation was made by two independent judges of TAT, SCT, and Projective questions.

FURTHER REFERENCES

For further references on Differences Among Clergymen, see also: **A1:** Dodson; **A2:** Lenski; **A2:** Tumblin; **A4:** Forest; **A4:** White; **B3:** Johnstone; **G:** Jamieson.

BAER, P.
Potential stress and individual adaptation: a study of a seminary.
Ph.D., University of Chicago, 1954.

Sample: 15 students, 3 faculty, and 12 graduates (selected as successful by denominational officials) of Meadville Theological School, University of Chicago.

Procedure: A questionnaire was sent to the 12 graduates. Students and faculty gave extended interviews. Students also took a Q-sort, Rorschach, TAT, and a sociometric questionnaire. Students were rated by the faculty.

Results: Data are integrated into a description of each student. Many stress situations in seminary life are identified (in fact, no aspect was found to be free from stress); the establishment of personal independence is primary in most situations. Means of adaptation vary widely. Students whose attitudes are positive to the administration (adaptation) are ranked by the faculty much more highly on success as a student (stress). Students as a group show high anxiety, withdrawal, perseverative and obsessive ideas, and illogical and confused thinking; yet most are capable of genuine introspection and appropriate, responsive, emotional contact with others. It is not clear how the questionnaires from graduates were used.

BLAIN, D.
Fostering the mental health of ministers.
Pastoral Psychol., 1958, *9*(84), 9-18.
Pp. 18-32 in **H:** Oates.

The author presents seven common hazards to the mental health of the minister stemming from the nature of his profession. The basic psychological principles upon which the minister can build a mentally healthy life for himself, his family, and his parish are discussed.

BLIZZARD, S. W.
Role conflicts of the urban minister.
The City Church, 1956, *7*(4), 13-15.

Sample: 345 urban parish clergy representing 21 Protestant denominations.
Procedure: Mail interview.
Results: Several themes emerge from the conflicts of urban ministers: (1) believer vs. prophet role: the minister feels he is expected to be a man of belief, but to withhold his judgments on social issues; (2) practitioner vs. scholar role: although the average time per day devoted to practitioner roles is 10 hours, 32 minutes, and to intellectual and sermon preparation activities is 65 minutes, the minister persists in admiring the scholar image; (3) specialist vs. general practitioner: lack of specialists forces the minister to perform a wide range of duties but his view of success in the denomination places a high value on his proficiency in one role; (4) effectiveness in the parish vs. success in the denomination: characteristics of these images are ranked differently; (5) professional vs. family man: the average urban minister spends 1 hour, 46 minutes daily with his family, 33 minutes less than his rural counterpart; (6) professional vs. extraprofessional role: though the min-

ister's primary responsibility is to his church, his membership in the community imposes certain requirements and expectations upon him.

"In the context of conflicting role expectations, the urban clergyman faces the problem of emotional maturity and the desire for self-understanding."

BRAUDE, L.
The rabbi: some notes on identity clash.
Jewish Soc. Stud., 1960, *22*, 43-52.

Sample: 17 randomly selected rabbis, representing all 3 denominations.
Procedure: Interview.
Results: The descriptive analysis finds "identity clash" at the time of decision for the rabbinate and again as the trained rabbi finds his own expectations for his role in conflict with those of his congregation.

BROOKS, R. M.
The ex-seminarian.
Ave Maria, 1960, *92*, 5-10. (a)

Reports some results from Brooks 1960b.

BROOKS, R. M.
The former major seminarian: a study of change in status.
Ph.D., University of Notre Dame, 1960. (b)
Dissert. Abstr., 1960, *21*, 694.
Natl Cathol. Educ. Ass. Bull., 1961, *58*, 45-52.

Sample: 200 former major seminarians.
Procedure: CPI and social adjustment profiles.
Results: The transition from seminary to lay life involves role discontinuity; three fourths experience postseminary "trauma" (akin to anomie). Postseminary adjustment problems are concentrated in the areas of occupations, social relations,

and spiritual life (in that order of importance). Three fifths are satisfactorily adjusted on all levels.

BURCHARD, W. W.
Role conflicts of military chaplains.
Amer. sociol. Rev., 1954, *19*, 528-535.

Sample: 36 chaplains and 35 ex-chaplains were interviewed.
Results: Some support for the hypothesis that the position of chaplain *does* lead to role conflicts which he seeks to reconcile either through rationalization or compartmentalization. Rationalization tends to strengthen the role of military officer at the expense of the role of minister.

CALPIN, T. F.
The concepts of introversion and extroversion and a study of their incidence among a group of seminarians.
M.A., Catholic University of America, 1939.

Sample: 134 lower and upper seminarians in 4 study houses of one order.
Procedure: Bernreuter and questionnaire.
Results: There was a slight, persistent trend toward the increase of introversion in the group as the years of life in the seminary atmosphere go on.

CHAMBERLAIN, D. B.
Communication problems in the parish ministry: an action research study of fifty Protestant ministers in a New England city.
Ph.D., Boston University, 1958.
Dissert. Abstr., 1958, *19*, 891-892.

Sample: ". . . a virtually complete sample of the professional Protestant ministers in a greater urban area of 150,000."
Procedure: Information about communications which took place on weekday and on Sunday in the life of each

minister was systematically collected by a self-recording technique. Follow-up interview.

Results: Minister's major role is pastor with administrator a close second. Ministers move away from administrative functions toward pastoral while parishioners call more frequently for the former. The organizational role is prominent but the minister is not well adjusted in it.

DeBoont, W.
The novice's crisis of identity. Explorations in a closed society.
M.A., University of Montreal, 1960.

See DeBoont 1962.

DeBoont, W.
Identity crisis and the male novice.
Rev. Relig., 1962, *21,* 104-128.
See also DeBoont 1960.

Sample: 28 male novices from 2 different communities.
Procedure: Rorschach, TAT, essay on "The ideal and the difficulties of my spiritual life," interviews.
Results: Novices showed many signs of tension as well as of attempts at synthesis. By uprooting the candidate from his former environment the novitiate deprives him of the support his identity enjoyed before. The imperfections of the novice should not be seen as faults which are exclusively in the moral order. These are rather phenomena normal to the effort of adapting to a new situation.

Erikson's views are recounted in some detail. Several case references are included.

DeMilan, Jean
Personality changes in religious life.
Cathol. Educator, 1956, *27,* 133-134; 173-174.

A religious does not want to destroy his personality but to consecrate it to God by putting it wholly at his service. Each of the vows of the religious is discussed.

Dittes, J. E.
Changes in TSI scores during seminary.
TSI Research Bull. #4. Dayton, O. (1810 Harvard Blvd.): Ministry Studies Board, 1963. 14 pages.

Sample: 204 students from 7 theological schools tested in 1959 and again in 1962.
Procedure: Changes in TSI scores calculated and correlated with characteristics of a particular school and its students, particular individual experiences during seminary, biographical information, postseminary vocational decision.
Results: Major changes in scale scores: decrease on natural leading, special leading, concept of the call, evangelical witness, self-fulfillment; increase on acceptance by others and leadership success. Seminaries seem to exert a homogenizing influence on their relatively extreme students. Effects of internship, clinical training, and field work enhance score changes due to theological education. Students experiencing extensive personality counseling frequently change in a direction opposite to that of classmates.

Evoy, J. J., & Christoph, V. F.
Maturity in the religious life.
New York: Sheed and Ward, 1965.

General discussion of maturity and mental health, with special attention to particular circumstances of the female religious, including such problems as privacy, uniformity, group relations, and relations with a superior.

Falk, L. L.
The minister's response to his perception of conflict between self-expectations and parishioners' expectations of his role.

Ph.D., University of Nebraska, 1962.
Dissert. Abstr., 1963, *23,* 2611-2612.

Sample: Not reported in abstract.

Procedure: Types of role conflict are examined in relation to types of responses to conflict. Both the actual conflict and the minister's perception of the conflict are considered in each of the relationships. The instruments used are not discussed.

Results: When there is increased disagreement among parishioners' prescriptions, ministers tend to repudiate unacceptable expectations or redefine their roles. However, when parishioners consensually disagree with their minister, he tends to become depressed rather than to react in an overt fashion. Generally the ministers tend to underestimate the amount of disagreement between themselves and their parishioners. The specific relation between conflict and responses is not clear, suggesting that the ministers' responses to conflict are only partially a function of the degree of conflict, even when the ministers' perceptions of conflict are taken into account.

FALK, L. L.
The minister's response to role conflict.
Discourse, 1963, *6,* 216-228.
Based on Falk 1962.

Categories are presented for a theoretical analysis of role conflict and resolution. "Changing activities have introduced ambiguity and conflict into the ministerial role. . . . The minister refers his activities to a number of groups: his parishioners, his denominational leaders, his fellow ministers, and other community members. Inconsistencies may occur within and among these reference systems. . . . [The minister] may identify more closely with one, thereby ameliorating the dilemma. Responses to conflict include norm repudiation, delegation of authority, stalling, norm redefinition, behaving inconsistently, leav-

ing the ministry, and becoming ill or depressed. It is suggested that the response selected is in part determined by the ethical and religious values of the minister. Other problems considered are those of role competition, such as minister vs. father roles; insufficient time for role performance; and conflict in origin of authority . . . it is not clear which precise conflict situations lead to which particular responses."

FECHER, C. J.
The longevity of members of Catholic religious sisterhoods.
Ph.D., Catholic University of America, 1927.

Sample: About 25,000 questionnaires from more than 50 religious communities during the period 1900-1925.

Results: A sister of age 20 during the period 1920-1924 has an advantage of 3½ years of additional life over white females. After age 50 the difference gradually decreases. Causes of death, mortality rates of teaching sisters, and improvement in longevity during the quarter century are also reported.

FOLEY, A. S.
United States colored priests: hundred year survey.
America, 1953, *89,* 295-297.

Discussion of the careers of the colored priests ordained in the U.S. See Foley 1955.

FOLEY, A. S.
The status and role of the Negro priest in the American Catholic clergy.
Amer. Cathol. sociol. Rev., 1955, *16,* 83-93.

Sample: The 72 Negro priests ordained in the U.S. since 1854.

Procedure: Documents, questionnaires, interviews.

Results: Discussion is given of social status, social role, and role conflict.

GRÜNEWALD, E.

Zur Frage der Berufsneurose beim Theologen (The problem of occupational neurosis in the theologian).

Jhb. Psychol. Psychother., 1955, *3*, 405-411.

The importance of oral wishes and conflicts are suggested as factors in abandoning the priesthood by young men. The theologian, through his representative relation to an order transcending the individual self, is more likely than persons in other professions to experience tensions between id impulses and infantile superego residues. (Abstract by Meissner.)

HAGMAIER, G.

Today's religious candidate: psychological and emotional considerations.

Natl Cathol. Educ. Ass. Bull., 1962, *59*, 110-118.

The role of the minor seminary in the emotional life of the candidate is discussed. Consequences of vows of chastity are considered in some detail. Use of psychological tests by counselors is helpful.

HOYER, L. B.

Theory of ego identity with reference to the young pastor in clinical training.

Ph.D., Boston University, 1962.

Dissert. Abstr., 1962, *23*, 1809-1810.

Uses questionnaire responses of students in clinical training and the ego identity theory of Erikson to formulate a theoretical approach to pastoral identity. Uses logical analysis rather than empirical procedure. Four identity problems are discussed in detail: intimacy, ideology, value

and virtue, role. Implications for further study are made.

KELLY, G.

Guidance for religious.

Westminster, Md.: Newman, 1957.

Part I discusses emotional maturity with emphasis on the adjustment from one's own family to the religious family and adjustment to the chastity vows. Most of the book's contents had previously appeared in *Rev. Relig.*

KENDALL, J. S.

The concept of the minister—a study of certain relationships between occupational stereotype, self concept and selected variables.

Ph.D., University of Minnesota, 1959.

Dissert. Abstr., 1959, *20*, 2377-2378.

Sample: Seminarians, parish pastors, and laymen associated with the Lutheran Church.

Procedure: Two adjective checklists (each 120 items) were used: "self-description" and "the typical minister." Three indices were developed: (1) agreement between self-description and description of typical minister; (2) agreement between self-description and the minister stereotype held by the group; (3) agreement between individual stereotype of the minister and the stereotype held by a group.

Results: There does exist an occupational stereotype associated with the ministry by persons significantly related to the ministry. The relations between occupational stereotype and self-concept are suggestive but incomplete.

KENOYER, SISTER MARIE F.

The influence of religious life on three levels of perceptual processes.

Ph.D., Fordham University, 1961.

Dissert. Abstr., 1961, *22*, 909.

Sample: 500 Catholic women divided into 3 groups according to level of religious life. A subgroup representing religious experience and a matched lay group were formed at each of the 3 levels.

Procedure: 3 levels of perception were assessed: self (GZTS), complex verbal material (Watson-Glaser Critical Thinking Appraisal), and sensory (tests of flexibility and speed of closure).

Results: The influence of religious life on perception was clearly evident only in the areas of ascendance and sociability on the GZTS. Sensory perception and perception of complex verbal material were related in their common distinction from self-perception.

KLAUSNER, S. Z. (Ed.)

Annotated bibliography and directory of workers in the field of religion and psychiatry.

New York: Columbia University, Bureau of Applied Social Research, 1958.

Entries are books and articles which have tried to bridge religion and psychiatry. Arrangement is alphabetically by author. This is considered to be volume 2 of a set of which volume 1 is Klausner 1964a.

KLAUSNER, S. Z.

Role adaptation of ministers and psychiatrists in the religio-psychiatric movement.

Ph.D., Columbia University, 1963.

Same as the first part of Klausner 1964a.

KLAUSNER, S. Z.

Psychiatry and religion.

New York: Free Press of Glencoe, 1964. (a)

The relation of religion and psychiatry is studied through the literature of each discipline which has bearing on the other.

From 1,347 books and articles whose authors could be identified (see Klausner 1958), the history and interests of the religio-psychiatric movement can be traced. The Peale-Blanton clinic in New York City is examined as a case study (see **A4:** Klausner 1957). Ministers in the movement tend to be from denominations of relatively high socio-economic status or are highly educated individuals serving in low-prestige denominations. When ministers, traditionally concerned with the individual in community, join with psychiatrists, traditionally concerned with individuals in relation to personal fulfillment, their joint endeavor suffers from these conflicting norms.

KLAUSNER, S. Z.

The religio-psychiatric movement: participation by Protestant, Catholic and Jew.

Rev. relig. Res., 1964, 5, 63-74. (b)

Procedure: This paper adds to the data of Klausner 1964a content analysis of an additional 506 books and articles published through 1962.

Results: There is some evidence that the movement is becoming stabilized and may be on the decline. It is less radical than during its initial phases and more homogeneously Protestant. While the movement's center remains in the U.S., a second focus seems to be emerging in Germany. Practical theologians in seminaries and psychoanalytically oriented ministers in the chaplaincy and in psychiatric clinics are gaining in numerical import.

KLAUSNER, S. Z.

The religio-psychiatric movement: changing ideology of the movement.

Rev. relig. Res., 1964, 6, 7-22. (c)

Continues the analysis of Klausner 1964b. Based largely on analysis of 100 authors who wrote throughout the period 1948-1962. Opposition to the movement is waning with the movement's increasing institutionalization. There is general agreement that primary admission to the counseling role should be contingent upon training, especially training in psychological counseling techniques. Because of its increasing Protestant character, the movement will less often bring men of various faiths together, but it will continue to serve as a meeting place for religion and science.

LANDIS, B. Y.
Incomes of ministers.
Pastoral Psychol., 1965, *16*(152), 9-13.

The author makes comparisons between salaries of ministers and those employed in other occupations. Ministers' cash salaries closely approximate salaries of factory workers. Salaries vary with size of church, years of service, and size of the community.

MASTEJ, SISTER MARY M.
A study of the influence of the religious life on the personality adjustment of religious women as measured by a modified form of the MMPI.
Ph.D., Fordham University, 1954.

Sample: 100 women in each stage of religious life: postulants, novices, junior professed, senior professed I, senior professed II. 100 religious aspirants served as controls.
Procedure: Bier's MMPI.
Results: The experimental groups tended to deviate toward higher scores. Mean scores increased with age and with time in religion. The tendencies found in the control group were emphasized in the experimental groups. The areas of adjustment affected most were the neurotic and psychotic portions of the inventory (Hs, D, Pt, Sc, and Ma).

McCARTHY, T. N.
Personality trait consistency during the training period for a Roman Catholic congregation of teaching brothers.
Ph.D., University of Ottawa, 1956.

Sample: 81 men in one brotherhood.
Procedure: Subjects were divided into 5 groups: (1) $N = 20$: tested as postulants and 1 year later; (2) $N = 13$: tested as postulants and 2 years later; (3) $N = 23$: tested as postulants and 3 years later; (4) $N = 16$: tested at first-year novitiate and 3 years later; (5) $N = 9$: tested at second-year novitiate and 3 years later. The first testing used a battery including ACE and Cattell 16; second testing used only the Cattell 16.
Results: Only group 3 showed systematic personality trait changes: more schizothymic, more concerned about the correctness of behavior, and decrease in nervous tension. Although none of the other groups showed personality trait changes for the period studied, it was found that the groups did respond in a systematic way. Differential effects on the traits measured were found; thus the idea of over-all tendency to change was rejected in favor of specificity of trait change. Findings are discussed in light of Super's theory of vocational development.

McCARTNEY, J. L.
The call to foreign missions; its effect on unstable personalities.
Ment. Hyg., N. Y., 1928, *12*, 521-529.

Author speculates from his own experience on the effects of climate, food, economics, and interpersonal problems which missionaries encounter. He concludes that neurotic and psychotic reactions are conditioned by repressed emotional states and unconscious motives similar to those found among such cases in America.

MOORE, J.

Why young ministers are leaving the church.

Harper's, 1957, *215*(1286), 65-69.

It is not only the multiplicity of roles which causes breakdowns, but also the conflict between the role the minister is expected to play as a minister and the kind of life he wants to live as a human being.

MURPHY, L.

Changes in MMPI scores of three groups of seminarians retested after one, two, and three years.

M.A., Fordham University, 1962.

Sample: 3 groups of seminarians: one (N = 15) retested after 3 years, one (N = 12) retested after 2 years, and one (N = 16) retested after 1 year. There was also a group (N = 26) to control for reliability, retested after 16 days.

Procedure: MMPI.

Results: Significant changes over time in the direction of "healthy" adjustment were found on Hs, D, and Hy scales.

NICHOLS, W. C., JR.

The minister as a family man: a study of role expectations and behavior.

Ed.D., Columbia University, Teachers College, 1960.

Sample: 17 Baptist ministers and their wives in the New York area.

Procedure: Intensive structured interview.

Results: Pertinent results include discussion of time schedule, privacy, work tension, theological position. Ministers can be ranked on a scale from "servant of the congregation" to "professional man of the congregation."

NODET, C.-H.

Psychological factors affecting vocation.

In *A manual for novice mistresses.* Lon-

don: Blackfriars, 1958. Pp. 11-23. (Religious Life Series, IX.)

From a psychological view we can say that life is love, that love is not full and mature until it has become giving, and such love necessarily leads to balance. The first selfish loves of the child are transformed gradually into a love which is conscious, moral, voluntary, and generous. Often vocation's difficulties in the development of love occur in the following areas: history of the vocation, family love, sex, and penitence.

ROBERTS, H. W.

The rural Negro minister: his work and salary.

Rural Sociol., 1947, *12*, 284-294.

Sample: 141 Negro ministers who attended the summer school for ministers at Virginia State College from 1943 to 1946. 117 of them pastor rural churches (about 21% of all rural ministers in the state).

Procedure: Interviews and questionnaires.

Results: The average rural Negro minister pastors more than 1 church and conducts services at each church only 1 or 2 Sundays a month. Data are given on the number of members per church, amount of Sunday travel, salary, parsonages, secular employment, and its effects on the man and his task.

ROBINSON, CLARICE M.

An analysis of the business activities of 120 Protestant ministers.

Ed.D., Indiana University, 1949.

Sample: 120 ministers filled out checklists.

Results: Business activities of ministers were enumerated in such categories as use of office machines, budgeting, purchasing, income. Stresses the importance of busi-

ness education for those who are to become ministers.

SCHERER, R. P.

Income and business costs of the Protestant clergy in 1963: a preliminary report of a National Council of Churches'
survey of clergy support.

Information Service, 1964, *43*(19), 1-8.

Sample: 5,623 parish ministers, a 66%
return from 8,492 randomly selected from
a population of 110,000 parish ministers
in 15 Protestant denominations.

Procedure: 52-item mailed questionnaire covering professional and family
background, income, expenses, and opinions concerning relative importance of
various factors in determining salaries.
One item asks for opinion concerning relative importance of 24 different clergy
activities.

Results: Median salary was $5,158, plus
approximately $1,848 additional benefits.
Salary is correlated closely with church
size, less so with amount of training and
experience. Variation within denominations is much greater than between. Ministers receive little in additional gifts or
fees, are not likely to work outside their
parish, nor have employed wives. Few receive annual increase.

SCHERER, R. P.

Compensation of the Protestant clergy in
1963.

Seminary Quart., 1965, *6*(3), 1-3.

Data from Scherer 1964.

SHRADER, W.

Why ministers are breaking down.

Life, 1956, *41*(8), 95-104.

Numerous anecdotes are recounted in
the contention that too much work at too
many kinds of jobs makes the clergyman's role impossible.

SMITH, L. M.

Parish clergymen's role images as pastoral
counselors.

J. pastoral Care, 1960, *14,* 21-28.

Sample: 22 clergymen: Conservative
Jews, Roman Catholics, Episcopalians,
Southern Baptists, Congregationalists.

Procedure: Intensive interviews.

Results: Emphasis on counseling decreased minister's perception of strains between counseling and his other activities.
Where "clients" are marginal or nonpar-
ticipant in the parish, and where permis-
sive techniques are used, emphasis on
counseling will not result in role strains
for the clergy.

STEWART, C. W.

What frustrates a minister.

Christian Advocate, 1965, *9*(1), 9-10.

Sample: Alumni (N not given) of the
Institute for Advanced Pastoral Studies.

Procedure: Questionnaire on sources of
frustration.

Results: Tabulation of frustrations: (1)
difficulty in fulfilling professional functions
(35%); (2) indifference, irresponsibility,
and lack of integrity of people with whom
the minister works (24%); (3) personal
inadequacy, such as lack of discipline, im-
patience, hostility (13%); (4) personal
life: family, salary, etc. (12%); (5) conflict between role and the present "state
of the church" (8%).

Discussion is included of causes of these
frustrations and their relation to the concepts of ministry the frustrated ministers
hold. Especially noted are the dislike of
administrative duties, the lack of effectiveness in communication, and the minister's
self-perception of his centrality. Frustration can be alleviated as the task of ministry is understood as that of the layman
as well as the minister.

THOMAS, O. C.
Psychological pressures on the seminarian.
J. pastoral Care, 1962, *16,* 95-97.

That seminary students comprise the largest group to use the psychiatric clinics of the Harvard Health Service is explained by three reasons: (1) continued dealing with humanity's deepest and most essential questions; (2) the church in contemporary society is an "irrational anomaly"; (3) theology students have unusually intense doubts about their vocation to the ministry.

WALKER, D. D.
The human problems of the minister.
New York: Harper, 1960.

Anecdotal accounts, interpretation, and recommendations. Typical chapter titles: "Condemned to sin piously," "The struggle to love our enemies," "Competing with our brothers," "The professional family man," "Disciplined disorder," "Afraid to be radical," and "The right thing at the right time."

WILSON, B. R.
The Pentecostalist minister: role conflicts and status contradictions.
Amer. J. Sociol., 1959, *64,* 494-504.

Procedure: Participant observation and some interviews.
Results: In Great Britain the Pentecostal movement has accepted paid, permanent ministers. The minister suffers role conflicts not suffered by other ministers because he is the guardian of a sectarian ethic in a denominationalizing organization, in which the ministry is structurally one of the most distinctly denominational elements.

FURTHER REFERENCES

For further references on Consequences, see also: **A1:** Wagoner; **A1:** Wheelis; **A2:** Carper; **A2:** Fichter 1961; **A4:** Hibbard; **A4:** Klausner; **A4:** Moore; **B1:** Bamberger; **B1:** Blizzard 1956a; **B1:** Blizzard 1956b; **B1:** Blizzard 1958a; **B1:** Blizzard 1958b; **B1:** Blizzard 1960; **B1:** Hiltner; **B1:** Plyler; **B2:** Hudson; **B2:** Whitcomb 1957; **B4:** Kennedy; **C:** Gold; **C:** Maurer; **E:** Bowers 1963a; **F:** Meiburg; **G:** Scanzoni 1964 and 1965; **I:** Bier 1960b.

COUNSELING AND THERAPY

ARNOT, R.
Some observations on mental health based on the psychiatric treatment of the religious.
Bull. Guild Cathol. Psychiat., 1960, 7, 158-163.

Discusses the treatment of religious suffering from psychoneuroses in their relationship to the superior, parents, peers, sexual incidents, and the practice of the religious life.

BEIRNAERT, L.
Immaturité affective et problèmes de vocation.
Suppl. Vie Spir., 1958, *11*(46), 323-327.

Affective maturity must be kept distinct from spiritual maturity. Affective immaturity lies at the root of many vocation problems. Some suggestions are made for recognizing affective immaturity and the help of psychological specialists is advised. (Abstract by Meissner.)

BIER, W. C.
The guidance counselor and the spiritual director: the distinct role of each.
Natl Cathol. Educ. Ass. Bull., 1964, *61*, 112-121.

The spiritual director is a teacher and guide of the seminarians in their spiritual life and the guidance counselor is a source of psychological help needed to adjust satisfactorily to seminary life. The latter generally uses nondirective techniques. Neither functions as a psychotherapist.

BOWERS, MARGARETTA K.
Conflicts of the clergy: a psychodynamic study with case histories.
New York: Thomas Nelson & Sons, 1963. (a)

A report based on experience in therapy with 37 ordained and 28 unordained patients, most of them Anglican, in church occupations. Discusses the special nature and goals of clerical psychotherapy. Success is to be judged in "reconciling the patient's unconscious religious attitudes with his conscious theological attitudes, achieving a state where theological truth and psychological truth coincide." Presents 13 case histories illustrating individual and group therapy of religious conflicts.

BOWERS, MARGARETTA K.
Psychotherapy of religious personnel: some observations and recommendations.
J. pastoral Care, 1963, *17*, 11-16. (b)
Also in S. W. Cook (Ed.), *Research plans.* New York (545 W. 111th St.): Religious Education Association, 1962. Pp. 123-127.

Psychiatric disturbances displayed by patients dedicated to religious work are "empirically" outlined to suggest research. 2 recommendations are made to the Protestant Episcopal Church re: (1) selection of therapists for psychotherapeutic care of seminarians and clergy, and (2) establishment of rehabilitation centers for such work.

BOWERS, MARGARETTA K., BERKOWITZ, B., & BRECHER, SYLVIA
Therapeutic implications of analytic group psychotherapy of religious personnel.
Int. J. group Psychother., 1958, *8*, 243-256.

A report of 5 years' experience with 12 clergymen, most of them Anglican, who had undergone from 1 to 4 years in group therapy. Analytically oriented group therapy presents at the current time an excellent technique for the analysis of magical omnipotent thinking of severe authoritarian attitudes among people whose professional life provides a socially accepted façade for these attitudes. The peer group relationship not only makes it possible for them to overcome the essential loneliness of their set-apartness, but helps to overcome problems of revolt against authority so that the authority of the peer group can be accepted in the working through of many behavior problems.

BOYD, R. W.
The use of group psychotherapy in the professional training of ministers.
Ph.D., Boston University, 1952.

The effect of group therapy was measured in 2 groups of ministers training at the Boston Psychopathic Hospital. After therapy, subjects became more stable and less authoritarian in social attitudes. The therapy process is analyzed according to the problem-solving ability of the group, group goals, member role functions, dynamic personality changes, and patterns of identification and rejection.

CARRIER, BLANCHE
Counseling pre-ministerial students.
Pastoral Psychol., 1951, *2*(18), 21-25.

The personality conflicts of ministerial students follow the range found in other vocations, but they have certain emphases due to the religious background and vo-

cational situations faced. Problems of guilt may be more acute and often displaced. Church teaching tends to keep ideals in abstract and generalized terms, leading to absolute codes which are isolating and disillusioning. Counseling will provide the emotional release, discover the inadequacy of some motivations for entering the ministry, reduce pseudo-guilt, find more realistic ways of defining ideals, and provide healthy attitudes through emotional understanding. The time to discover immature motives is prior to seminary enrollment.

CURRAN, C. A.
Counseling in the minor seminary program.
Natl Cathol. Educ. Ass. Bull., 1958, *55*, 91.

Counseling increases self-knowledge and self-reorganization as well as control over conflicting emotions and instincts.

CURRAN, C. A.
Counseling and guidance.
In J. E. Haley (Ed.), *Proceedings of the 1960 Sisters' Institute of Spirituality.* Notre Dame, Ind.: University of Notre Dame Press, 1961. Pp. 101-194.

These sessions were designed to present the theory and practice of counseling and guidance skills applied to the superior in her relationships with the individual members of the community. Practice in role-playing was given. Chapters include extracts from counseling interviews, and a supplement of quotations from St. Thomas is included.

ERIKSON, E. H.
The nature of clinical evidence.
Daedalus, 1958, *87*, 65-87.
Also in D. Lerner (Ed.), *Evidence and inference.* Glencoe, Ill.: Free Press, 1959.
Revised in E. H. Erikson, *Insight and*

responsibility. New York: W. W. Norton and Company, 1964. Pp. 47-80.

This lecture illustrates the processes of therapeutic inference with an extended analysis of a dream reported midway during the first year of therapy by a Protestant seminary student training for missionary work in Asia. The theme of the dream, explicitly related by the author to the patient's religious faith but not to his vocation, is: "Whenever I begin to have faith in somebody's strength and love, some angry and sickly emotions pervade the relationship, and I end up mistrusting, empty, and a victim of anger and despair. ... The patient's father images [absent from the dream] became dominant in a later period of the treatment and proved most important for the patient's eventual solution of his spiritual vocational problems."

FORD, J. C.
Religious superiors, subjects, and psychiatrists.
Westminster, Md.: Newman, 1963.

Discusses how to protect simultaneously the mental health of religious, the principles of religious government, the right of religious to psychic privacy, and the filial confidence of religious subjects to their superiors. "The principal problem is that of harmonizing, in a family setting, the right of the individual religious to the secrets of his interior life with his essential dependence on superiors."

GALLEZ, E., & NASSAUX, X.
Hygiène mentale et apostolat.
Rev. Dioc. Tournai, 1955, *10*, 256-265.

The importance of advances in mental hygiene for the effectiveness of the priest's own apostolate and for his adaptation to the demands of his vocation are discussed. (Abstract by Meissner.)

HARVEY, J. F.
Counseling the invert in religious life.

Bull. Guild Cathol. Psychiat., 1962, *9*, 210-221.

Pastoral advice on the counseling which a superior may give to male religious and priests, nuns, and teachers when homosexuality is an issue.

HOLT, H., & WINICK, C.
Group psychotherapeutic experiences with clergymen.
J. Relig. Hlth, 1962, *1*, 113-126.

Sample: 10 Protestant ministers, 13 rabbis, 6 priests in separate therapy groups.
Results: The most important characteristic of all the groups was the honesty and courage of the members in seeking and facing a new and unknown experience.

HOWE, R. L.
Counseling the theological student.
J. clin. pastoral Wk, 1947, *1*, 11-17.

Today's theological education emphasizes training *men* for the ministry rather than teaching subject matter as an end in itself. Students with and without pastoral training differ in their need for and response to counseling. Counseling is essential when clinical training is part of the curriculum.

HULME, W. E.
Pastoral care of the pastor.
Pastoral Psychol., 1963, *14*(136), 31-37.

There need be no sense of failure in recognizing that there are times when the minister, just like everybody else, is in need of help by a specialist—whether this be a fellow minister or some other professional counselor—to help him with his own inner feelings, his relationships with his people, as well as his relationship with God.

KALTHOFF, R. J., & GUNTER, F. L.
Collaboration of psychiatrist and super-

vised psychotherapist in the treatment of people in religious life.

Bull. Guild Cathol. Psychiat., 1963, *10,* 18-28.

Description of 6 years of experience collaborating on treatment of certain kinds of religious patients.

KINNANE, J. F., & TAGESON, C. F.
Psychology can serve religious life.
Homil. Pastoral Rev., 1961, *61,* 343-349.

A description is given for priests of the need for psychological services in the religious life. The following services are discussed: psychologist, diagnostician, therapeutic counselor, scientist-practitioner.

KNIGHT, R. P.
Practical and theoretical considerations in the analysis of a minister.
Psychoanal. Rev., 1937, *24,* 350-364.

Report of an analysis of a minister. Concludes that "the individual religious beliefs of a person will take a form which is for him the best solution of his own Oedipus conflict. At least in some cases, the patient can be relieved, by analysis, of his disabling neurotic symptoms without dissipating a strong religious faith which also has evident neurotic origins."

LABOUCARIE, J.
Problèmes posés par le traitement des états névrotiques dans les états de vie religieuse.
In *Conducta religiosa y salud mental.* Madrid: VII Congreso Catolico Internatl. de Psicoterapía y Psicología Clinica, 1959. Pp. 191-195.

Some problems which arise in the treatment of neurotic religious are discussed. Problems relative to diagnosis and therapy are touched on. Ignorance, failure to recognize early stages of maladjustment, and defensive attitudes of superiors are pointed

to as prominent factors. (Abstract by Meissner.)

LYON, W. H., & RIGGS, M. D.
An experience of group psychotherapy for the parish minister: I. A process of selection and motivation.
J. pastoral Care, 1961, *15,* 172-173.

Description of a 1-day retreat of 9 Protestant ministers and 2 psychologists. Program was described in advance as focusing on "use of self" and some of the practical, personal, and professional problems of the ministry. "As the sessions continued, 'felt need' emerged and much time was spent on the clarifying and understanding of the strengths and weaknesses of the men represented in areas such as preaching, pastoral work, the minister and his family, and the minister's participation in community life."

LYON, W. H., & RIGGS, M. D.
An experience of group psychotherapy for the parish minister: II. The experience itself—and a look to the future.
J. pastoral Care, 1964, *18,* 166-169.

Follow-up report on Lyon 1961.
Sample: Ministers (N not given) in group therapy programs.
Procedure: 1 group was tested at the beginning of therapy, after 1 year, and at the end of therapy; 3 other groups were tested at the beginning and end. Instruments: Taylor Manifest Anxiety Scale, Security-Insecurity Inventory, Barron Ego-Strength Scale, and Edwards Personal Preference Schedule.
Results: There were no statistically significant changes with successive testings in any of the groups. No pathology was indicated in any member at any testing. Nevertheless, benefits were reported by participants (N = 23): recognition and acceptance of "humanness" of themselves and fellow ministers, self-insight, and labo-

ratory experience in counseling methods. Changes in the program are discussed including groups for wives, a new test battery (MMPI for the women, IPAT Neuroticism Scale for the men), and elimination of a 24-hour retreat.

NODET, C.-H.
Psychanalyse et vocation religieuse.
Psyché, 1949, *30-31*, 399-412.

NODET, C.-H.
Psychiatrie et vie religieuse.
Encyclopédie médico-chirurgicale. Paris: 1955.

PARROT, P.
Point de vue du médecin psychologue sur les aptitudes psychiques à une vocation religieuse.
Suppl. Vie Spir., 1960, *13*(52), 99-108.

A psychiatrist presents some observations on his experience in treating religious patients in reference to the determination of suitability for religious life. The psychological means at his disposal for making such a judgment and some of the practical problems which arise in the handling of such cases are discussed. (Abstract by Meissner.)

PARROT, P., ROMAIN, R. P., MABILLE, M., & COURTELARE, M.
Réflexions après trois ans de fonctionnement d'une maison médico-psychologique reservée à des prêtres.
Suppl. Vie Spir., 1958, *11*(46), 355-368.

A clinic for the care of disturbed priests is described.

SMITH, D.
The problem of professional courtesy in the treatment of religious.
Bull. Guild Cathol. Psychiat., 1963, *10*, 28-32.

The religious patient is no more exempt from some kind of fee arrangement with the therapist, despite his vow of poverty, than he is exempt from discussing his sexual feelings because of his vow of chastity.

VAUGHAN, R. P.
Counseling the former seminarian.
Cathol. Counsel., 1957, *2*, 3-5.

VAUGHAN, R. P.
Religious and psychotherapy.
Rev. Relig., 1958, *17*, 73-81. (a)

The usually unfounded distrust of psychiatry causes many of the religious to continue suffering from mental or emotional illness instead of seeking treatment. Some consideration is given to how to choose a psychiatrist.

VAUGHAN, R. P.
The neurotic religious.
Rev. Relig., 1958, *17*, 271-278. (b)

The neurotic priest, brother, or sister is not a second-rate religious but rather a sick religious needing care and understanding. Characteristics of neuroses are discussed.

FURTHER REFERENCES

For further references on Counseling and Therapy, see also: **B2:** Choisy; **B4:** Scholefield; **I:** Dondero.

MENTAL HEALTH AND ILLNESS

ARGYLE, M.
Religious behaviour.
Glencoe, Ill.: Free Press, 1959.

Chap. 9, pp. 109-112: Summary of the speculative literature on mental disorder among religious leaders.
P. 105: Tabular summary of 6 personality studies of theological students. **A1** and **B2:** Cockrum; **A1:** Johnson 1943; **A1:** Kimber; **A1:** McCarthy 1942; **A1:** Peters; **A1:** Sward.

BIOT, R.
Psychonévroses et séminaires.
Bull. anc. Élèves Saint-Sulpice, 1932.

BISSONIER, H.
Some conflicts and psychological motivations in the life of the active religious.
In *Apostolic Life.* London: Blackfriars, 1958. Pp. 178-191. (Religious Life Series, X.)

This is a discussion of the motivations and personality maladjustments of the active religious. Motives of candidates to the religious life must be given a thorough psychological scrutiny. Occasional warnings can profitably be given the religious about the singularity in apostolic activity. Apostolic activity, even when inspired by partially defective motives, can be effective.

CHRISTENSEN, C. W.
The occurrence of mental illness in the ministry: introduction.
J. pastoral Care, 1959, *13,* 79-87.
Also pp. 245-257 in **H:** Oates.

Sample: 100 individuals associated with religious professions seen for intensive (N = 44) or brief (N = 56) psychotherapy over a five-year period. Includes Baptists, Lutherans, Episcopalians, Methodists, and Unitarians.
Procedure: Material was gathered in the course of therapy rather than as a part of specific research. No statistical analysis is attempted.
See other Christensen entries for results.

CHRISTENSEN, C. W.
The occurrence of mental illness in the ministry: family origins.
J. pastoral Care, 1960, *14,* 13-20.

A description of some family backgrounds and relationships of a group of ministers under study. See Christensen 1959.

CHRISTENSEN, C. W.
The occurrence of mental illness in the ministry: psychotic disorders.
J. pastoral Care, 1961, *15,* 153-159.

16 of the 100 ministers involved in this study (see Christensen 1959) were diagnosed as psychotic. Several generalizations are made and one case is discussed in detail.

CHRISTENSEN, C. W.
The occurrence of mental illness in the ministry: psychoneurotic disorders.
J. pastoral Care, 1963, *17,* 1-10. (a)

Of 100 ministers, 33 are considered psychoneurotic. Several cases are described and briefly analyzed. See Christensen 1959.

CHRISTENSEN, C. W.

The occurrence of mental illness in the ministry: personality disorders.

J. pastoral Care, 1963, *17,* 125-135. (b)

Several generalizations and case histories are presented from 51 cases in sample of 100 (see Christensen 1959). The trend seems to be changing from rural to urban backgrounds, from lower to middle class. Presence of intrafamily disharmony was a persistent finding. Diagnostic categories tended to reflect incidence of mental illness as found in the general population.

D'ARCY, P. F.

Underachieving and vocation.

Natl Cathol. Educ. Ass. Bull., 1963, *60,* 512-514.

Chronic underachieving—a student's grades significantly lower than expected from a person of his ability—is often a clue to personality disturbance. Because teachers can easily recognize this condition, they should offer help with study habits and look into the candidate's personal and social life and perhaps arrange for further counseling.

GODIN, A.

Problems of mental health before and after entering religious life.

Sister Formation Bull., 1959-60, *6*(2), 1-5.

KELLEY, SISTER MARY W.

The incidence of hospitalized mental illness among religious sisters in the United States.

Amer. J. Psychiat., 1958, *115,* 72-75.

Sample: All nuns with discoverable mental illness in 1956. 357 (94%) of 378 private and public hospitals contacted provided usable information.

Procedure: Comparison with rates of U.S. women in general.

Results: Statistically significant findings: Occurrence of mental illness is higher in women in general (358.3 per 100,000) than for sisters (319.6); rates have come closer to each other, however, since report of **F:** Moore in 1936. Sisters have higher proportion of psychotic (particularly schizophrenic) and psychoneurotic disorders, but lower rates of alcoholism, syphilitic psychotic reaction, and mental deficiency. Rate of schizophrenia for women in general is 259.6 per 100,000 and for sisters is 193.67. Lower-class sisters had more psychoses, higher-class sisters more psychoneurotic disorders.

KELLEY, SISTER MARY W.

Depression in the psychoses of members of religious communities of women.

Amer. J. Psychiat., 1961, *118,* 423-425.

Case histories of 50 hospitalized religious were examined. They revealed high incidence of insecurity, depression, self-accusation. Rates increase from the most absorbing occupations to those which "leave the greatest freedom to the mind."

KOBLER, F. J.

Casebook in psychopathology.

New York: Alba House, 1964.

Chap. 14, "Neurotic depression in a religious," pp. 177-205. Case study of a 23-year-old woman in treatment after being asked to leave a convent after 15 months because of repeated states of depression. Clinical diagnosis: psychoneurosis with a depressive reaction in a basically obsessive-compulsive type of personality with mild paranoid features. Included are excerpts from therapy sessions and test information, appending Rorschach and TAT protocols.

McALLISTER, R. J., & VANDERVELDT, A.

Factors in mental illness among hospitalized clergy.

J. nerv. ment. Dis., 1961, *132,* 80-88.

Analysis of the case histories of 100 Catholic priests consecutively discharged from a private psychiatric hospital was made in comparison with a group of 100 Catholic seminarians approaching ordination and 100 male patients discharged from the same institution. The two patient groups differed in diagnosis, major symptomatology, age of onset, socioeconomic background, school achievement, and parental influence.

MEIBURG, A. L., & YOUNG, R. K.
The hospitalized minister: a preliminary study.
Pastoral Psychol., 1958, 9(84), 37-42.
Pp. 237-244 in **H:** Oates.

Sample: 113 ministers, selected at random from in-patients and out-patients at a general hospital, 1944-57.
Procedure: Hospital records consulted.
Results: 18% (greatest frequency) of diagnoses were of mental illness. Frequencies of other diagnoses reported. 22 cases suggested a relationship between vocational pressures and illness categorized by authors as relating to overwork (13), special problems connected with evangelism (5), or vocational uncertainty (4). The study is considered exploratory by the authors.

MIDLEFORT, C. F.
Christian prophets and mystics in history and today.
Pp. 1-12 in **H:** Southard.

Sample: 35 pastors, wives, or other close relatives seen as psychiatric patients.
Results: Interpretations are offered of the relation of symptoms to religious traditions and to some extent to vocational conditions. Emphasis on "the past . . . and the prophetic and transcendental side of Christianity" was found related with depressive, paranoid, schizophrenic, and compulsive disorders. Emphasis on "the

present . . . and the mystical and immanental side" was found related with hysterical, schizophrenic, and character disorders.

MOORE, T. V.
Insanity in priests and religious: I. The rate of insanity in priests and religious.
Amer. eccl. Rev., 1936, 95, 485-498.

The rates of diagnostic categories among priests and religious are presented:

	Nuns	Women in general	Priests	Men in general
Dementia praecox	44%	21%	28%	17%
Manic-depressive	18%	17%	—	—
Alcoholic	—	—	21%	7%

He concludes that prepsychotic personalities may be attracted to the religious life. That the total incidence of insanity is so much lower than in the general population is due to the fact that the syphilitic types are absent.

MORGAN, L.
Mental illness among the clergy: a survey of state mental hospitals in America.
Pastoral Psychol., 1958, 9(84), 29-36.

Sample: 26 completed questionnaires regarding hospital patients in 1946 and 1956.
Results: Suggest that the proportion of ministers suffering from mental illness corresponds to the proportion of the population identified with their faith group.

NODET, C.-H.
Troubles nerveux et vocation.
Suppl. Vie Spir., 1957, 10(40), 17-23.

A psychiatrist discusses problems relating to attitudes toward the religious or seminarian who suffers mental illness.

NURNBERGER, J. I.
Personality disorders and procedures:

early indicators and the role of the superior and professional counselor.
In J. E. Haley (Ed.), *Proceedings of the 1959 Sisters' Institute of Spirituality.* Volume 7. Notre Dame, Ind.: University of Notre Dame Press, 1960. Pp. 301-342.

Early environment is very important for healthy personality development. Some disorders are related to life epochs and vocational phases and should be approached in those contexts. Emotional disorder should be dealt with within the community when possible, but if the life of the community is seriously threatened, outside consultation should be called.

NUTTIN, J.
Séminaire et équilibre psychique.
In *Cardinal Mercier, fondateur de séminaire.* Louvain: 1952. Pp. 133-149.

SOUTHARD, S.
The mental health of ministers.
Pastoral Psychol., 1958, *9*(84), 43-48.
Pp. 229-236 in **H:** Oates as An overview of research on the mental illness of the minister.

On the basis of research encountered by the author, there is no reason to believe that mental breakdowns occur among ministers in any greater proportion than among other professional groups.

VANDERVELDT, J.
Mental health in the religious and spiritual spheres.

Sister Formation Bull., Spring, 1956, *2* (3), 10-11.

VAUGHAN, R. P.
Severe mental illness among religious.
Rev. Relig., 1959, *18,* 25-36.

Discusses the characteristics of schizophrenia, paranoia, and severe depression as they manifest themselves in psychotic religious. Emphasis is placed on the need for understanding and loving support from the psychotic's fellow religious.

VAUGHAN, R. P.
Mental illness and the religious life.
Milwaukee: Bruce Publishing Company, 1962.

A book written for religious about religious, to help them understand a mentally ill priest, brother, or sister. This expands articles which have appeared in *Rev. Relig.* Author pictures the inner strife of those who are mentally ill, to show how those experiences hinder the leading of a full religious life, and explains how the religious can be helped through the medium of psychiatric treatment.

WILLIAM, SISTER MARY
Maladies mentales des religieuses.
Suppl. Vie Spir., 1959, *12,* 295-305.

A survey, conducted in 1957, revealed that 783 religious women were hospitalized in 1955-56 for psychiatric reasons in the U.S. This represents a rate of 490.77 per 100,000. The study concludes that religious life attracts candidates liable to have psychiatric difficulties rather than causing these difficulties of itself. (Abstract by Meissner.)

FURTHER REFERENCES

For further references on Mental Health and Illness, see also: **B1:** McCarthy 1963b; **B3:** Biot; **D:** Evoy; **I:** Bier 1953.

WIVES AND FAMILY

BLOUNT, LOUISE F., & BOYLE, J. H.
The theological seminary and the pastor's wife.
Pastoral Psychol., 1961, *12*(119), 40-45; 66.

Sample: 122 theological seminaries and schools listed by the AATS. 101 (83%) replied.

Procedure: Survey questionnaire.

Results: Wide variations were found in what theological seminaries are doing and/or planning to do in instruction and guidance for seminary wives. Much of what is available is "social" in nature rather than formally structured.

DENTON, G. W.
Role attitudes of the minister's wife.
Ed.D., Columbia University, Teachers College, 1958.

Sample: 30 ministers' wives selected at random from denominational handbooks (8 Baptist, 4 Methodist, 7 Lutheran, 10 Presbyterian, 1 Episcopalian).

Procedure: Structured interviews.

Results: Reported in terms of role theory: role attitudes toward husband's work, toward family life, and toward church and community. It is concluded that there are 3 types of wives in the sample: aloof-participant (N = 3), supportive-participant (N = 23), and incorporated-participant (N = 4).

DENTON, [G.] W.
Role attitudes of the minister's wife.
Pastoral Psychol., 1961, *12*(119), 17-23.
Pp. 167-178 in **H**: Oates.

These are conclusions from research, which is not described here (see Denton 1962), with ministers' wives. The author discusses attitudes toward husband's work, toward family life, and toward church and community.

DENTON, [G.] W.
The role of the minister's wife.
Philadelphia: Westminster, 1962.

Sample: 30 ordained ministers' wives (see Denton 1958). Includes a review of the literature and a comparative analysis with the wives of other business and professional men.

DOUGLAS, W. G. T.
A selected annotated bibliography: the American minister's wife.
Unpublished. Boston: Boston University School of Theology, 1960. 29 pp.

DOUGLAS, W. G. T.
Ministers' wives: a tentative typology.
Pastoral Psychol., 1961, *12*(119), 11-16.

Sample: 4,000 parish ministers' wives (5% national sample) from 38 Protestant denominations.

Procedure: Questionnaires, some interviews and situational ratings.

Results: Preliminary analysis suggests these types: (1) fulfillment through natural growth, 20%; (2) fulfillment through hard struggle, 60%; (3) frustration through their demands and denials, 20%;

(4) frustration through inadequacy and insecurity, 20%.

DOUGLAS, W. G. T.
Role orientation of future ministers' wives.
In S. W. Cook (Ed.), *Research plans.* New York (545 W. 111th St.): Religious Education Association, 1962. Pp. 189-195.

Summarizes procedure of research project on ministers' wives. Proposes a training program and evaluation of training for ministers' wives: 25 wives of theological students would meet in small groups of 8 or 9 to discuss typical problem cases. Groups would be led by ministers' wives and would meet in churches or parsonages. Participants would complete initially the following instruments: Guilford-Zimmerman Temperament Survey, Edwards Personal Preference Schedule, a sentence completion test, Rosenzweig Picture Frustration Study, a role attitude and perception test. Initial test results are to be correlated with performance in the groups.

GOLD, R. L.
The minister's wife: a case of structurally induced ethnicity.
Unpublished paper. Missoula, Mont.: Author, Montana State University, 1962. 14 pp.
Delivered at 1962 meetings of the Pacific Sociological Association, Sacramento, California.

Abstracts and interpretations from interviews with an unspecified number of ministers' wives in western Montana. Emphasis on the process by which the wife becomes an "ethnic," "in but not of society," and on her reaction.

GUTHRIE, H.
Group therapy and seminary wives.
J. pastoral Care, 1961, *15*, 101-104.

This is a report of observations from 21 two-hour group therapy sessions of seminary wives. 6, about half, attended particularly regularly.

JAMIESON, H. M., JR.
Relationships between a United Presbyterian minister's family situation and his work.
Ph.D., University of Pittsburgh, 1962.
Dissert. Abstr., 1963, *23*, 4613.

Sample: Stratified random sample of 500 Presbyterian ministers.
Procedure: 413 ministers (83%) returned the questionnaire. Correlations were made between characteristics of the family situation and items of factual information in the following areas: scholarly activity, community activity, pastoral activity, activity in Christian education.
Results: Activity of minister's wife is related (.01 level) to scholarly, community, and Christian education activity. Discussion of work and family life is related (.01 level) to scholarly, pastoral, and Christian education activity. Of no significance when related to the 4 areas: employment of wife, college degree of wife, time spent with family, encouragement of pastoral activity by family.

KOEHLER, J. G.
The minister as a family man.
Pastoral Psychol., 1960, *11*(106), 11-15. Pp. 159-166 in **H:** Oates.

Sample: 150 wives of American Baptist clergy. 119 (79%) returned the questionnaire.
Results: Ministers spend, on the average, 25 hours a week with their families; the

total time is not related to the number of children in the family. Wives complain less about the amount of time than about the inability to count on the time.

MORENTZ, P. E.
The image of the seminary wife.
Pastoral Psychol., 1961, *12*(119), 46-52.

Sample: 196 wives of seminary students from 3 seminaries (of different denominations) in the San Francisco area.
Procedure: MMPI, profiles analyzed as wholes.
Results: There were 2 dimensions of particular interest to the author: relationship to the social order and self-image. Profiles were grouped at the extremes of each dimension. Results are discussed in terms of specific scales. Implications for seminaries are noted.

RANKIN, R. P.
The ministerial calling and the minister's wife.
Pastoral Psychol., 1960, *11*(106), 16-22.

The concept of the ministerial call is confronted today with a changing social situation which is felt even in the life of the parsonage. Churches need to face the situation realistically, making use of pertinent research in church and family.

SCANZONI, J.
Resolution of role incompatibility in church and sect clergy marriages.
Ph.D., University of Oregon, 1964.

Church-type clergymen allow occupational roles to go unfulfilled during periods when they express conjugal behaviors. In contrast, sect-type clergy tend to carry out occupational behaviors to the extent that their conjugal interaction is reduced. Sect-type clergy and their families also tend to conform to subgroup expectations in cases of conflict, whereas church-type clergy couples do not fill these expectations but act in terms of conjugal norms. It is suggested that interpretation of findings be done in terms of values analogous to church and sect orientations.

SCANZONI, J.
Resolution of occupational-conjugal role conflict in clergy marriages.
J. Marr. & Fam., August, 1965.

Summary of Scanzoni 1964.

SUPUT, M. G. H.
A study of the emotional conflicts of student ministers' wives.
M.A., Northwestern University, 1953.

Sample: 67 wives of ministerial students at Garrett during 1949-50.
Procedure: 52 wives (77%) returned the mailed questionnaire.
Results: Background: Average age 29.8, 27% finished college. Marital relationships: 19% felt the sexual aspect of marriage was as enjoyable to them as to husband. All but 3 were mothers. 57% were favorable to husband's career. 55% work. Aspects of role disliked: being expected to serve as an example, personal lack of "religion," husband's activity in community.

TROUTNER, E. J.
Optimal factors in marital decision making with one hundred forty Methodist ministers and their wives.
Th.D., Boston University School of Theology, 1961.
Dissert. Abstr., 1961, *22*, 1295-1296.

Sample: 140 ministers and wives with 2 or more children in California-Nevada Conference of the Methodist Church.
Procedure: Questionnaire.
Results: Authoritarian patterns in the home have been and are diminishing.

There is an increasing amount of shared responsibility in such things as finances, family size, and religious practices. 93.5% of women and 87.8% of men believe that Christianity supports their positions regarding their marital roles.

FURTHER REFERENCES

For further reference on Wives and Family, see also: **B1:** Fairchild.

BENSON, J. V. (Ed.)

Papers presented at a conference on psychological research.

New York (231 Madison Ave.): Lutheran Church in America, Board of Theological Education, 1962.

See: **I:** Booth 1963; **I:** Brown; **B2:** Harrower 1963.

COLWELL, C. A.

Roles and role conflicts of the parish minister: a study of roles and role conflicts as perceived by ministers selected from the Connecticut Conference of Congregational Christian Churches.

Ph.D., Hartford Seminary Foundation, 1964.

Dissert. Abstr., 1965, *25,* 4271.

The literature dealing with roles and role conflicts of the functionaries of the three major religious traditions in America is summarized and critiqued. Extensive and detailed typologies of role and role conflict are then developed inductively.

D'ARCY, P. F.

Review of research on the vocational interests of priests, brothers and sisters.

Pp. 149-203 in **B2:** Arnold *et al.* 1962.

Reviews studies which attempt to gain knowledge helpful to youth of high schools and college age in selecting more satisfying and self-fulfilling vocations. The report is concerned only with vocational interests and presents an integrated summary

of that research. Future needs for research are discussed.

The following are reviewed, in addition to some unpublished research. **B2:** Burke; **A1:** D'Arcy; **A1:** Friedl; **A1:** Gorman; **A1:** Kennedy 1958; **A1:** Kenney; **A1:** Kolb; **A1:** Lhota; **A1:** McCarthy 1952; **A1:** McDonagh; **I:** Moore; **A1:** Murray 1957; **A1:** Sutter; **B2:** Wauck.

Among conclusions: ". . . The need for the Diocesan Priest scale . . . and for specialized scales within the Catholic priesthood. . . ." "On the Kuder, seminarian groups are uniformly high in 'social service, literary, and musical' interests, low in 'mechanical, scientific, and clerical' interests, average in 'artistic' interests. In 'outdoor, computational, and persuasive' interests different seminarian groups have scored both high and low. On the Strong, seminarians and priests . . . generally attain the highest mean score for any group scale on Group V: Social Service." "The interest pattern of seminarians . . . changes systematically with age." "Certain environmental factors . . . modify the interest scores of seminarians." "Interests characteristic of the priesthood are already identifiable for many in their early teens. The perseverance . . . of those scoring high in Interest Maturity on the Strong is predictable on the basis of their other interests."

DITTES, J. E.

Facts and fantasy in (the minister's) mental health.

Pastoral Psychol., 1959, *10*(92), 15-24.

Pp. 209-222 in **H**: Oates.

The paucity of empirical research on mental health of the clergy is deplored. Problems in such research are discussed, including fallacious causal reasoning, researcher biases, cross-validation, and sampling.

DITTES, J. E.

Research on clergymen: factors influencing decisions for religious service and effectiveness in the vocation.

Relig. Educ., 1962, *57*(4), Research Supplement, S-141-165.

Most research has proceeded to collect data and to draw conclusions without first solving important methodological problems. Where such problems have been successfully solved, the results have not yet been applied to full-blown research.

Two criteria for the effective minister, being a healthy person and being effective in those performances unique to the clergy, are often confused.

The use of secondhand measures borrowed from other research problems is futile. Better would be an item analysis of existing measurement devices when used on a clergy population or a survey of existing personality measures to see which appear to be theoretically relevant. About all that has been empirically demonstrated is that general norms do seem applicable to clergymen. All this reflects the existing paucity of theory. Research generally ignores differences between groups of clergy.

KLING, F. R.

A study of testing as related to the ministry.

Relig. Educ., 1958, *53*, 243-248.

A general introduction to the Educational Testing Service Ministry Study begun in 1956 as a program for evaluating tests used by schools and churches in selecting candidates for the ministry. The relation of these tests is to be determined by their correlation with success in the ministry as revealed by ratings of ministers by themselves and by laymen. This survey is expected to provide more precise information about the nature of the ministry, and eventually it is hoped that new tests will be developed specifically for selecting ministerial candidates.

McCARTHY, T. N., & DONDERO, E. A.

Predictor variables and criteria of success in religious life: needed research.

Cathol. psychol. Rec., 1963, *1*(1), 71-80.

In addition to screening out pathology in applicants to the religious life, psychometricians should be concerned with predicting who among the healthy will be successful. First, criterion categories according to performance must be established; then any other related attributes (intelligence, personality, social) may be searched for.

Criteria may be determined using a job analysis (there is no literature in this area) or with the use of comparison groups. Literature in the latter area is reviewed: (1) Compare those who enter religious life with those who don't. (2) Compare those who remain in seminaries with those who drop out, and those who are accepted with those later rejected. (3) Compare successful perseverers with poorly adjusted perseverers.

MEISSNER, W. W.

Annotated bibliography in religion and psychology.

New York: Academy of Religion and Mental Health, 1961. 235 pp.

Exhaustive listing of Roman Catholic and Protestant, English- and non-English-language studies which bridge religion and mental health. Topical classification. 2,905 entries. 58 entries under "Psychology of Religious Vocation," and 71 entries under "Psychology of Religious Personnel."

MOBERG, D. O.
The church as a social institution.
Englewood Cliffs, N. J.: Prentice-Hall, 1962.

Chap. 18, "The Clergy" (pp. 481-511), surveys sociological research on ministers, priests, and rabbis. Such topics as recruitment, education, roles, duties, and status are discussed.

OATES, W. E. (Ed.)
The minister's own mental health.
Great Neck, N. Y.: Channel Press, 1961.

An anthology of 29 articles, most of which have appeared in *Pastoral Psychology*. Those abstracted here are: **B2**: Anderson; **D**: Blain; **B1**: Blizzard 1958 a and b; **I**: Booth 1958; **F**: Christensen 1959; **G**: Denton 1961; **H**: Dittes 1959; **A3**: Kemp; **B2**: Kildahl; **A4**: Kling; **G**: Koehler; **A1**: Leslie; **I**: Masserman 1961; **F**: Meiburg; **C**: Ranck 1961; **B4**: Scholefield; **B2**: Southard 1961; **F**: Southard.

SALISBURY, W. S.
Religion in American culture: a sociological interpretation.
Homewood, Ill.: Dorsey, 1964.

Chap. 10, "The Clergy" (pp. 206-245), summarizes sociological research on techniques of recruitment, patterns of training, and roles for Protestants, Catholics, and Jews. The typical Protestant minister enjoys the preaching and counseling roles, but tends to be unhappy and ill at ease in the administrative role. Although priestly and liturgical roles are first in importance for the priest, the roles of educator and counselor are increasing in importance.

The traditional Orthodox rabbi strives to play the scholar-saint role; the Reform rabbi is more like the liberal Protestant minister than like traditional Judaism; the Conservative rabbi stands midway between the Orthodox and Reform rabbis.

SOUTHARD, S. (Ed.)
Conference on motivation for the ministry.
Louisville, Ky.: Southern Baptist Theological Seminary, 1959.

Papers from a conference supported by Lilly Endowment, Inc., and attended by 24 pastors, theologians, sociologists, psychiatrists, and psychologists. Free and creative discussion was encouraged; there was no task orientation. The emphasis was on interdisciplinary conversation. Summaries of discussion are presented by Paul Irion, Thomas Bennett (see **A2**: Bennett), O. Mowrer, and Samuel Southard (see **B2**: Southard 1961).

Papers abstracted here are **A2**: Bennett; **B1**: Blizzard 1959a; **I**: Booth 1958; **A1**: Hudson; **A2**: Leiffer 1959, **A1**: Leslie; **F**: Midlefort; **A2**: Pipes.

WISE, C. A.
The call to the ministry.
Pastoral Psychol., 1958, *9*(89), 9-17.

Psychology can study the processes within a person and in his interpersonal relations, which make up the configuration of experiences which are interpreted religiously as a call. A call is psychologically a decision. Psychological aspects of vocational decision including the role of tests and counseling are discussed.

FURTHER REFERENCES

For further references on Surveys of Research, see also: **A1** and **F**: Argyle; **A1**: McCarthy 1960a; **A1**: McCarthy 1962; **A2**: Fichter 1959; **I**: Johnson.

SURVEYS OF PSYCHOLOGICAL TESTING

BARBEY, L.
Apports de la psychologie au problème de la vocation.
L'Ami du Clerge, 1961, *71*, 88-92.

BIER, W. C.
Psychological testing of candidates and the theology of vocation.
Rev. Relig., 1953, *12*, 291-304.
Translated in *Suppl. Vie Spir.*, 1954, 7 (29).

A theological justification for the use of psychological tests with religious and a discussion of the types of illnesses to which the religious seem subject.

BIER, W. C.
L'examen psychologique.
Suppl. Vie Spir., 1954, 7(29), 118-151. (a)

The nature of a vocation is discussed under St. Thomas' distinction of internal and external vocation. The psychological examination for admission to candidacy is for the most part negative, but it plays a positive role in the detection of abnormalities. Various aspects of the examination are discussed: doubtful cases, practical conditions, types of tests, cross-checking by consultation. It is important for many reasons that the examination be given prior to admission. (Abstract by Meissner.)

BIER, W. C.
Practical requirements of a program for the psychological screening of candidates.
Rev. Relig., 1954, *13*, 13-27. (b)

Practical aspects of implementing a program of psychological testing for the selection of candidates to religious life are discussed. The author recommends that such tests be administered prior to admission to the institution and that personnel for such a program be well trained. General characteristics of useful tests are listed. Group tests are to be supplemented by individual counseling.

BIER, W. C.
Psychological tests in the screening of candidates in the minor seminary.
Natl Cathol. Educ. Ass. Bull., 1954, *51*, 128-135. (c)

The use of psychological tests with religious candidates is justified. General requirements of such a program, especially as applied to a minor seminary, are discussed.

BIER, W. C.
Psychological evaluation of religious candidates.
Natl Cathol. Educ. Ass. Bull., 1959, *56*, 341-345.

Discusses the need and theological justification for psychological evaluation of religious candidates. The technique is neither simple nor automatic and no substitute for good judgment, but the mistakes made will be fewer and less serious.

BIER, W. C.

Testing procedures and their value.

In J. E. Haley (Ed.), *Proceedings of the 1959 Sisters' Institute of Spirituality.* Volume 7. Notre Dame, Ind.: University of Notre Dame Press, 1960. Pp. 263-295. (a)

A series of lectures which gives the rationale for psychological testing of religious. Such tests may be used for "supplementing traditional sources of information on applicants for the religious life to insure their psychological suitability for such a way of life." Calls for more research on matters of validity.

BIER, W. C.

Basic rationale of screening for religious vocations.

In W. C. Bier and A. A. Schneiders (Eds.), *Selected papers from the American Catholic Psychological Association meetings of 1957, 1958, 1959.* New York: American Catholic Psychological Association, Fordham University, 1960. Pp. 7-16. (b)

It is on the natural side of vocation that psychology can make its best contributions. The information supplied by psychological instruments is useful because: (1) psychological problems are characteristic of our age; (2) disturbed individuals are attracted to the religious life; (3) psychological demands are greater in religious life than in life in the world.

BOOTH, G.

Unconscious motivation in the choice of the ministry as vocation.

Pastoral Psychol., 1958, *9*(89), 18-24.

Also pp. 76-85 in **H:** Oates.

Similar paper in **H:** Southard.

Presents a favorable opinion on the use of psychological tests as a method which provides part of an answer to the problem of vocation. Discusses the Szondi test in some detail. Offers the following safeguards: (1) Psychological examinations should not be used primarily for screening out psychotic cases. (2) Psychological tests should not be of the questionnaire type. (3) Psychological tests should be interpreted in light of self-images. (4) Deviant results should be discussed with the candidate.

BOOTH, G.

Tests and therapy applied to the clergy.

J. Relig. Hlth, 1963, *2*, 267-276.

Also in **H:** Benson as Practical conclusions from twenty-four years of testing and psychotherapy with seminarians and clergymen.

A description of the author's approach to testing and therapy with ministers and seminarians at General Theological Seminary over a 24-year period. His practice is to discuss with the candidates the differences between their reported self-image and the image reported by the tests.

BROWN, F.

Some observations upon the use of psychological tests in the selection and assessment of candidates for ministerial training.

In **H:** Benson.

Conclusion: "The main point to be emphasized at this time is that we possess imperfect tests with which to evaluate complex individuals against criterion settings about which we know too little."

BURKE, H. R.

Tests and measurements in the minor seminary.

Cathol. Educ. Rev., 1955, *53*, 455-466.

A review of methods for intelligence and achievement testing which might be useful in a minor seminary. Reviews of several tests are included. The following minimum program is recommended: Terman-McNemar Test of Mental Ability, Differential Aptitude Test, Stanford Achievement Test, Iowa Grammar Information Test.

BURKE, T.
The use of the questionnaire in vocation work.
In *Proc. 8th annu. Convocation of the Voc. Inst.* Notre Dame, Ind.: Notre Dame Press, 1955. Pp. 47-50.

CASTELVI, M.
Subsidia quae provenire possunt ex diversis scientiis in selectione vocationum.
Acta et Documenta Congressus Generalis de Statibus Perfectionis. Rome: Pia Società S. Paolo, 1952, *2,* 792-799.

CLAUDIA, M.
A sister looks at the psychological screening of candidates.
Cathol. Counsel., 1964, *8,* 57-59.

The person using psychological tests makes decisions which result from far more than test results. When refusals are made, care must be taken to announce the decision with gentleness and compassion.

COMBES, A.
Vocation surnaturelle et investigation scientifique.
La Pensée Catholique, 1960, *66,* 23-43.

CORCORAN, C. J. D.
Y a-t-il des "types" humains inaptes à la vie religieuse?
Suppl. Vie Spir., 1955, *8*(33), 171-183.

Psychological tests and other psychiatric helps enable those who select candidates for religion to render a much more certain judgment of the suitability of a given candidate. But the effect of grace and the therapeutic aspects of virtue should not be overlooked. Unsuitable candidates should be rejected, but the superior should also not be afraid to take risks and have confidence in his own judgment. (Abstract by Meissner.)

COVILLE, W. J.
The personality assessment of candidates for the priesthood and the religious life.
Natl Cathol. Educ. Ass. Bull., 1964, *61,* 396-409.

Spirituality, appropriate motivation, intelligence, emotional stability, and capacity for satisfactory human relationships are given as the qualities essential for the religious life. The author comments on the need for behavioral scientists to operate in these areas, so that the "obviously poor risks" can be eliminated from among the candidates. Steps in setting up an assessment program are discussed, and the New York Program (see **B2:** Coville) is given as an example (utilizing the College Qualification Test, MMPI, Sentence Completion, Draw-a-Person, and Personality Inventory for Religious, supplemented by a life history questionnaire and a clinical interview). Over a period of 4 years, 600 candidates have been tested and will be followed.

CZECHOWICZ, W. G.
A philosophical investigation of the principles underlying objective testing in relation to measurement and evaluation in religion.
Ph.D., Catholic University of America, 1962.
Dissert. Abstr., 1963, *23,* 3185-3186.

An investigation of the basic philosophical presuppositions concerning the nature of man upon which the measurement movement is founded. Evaluation is based on the Catholic teaching regarding the nature of man, his purpose in life, and his ultimate destiny. Sources analyzed are: Wundt, Darwin, Binet, Cattell, and Thorndike.

Catholic philosophy finds unacceptable those philosophical foundations of measurement procedures which aspire to the pretension that the entirety of human nature is measurable by these procedures.

DAVIS, C. E.
Psychological techniques in the enlistment work of the church.
AATS Bull., 1950, *19,* 122-130.

A review of the history of the acceptance of testing into Protestantism. The testing program of the Presbyterian Church U.S.A. uncovers about 5% of students with personality and academic problems which make the ministry inadvisable for them. About 33% have minor personality difficulties, many of which can be corrected.

DEWIRE, H. A.
Psychological   testing   in   theological schools.
Ministry Studies Board Newsletter (1810 Harvard Blvd., Dayton, O.), 1962, *1,* 2-4.

Sample: 110 (95%) of Protestant seminaries in the American Association of Theological Schools.
Procedure: Questionnaire.
Results: The average number of tests per school is 3.7. 19 use no tests at all. The MMPI and SVIB are the most frequently used tests, although test batteries are not static. Many schools requested coordinated research in the test instruments.

DIGNA, MARY
That God's will be better known: use of psychometrics in appraising candidates for the religious life.
Rev. Relig., 1949, *8,* 201-207.

A general discussion of those characteristics of a religious community which can be served by the psychological testing of applicants to the religious life.

DIGNA, MARY
A tentative testing program for religious life.
Rev. Relig., 1951, *10,* 75-81.

Applicability of the following as tests for applicants to the religious life is discussed briefly: CTMM, CTP, Bell, Bernreuter, MMPI, MPS, Kuder, SVIB.

DIGNA, MARY
Testing and screening.
In *Proc. 8th annu. Convocation of the Voc. Inst.* Notre Dame, Ind.: Notre Dame Press, 1955. Pp. 83-89.

DIGNA, SISTER MARY
Uses of information in a screening program.
Rev. Relig., 1963, *22,* 300-306.

Over the past 10 years the Sisters of St. Benedict have conducted a testing program. It now includes the California Short Form of Mental Maturity, which replaced the ACE and the Otis; MMPI, which replaced the Minnesota Personality Scale; SVIB. Research during this period (N not given) has shown a correlation between test data and subsequent religious adjustment; tests are now administered prior to admission. Several case studies illustrate the bases used in decision-making.

DONDERO, E. A., & McCARTHY, T. N.
Professional and theological problems in psychological assessment.
In A. A. Schneiders & P. J. Centi (Eds.), *Selected papers from the American Catholic Psychological Association meetings of 1960, 1961.* New York:

Fordham University Press, 1962. Pp. 66-70.

Problems in 2 areas are discussed—psychology and theology. The latter includes the need for the one who makes the referral to specify the scope of the investigation, the nature of the report in an unspecified referral, the problem of an involuntary manifestation of conscience in a required psychological examination, and the psychologist's right to withhold information from either the candidate or the superior.

DUFFEY, F. D.
Testing the spirit.
St. Louis: Herder, 1947.

EITZEN, D.
Counseling in the student personnel program, School of Religion, University of Southern California.
Report of the 2nd biennial meeting of the Association of Seminary Professors in the Practical Fields, 1952. Pp. 46-50.

Outlines a specific counseling program. Includes discussion of testing, use of results, and administration.

ETHIER, W.
Le rôle de l'orientation professionnelle dans le discernement des vocations.
Vie Comm. Relig., 1946, 5, 73-83.

FRISON, B.
Selection and incorporation of candidates for the religious life.
Milwaukee: Bruce Publishing Company, 1961.

An explanation and commentary on Articles 31-34 of the *Apostolic Constitution Sedes Sapientiae* which considers "the students, their selection, and their incorporation." Includes a brief discussion of psychological testing among other selec-

tion procedures. The use of tests is justified with the quotation, "the psychological fitness (of the candidate) must also be investigated."

FROYD, M. C.
Pre-testing for the ministry.
Christian Century, 1956, 73¹, 769-770.

Brief descriptions for the layman of psychological testing programs in the Diciples of Christ, Presbyterian U.S.A., and Protestant Episcopal Churches. Similar programs in the seminaries are characterized as follows: "considerable activity, great diversity, rugged individualism, and almost no cross-communication." The beginnings of the Educational Testing Service study are described.

GRATTON, H.
Quelques expériences d'investigation psychologique et de psychothérapie auprès des candidats au sacerdoce.
Suppl. Vie Spir., 1957, 10(42), 354-364.

The author offers his reflections on his own personal experience in the employment of psychological testing devices for the selection of candidates for the priesthood. Psychological techniques, however helpful and valuable, cannot replace but only supplement training and grace. (Abstract by Meissner.)

GREENWALD, A. F.
Psychological assessment of religious aspirants.
Rev. Relig., 1963, 22, 296-299.

Although no tests are infallible, projective techniques have demonstrated their effectiveness in the study of personality and in determining within limits the psychological suitability of persons seeking a religious vocation. Early detection and disposition of seminarians making a marginal adjustment can help to avoid major disturbances. More definitive concepts and norms for those aspiring to a religious life should be developed.

GREENWALD, A. F.
Utilizing the psychiatrist's report with seminarians.
Rev. Relig., 1964, *23*, 612-615.

The psychologist is responsible for informing the seminarian of his reporting procedures, securing his consent to the evaluation, and for presenting his findings in a meaningful way to the seminary authorities. It is generally preferable for the spiritual director to summarize and communicate the psychologist's findings to the seminarian. Control techniques for minimizing misunderstanding and misinterpretation of the data are discussed.

HARTSHORNE, H.
Report of the committee on personality and aptitude. Twelfth Biennial Meeting of the AATS.
AATS Bull., 1940, *14*, 54-56.

No personality test is of use in seminary admissions although some might be used in later counseling. No useful aptitude tests are known to the committee. Difficulties of constructing such tests are listed. Selection and guidance procedures would be strengthened by the use of case studies utilizing questionnaires and interviews.

The report concludes with a call for increasing the number of highly qualified applicants which would eliminate the problem of merely cutting off poorly qualified ones at the bottom.

HENNESSY, T., & BLUHM, H.
Using interest inventories in religious and sacerdotal counseling.
Cathol. Counsel., 1958, *2*(2), 46-69.

Reviews **A1:** Lhota, **A1:** Kolb, and **A1:** D'Arcy. It is suggested that since the work of religious of different orders differs so

much, each order should consider developing interest inventory scoring stencils for its own candidates.

HILTNER, S.
Psychological tests for ministerial candidates.
J. pastoral Care, 1957, *11*, 106-108.

This editorial maintains: (1) Psychological tests in unskilled hands are reduced to gadgets. (2) It has not been demonstrated that tests peculiar to their purpose are necessary for ministerial students. (3) If tests are for "screening out," why not use general tests? (4) Faculty members' skill in using these tests may be no more valuable than increased skill in interviewing and related techniques.
(See reply **I:** Saunders.)

JOHNSON, P. E. (Chm.), BILLINSKY, J. M., DeWIRE, H., MILLION, E. G., MORENTZ, P. E., & SAUNDERS, D. R.
A panel discussion: using the results of testing.
AATS Biennial Meeting, June 22, 1956, 135.

Generally informal comments on research problems in testing theological students, vocational guidance using tests, need to begin testing early, and the criterion problem.

KEMP, C. F., & HUNT, R. A.
Theological school checklist of study skills and attitudes.
St. Louis: Bethany, 1965.

Information for use in counseling theological students. Study habits and skills are described using the results of statistically analyzed research.

KENNEALLY, W. J.
Psychiatric tests for seminarians.
Natl Cathol. Educ. Ass. Bull., 1954, *51*, 89-95.

The author distinguishes between psychiatric and psychological testing, endorsing the latter. He feels that because of the present state of development of psychiatry, the strongest statement to be made is that *some* seminarians should be subjected to psychiatric tests during, not before, their seminary life.

KURTH, C. J.
Psychiatric and psychological selection of candidates for the sisterhood.
Bull. Guild Cathol. Psychiat., 1961, *8*, 19-25.

Discusses the problem of discovering and rejecting those psychologically-psychiatrically unsuited to the strenuous life of sisterhood. Heredity, environment, and motivation are treated briefly. A psychological screening examination is recommended for all candidates. The team approach using the Otis, MMPI, and personal interview is suggested. Minimum standards for rejection on psychiatric grounds are presented.

LONG, L. L.
Psychometric testing of candidates for overseas work.
Boston (14 Beacon St.): Personnel Secretary of American Board of Commissioners for Foreign Missions, 1948.

Sample: 118 people: 23 experienced missionaries, 95 new candidates.
Procedure: OSUPE, SVIB, A-V Study of Values, Kuder, Bernreuter, self-administered. No criteria of success were established.
Results: Tentatively concluded that this battery is adequate for the board's work. On the basis of 3½ years of experience, tentative norms and danger zones are suggested for the OSUPE, A-V Study of Values, Bernreuter.

MANDELL, W. S., & HODEL, G. H.
Psychological testing of seminarians.

In *Proceedings of the fourth annual Baguio Religious Acculturation Conference.* Manila: Baguio Religious Acculturation Conference, 1961. Pp. 74-85.

MARGARET LOUISE, SISTER
Psychological problems of vocation candidates.
Natl Cathol. Educ. Ass. Bull., 1961, *58*, 450-454.

Variations in intellectual ability and emotional adjustment must be considered in programs in religious orders. The contribution of psychological tests for screening is an important one but needs further research. Hypochondriasis is especially pertinent to screening for the religious life.

MASSERMAN, J. H.
The practice of dynamic psychiatry.
Philadelphia: W. B. Saunders, 1955.

Chap. 16, Psychiatric reports to nonmedical personnel, pp. 269-298. 14 complete reports are presented as examples of the author's approach. All have to do with candidates for overseas missionary service.

MASSERMAN, J. H., & PALMER, R. T.
Psychiatric and psychologic tests for ministerial personnel.
Pastoral Psychol., 1961, *12*(112), 24-33.
Similar article in **H:** Oates, pp. 278-298: Psychiatric and psychological tests for missionary personnel.

The authors report on their work as psychiatric-psychological consultants for several Protestant mission boards. A study (N = 364) by 1 board over a 15-year period produced highly significant results. A sample personnel evaluation report is included. The authors conclude with a call for more intensive testing and reporting programs.

McCARTHY, T. N.
Psychological assessment in the religious
vocation.
Natl Cathol. Educ. Ass. Bull., 1958, *55*,
94.

The psychologist does not deal with the
spiritual aspects of the vocation. His contribution is in screening out those who are
lacking in psychological qualifications and
in identifying those who might profit from
counseling or remedial work.

MILLION, E. G.
Psychological testing in the seminaries.
AATS Bull., 1954, *21*, 85-99.

Sample: 107 theological schools in the
U.S. and Canada.
Procedure: 80 responded to 3 open-
ended questions sent by letter.
Results: 53 schools report using 46 different psychological tests. Programs in use
by certain seminaries and denominations
are briefly described. Achievement tests
are seen as superfluous, attitude and intelligence tests as useful, and personality
tests as counseling aids.

MOORE, T. V.
Insanity in priests and religious: II. The
detection of prepsychotics who apply
for admission to the priesthood or religious communities.
Amer. eccl. Rev., 1936, *95*, 601-613.

Suggests that a set of questions should
be formed into a booklet to be filled out
by the applicant, a member of his family,
and a priest. Questions concern personal and family history, character, and
emotional traits. (See **F:** Moore.)

NELSON, J. O.
Vocation, theism, and testing.
Pastoral Psychol., 1959, *9*(89), 33-40.

Discusses the call, whether "religious"
vocation differs qualitatively from other

vocations, and how psychometric data can
be helpful. Tests are seen as an aid rather
than an intrusion into the matter of vocation.

O'CONNER, L. L.
Use of testing programs in the selection of
personnel for the church vocations.
M.A., Austin Presbyterian Theological
Seminary, 1948.

A survey of church institutions to determine existing practices used in the selection of personnel for church work.

OLIVAUX, R.
Possibilités et limites de la graphologie
dans l'étude des vocations religieuses.
Suppl. Vie Spir., 1958, *11*(45), 197-214.

The same limits must be imposed on
graphology as on psychological tests; its
value depends on the competence and
balanced judgment of the graphologist.
Respect for the rights of the person is the
essential which must be observed. (Abstract by Meissner.)

ORAISON, M.
Niveau psychologique nécessaire à l'en-
gagement dans une 'vocation.'
In *Psychologie moderne et réflexion chré-
tienne.* Paris: Fayard, 1953. Pp. 109-
126.

PLÉ, A.
An experiment in discernment of voca-
tion.
J. Relig. Hlth, 1962, *1*, 165-179.

General discussion of rationale and of
procedures, now conducted for 3 years,
used in detecting psychological maladjustment among applicants for admission to
the novitiate. A priest, psychiatrist, and
clinical psychologist interview the candidate separately, and the psychologist ad-
ministers tests. The 3 interviewers then
confer and make a common recommenda-

tion which is communicated personally to the candidate and in writing to the novice master.

REED, K. E.
Psychological testing in supervision of clinical pastoral training.
Ph.D., Boston University, 1963.
Dissert. Abstr., 1963, *24*, 2595-2596.

39 students and 7 supervisors were involved in a study on how test information influences the work of supervisors. Tests used: EPPS, SCT, Listening Test. Results of the testing are not reported in the abstract. A historical and questionnaire survey of the clinical training movement revealed that interviews, autobiographies, and references are used for selection more often than psychological tests by the Council on Clinical Training and the Institute of Pastoral Care.

REH, F. F.
Use of the psychologist's report in a diocesan seminary.
In A. A. Schneiders & P. J. Centi (Eds.), *Selected papers from the American Catholic Psychological Association meetings of 1960, 1961.* New York: Fordham University Press, 1962. Pp. 71-76.

A review of Church pronouncements and Canon Law reveals encouragement for psychological assessment in seminaries. Results should be used in validity studies and counseling as well as screening. The rector must assume standards of absolute secrecy of the examination results. If the candidate makes any damaging admissions, he must understand that such information will be revealed to the seminary administration only with his permission.

RISTUCCIA, B. J.
The psychologist's report and canon law.

In A. A. Schneiders & P. J. Centi (Eds.), *Selected papers from the American Catholic Psychological Association meetings of 1960, 1961.* New York: Fordham University Press, 1962. Pp. 77-81.

The religious candidate has basic rights conferred on him by the Canon Law which states, "All religious superiors are strictly forbidden to induce in any manner persons subject to them to make a manifestation of conscience to them." The subject must never be forced to make a revelation of his conscience to anyone. He has a right to be informed as to both the extent and the depth of the manifestation of conscience that might be involved in the use of any psychological procedure. He may demand that what he reveals to the psychologist be told no one without his consent. Additional permission must be given if such information is to be used by others when harm or inconvenience to the subject could result.

ROBITAILLE, H. J., & SULLIVAN, A. A.
Some helps in discovering personality traits in minor seminarians.
Natl Cathol. Educ. Ass. Bull., 1950, *47*, 117-125.

An introduction to the evaluation techniques of self-inventory and rating scales. Brief reviews are given of the following: Rorschach, MMPI, TAT, Guilford-Martin Temperament Profile Chart, Guilford-Martin Inventory (GAMIN), Guilford's Inventory STDCR, Bernreuter, California Test of Personality, Mental Health Analysis, Burke's rating scale (see **B2:** Burke), Religious and Disciplinary Home Environment Questionnaire (see **B2:** Burke).

RYAN, T. A.
Vocational guidance as a means of determining aptitudes for ordination.

M.A., Catholic University of America, 1933.

Sample: 14 of 29 major seminaries replied to a questionnaire.

Results: Aside from the routine letters of health and character recommendations, no attempt in an organized manner was made to learn about the seminarian or to learn about his individual aptitudes, interests, and abilities. The uniform procedure for determining the candidate's aptitude for ordination is majority vote of the faculty.

SALMAN, D. H.
Le discernement des vocations religieuses.
Suppl. Vie Spir., 1960, *13*(52), 81-98.

Psychological devices such as the MMPI and Rorschach are useful but still imperfectly adapted to the demands of candidate selection, and should therefore be used with caution. (Abstract by Meissner.)

SAUNDERS, D. R., & WEBB, S. C.
A reply to Dr. Hiltner.
J. pastoral Care, 1957, *11,* 108-110.

Reply to **I:** Hiltner. (1) " . . . it seems premature to quibble over whether to use special tests . . . or general tests. Rather we should concentrate our energies systematically on identifying the various kinds of qualities that are necessary or desirable for effective performance in the several aspects of the ministry." (2) Such techniques as the interview have not been shown to surpass tests in validity.

SAXE, R. H.
Psychometric testing and missionary selection.
Bibliotheca Sacra, 1959, *116,* 249-258.

Sample: 30 denominational and interdenominational mission boards.

Procedure: 28 boards replied to a mailed questionnaire.

Results: 11 boards indicated regular use

and 9 occasional use of programs of psychometric testing. Most use a battery with the most common tests being Bernreuter, SVIB, Kuder. Fewer boards use psychiatric services; some of those which do, supplement their work with additional questions of their own. The one board with enough data to evaluate its program has decided to discontinue all but the OSUPE.

SEMINARY DEPARTMENTS OF THE NATIONAL CATHOLIC EDUCATIONAL ASSOCIATION.
Report on psychological testing, 1963-64.
Natl Cathol. Educ. Ass. Seminary Newsletter, 1964, *6*(1), 21-33.

"1. 390 institutions, 108 diocesan and 282 religious, or 88% of all institutions, replied to this section of the annual questionnaire.

"2. Intelligence tests are most frequently administered in the high school and college years. After sophomore year administration of intelligence tests diminishes sharply. The majority of institutions give only one or two intelligence tests and administer a given test for a variety of purposes.

"3. Interest or vocational tests are very seldom employed. Kuder Preference and Strong Vocational Interest Blank are the only two tests reported in use.

"4. Personality tests are sometimes given only for special cases, but most frequently they are administered to all students. Only one test is used; usually no indication is given of who interprets the tests, which are usually administered in grades 12, 13 and 14, for the purpose of counseling as well as screening. Personal interview with a trained psychologist is sometimes mentioned with a testing program. Most of those not now testing did not indicate why they are not, but some indicated that testing is done earlier and results are available to them, and a few institutions are beginning testing soon." The MMPI is, by far, the most used test.

TEPE, V.
A psicotécnica a serviço das vocaçóes.
Revista Eclesiástica Brasileira, 1959, *19,* 569-578.

VAUGHAN, R. P.
Moral issues in psychological screening.
Rev. Relig., 1957, *16,* 65-78.

A discussion of such subjects as purpose of psychological testing, confidentiality, professional secrecy, and decision-making. It is concluded that a well-conducted, cautious screening program can be extremely valuable and morally justifiable.

VAUGHAN, R. P.
Ethical aspects of screening programs.
In W. C. Bier and A. A. Schneiders (Eds.), *Selected papers from the American Catholic Psychological Association meetings of 1957, 1958, 1959.* New York: American Catholic Psychological Association, Fordham University, 1960. Pp. 27-32.

The principles of moral theology and ethics require that psychological data should not be used for any purposes except those for which they were secured. Neither can they be revealed to anyone else without the express consent of the person himself.

Superiors bear certain obligations to the members of their communities, in that they must decide who is not suited for religious life. The superior may use any means to carry out these obligations, including requiring that a candidate submit to testing under threat of exclusion from the community if he or she does not comply.

If a candidate is found to be seriously disturbed, it is not safe to assume religious life will improve his condition. Rather, the stresses are greater in religious life, and such candidate should be judged not to have a vocation. In the case of milder disorders, it should be recognized that changes are likely to occur only during some form of psychotherapy.

VAUGHAN, R. P.
Specificity in programs of psychological examinations.
Bull. Guild Cathol. Psychiat., 1961, *8,* 149-155.

Warns that all religious should not be considered "pretty much the same." Outlines an apparently successful screening program which has been in use for the past 4 years. It consists of tests (SAT of College Entrance Examination Board, CTMM, and sometimes WAIS, MMPI, modified Rorschach, SCT, DAP) which are evaluated by 2 psychologists, and of an interview structured around the test results. Statistical results are inconclusive and the author questions the validity of the criterion.

WAUCK, L. A.
Organization and administration of a screening program for religious vocations.
In W. C. Bier and A. A. Schneiders (Eds.), *Selected papers from the American Catholic Psychological Association meetings of 1957, 1958, 1959.* New York: American Catholic Psychological Association, Fordham University, 1960. Pp. 19-26.

The most useful kinds of tests are briefly discussed. The importance of proper interpretation and the need for qualified psychologists as well as tests are stressed.

WERLING, H. F.
The student personnel programs in the

pretheological colleges and theological seminaries in the major Lutheran bodies.

Ph.D., University of Wyoming, 1962.

Procedure: 7-page printed questionnaires were completed by 33 of the 34 pretheological colleges and theological seminaries of the major Lutheran Church bodies. Interviews were conducted at 5 colleges and 5 seminaries.

Results: Among the findings, the following relate to testing and counseling: All colleges and all but one seminary had testing programs. Both scholastic ability and achievement tests were administered by all colleges, but only 5.5% of the seminaries used this combination. 50% of the seminaries used a battery including a scholastic ability test, an interest inventory (45% used the SVIB), and a personality inventory (61% used the MMPI). The percentage of drop-outs increased gradually from the first year of junior college to the last year of seminary. Courses in psychology and availability of various types of counseling are common in most of the institutions but only since World War II.

WILLIAMS, M. O., JR.

The psychological-psychiatric appraisal of candidates for missionary service.

Pastoral Psychol., 1958, *9*(89), 41-44.

Preliminary, nonstatistical report of research by the Methodist Board of Missions which concludes that psychological and psychiatric data are valuable aids in appraising and guiding candidates. Questions given to psychiatrists and psychologists to answer in their report are listed.

WOODROOFE, R. W.

The selection of candidates for the ministry.

J. pastoral Care, 1951, *5*(4), 23-28.

This paper defends the usefulness of psychological instruments in examining candidates for the ministry, calls for an open-minded study of the ministry's requirements in real life, and briefly describes plans for 2 research projects in the Diocese of Massachusetts.

ZELLNER, A. A.

Psychological testing and the religious life.

Sponsa Regis, 1959, *31,* 68.

ZELLNER, A. A.

Screening of candidates for priesthood and religious life.

Cathol. Educ. Rev., 1960, *58,* 96-105.

The contribution of psychological tests to the screening of religious candidates is discussed, some research is reviewed, and descriptions of intelligence, achievement, interest, and personality tests are given. "It does seem rather unreasonable to contribute knowingly to the difficulties of religious life or the problems of the faithful in parishes by admitting psychologically unstable persons to orders or to the seminary." Psychological testing has a function to perform in this regard.

FURTHER REFERENCES

For further references on Surveys of Psychological Testing, see also: **A1:** Sweeney 1964b; **A2:** Higdon; **D:** Hagmaier; **H:** Kling; **H:** McCarthy; **H:** Wise.

INDEX OF AUTHORS

The index cites, in bold face type, each category under which one or more abstracts of that author may be found. In the case of multiple authors, the index entry for a second author cites the category and the principal author.

INDEX OF INSTRUMENTS AND METHODS

Each entry of this index gives the category, the first author's name, and year (if more than one abstract for that author appears in that category).

The name of a test's developer is included as part of the name of the test, and the test is alphabetized accordingly, if the instrument is conventionally known in this way or if the abstracted author has so referred to it.

INDEX OF SAMPLES

This index is divided into four major sections, and each section subdivided into appropriate categories, without regard to alphabetical arrangement. Many abstracts are, of course, indexed in more than one of these categories. The four major categories are: Clergy, religious, and seminary students; Denominational affiliations (for Protestants only); Control groups (non-clergy samples used for comparison); Location of samples, when this is distinctive.

190

INDEX OF TOPICS

Each entry of this index gives the category, the first author's name, and year (if more than one abstract for that author appears in that category).

B2: Bier 1963; **B2:** Billinsky; **B2:** Burke; **B2:** Cesar Vaca; **B2:** Corcoran; **B2:** McCarthy 1958; **B2:** Nabais 1955; **B2:** Nabais 1956; **B2:** Pertejo; **B2:** Philip; **B2:** Troisfontaines; **B2:** Wauck; **B3:** Cavanagh; **B3:** Dukehart; **B3:** Quigley; **B4:** Allport; **B4:** Wise; **E:** Parrot 1960; **H:** Kling; **H:** McCarthy; **I:** Bier 1954a; **I:** Bier 1954b; **I:** Bier 1954c; **I:** Bier 1959; **I:** Bier 1960a; **I:** Bier 1960b; **I:** Booth 1958; **I:** Castelvi; **I:** Corcoran; **I:** Coville; **I:** Davis; **I:** Digna 1955; **I:** Digna 1963; **I:** Ethier; **I:** Frison; **I:** Greenwald 1963; **I:** Hartshorne; **I:** Hostie; **I:** Kurth; **I:** Margaret Louise; **I:** McCarthy; **I:** Moore; **I:** O'Conner; **I:** Ple; **I:** Vaughan 1960a; **I:** Vaughan 1961; *also see* section **A3**
    of effective clergy: see section **B4**
self, actualization: **C:** Schultz
    esteem: **A1:** Sward
    ideal: **A1:** Gilbride; **A1:** Judy; **A1:** McCabe; **A2:** Hepple; **B1:** Jaquez; **B2:** McCabe; **B2:** Tageson
    image: **A1:** Gilbride; **A1:** Judy; **A1:** Kennedy 1962; **A1:** Linder; **A1:** McCabe; **A1:** Niebling; **A1:** Strike; **A1:** Whitlock 1963; **A2:** Mirse; **A4:** Fulton; **B1:** Blizzard 1956b; **B1:** Blizzard 1958a; **B1:** Blizzard 1958b; **B1:** Blizzard 1959b; **B1:** Blizzard 1960; **B1:** Clippinger; **B1:** McCann; **B1:** McCarthy 1963a; **B2:** Arnold 1962a; **B2:** Arnold 1962b; **B2:** Barnes; **B2:** Benton; **B2:** Fairbanks; **B2:** McCabe; **B2:** Tageson; **B4:** Atwood; **B4:** Gynther 1958; **B4:** Gynther 1962; **B4:** Swanson; **B4:** Thompson; **C:** Maurer; **D:** Kendall; **D:** Kenoyer; **G:** Morentz; **I:** Booth 1958; **I:** Booth 1963; *also see* identity

insight: **A1:** Johnson 1952; **B4:** Bonacker; **B4:** Keller; **B4:** Ramsden; **B4:** Swanson; **E:** Lyon 1964
    satisfaction: **A1:** Abrams; **A4:** Moore; **B2:** Ashbrook 1964; **B3:** Campbell 1963; **B3:** Rossman
sensitivity: **A2:** Smith 1947; **A2:** Smith 1948; **B4:** Keller
service: **A1:** Holland
sexuality: **A1:** Dodson; **A1:** Nodet; **A1:** Ple 1950; **B1:** McCarthy 1963b; **B1:** Rousset; **B2:** Bowes; **B2:** Hudson; **D:** Nodet
skills: **A1:** Hass; **B2:** Hamilton 1956; **B4:** Bonacker; **D:** Robinson; **I:** Kemp
sociability: **A1:** McCarthy 1942; **A1:** Peters; **A1:** Reindl; **A1:** Sweeney 1964a; **B2:** Becker; **B2:** Kelley; **B2:** Parrot; **B4:** Urschalitz; **D:** Kenoyer
social issues: **A1:** Sutter; **A2:** Lenski; **A2:** Roman; **A4:** Brown 1962; **A4:** Brown 1963; **A4:** Davis; **A4:** Glock; **A4:** Mitchell; **A4:** Olson; **B3:** Campbell 1959; **B3:** Johnstone; **B4:** Shissler; **C:** Johnson 1961/1962; **C:** Leslie; **C:** Northwood
socio-economic status: **A1:** Linder; **A2:** Bittinger; **A2:** Cassady; **A2:** Coxon; **A2:** Fichter 1959; **A2:** Fichter 1965; **A2:** Gaspar Mission Society; **A2:** Harte 1957; **A2:** Kelly; **A2:** Masson; **A2:** McCarrick 1963; **A2:** Pope; **A2:** Sadler; **A2:** Smith 1961; **A2:** Thompson; **A2:** Zerfoss; **A4:** Fichter 1960a; **A4:** Mitchell; **B2:** Cash 1954; **B2:** Cash 1962; **B2:** Ingram; **B3:** Campbell 1963; **B3:** Jackson; **B3:** Johnstone; **C:** Cumming; **C:** Maurer; **C:** Nameche; **D:** Foley; **D:** Klausner 1964a; **D:** Klausner 1964b; **D:** Klausner 1964c; **F:** Christensen 1963b; **F:** McAllister

specialization: **A4:** Fichter 1960b
    preference: **A1:** Dick; **A2:** Coxon; **A2:** Scherer 1963a; **A2:** Scherer 1963b; **B2:** Dittes; **C:** Mills
speech: **A4:** Anderson
spiritual director: **B2:** Bowes; **B2:** Marcozzi; **E:** Bier; **I:** Greenwald 1964
spiritual maturity: **B3:** Poehler
spirituality: **B2:** Kohls; **I:** Coville; *also see* religion, personal
stability: **A1:** Linder; **A1:** Scheuerman; **A2:** Gaspar Mission Society; **A2:** Sherman; **B2:** Kohls; **B3:** Murphy; **C:** Proctor; **D:** McCarthy; **E:** Boyd; **I:** Coville
success: **A1:** Godfrey; **A4:** Fichter 1960b; **B1:** Blizzard 1956c; **B1:** Blizzard 1958b; **B1:** Clippinger; **B1:** Jackson; **B1:** Klink; **B2:** Bier 1963; **B2:** Billinsky; **B2:** Douglas; **B2:** Ham; **B2:** Hamilton (undated); **B2:** Hamilton 1956; **B2:** Harrower 1964; **B2:** Hubbard; **B2:** Southard 1965; **B2:** Wright; **B3:** Allen; **B3:** Deegan 1963; **B3:** Deegan 1964; **B3:** Moxcey; **B4:** May; **C:** Rodehaver; **D:** Blizzard; **H:** Kling

testing: **A1:** Davis; **A1:** Hostie; **A1:** Johnson 1952; **A1:** Kling; **A1:** Kobler; **A1:** McCarthy 1960a; **A1:** McCarthy 1960b; **A1:** Stevaux; **A1:** Sweeney 1964a; **B1:** Vallejo-Nagero; **B2:** Arbaugh; **B2:** Bier 1963; **B2:** Bowes; **B2:** Digna; **B2:** Long; **B2:** McCarthy (undated); **B2:** McCarthy 1958; **B2:** Nabais 1956; **B2:** Philip; **B2:** Webb 1958a; **B4:** Allport; **E:** Kinnane; **E:** Parrot 1960
    general surveys: **B2:** Atwater; **B2:** Beirnaert 1960; **B2:** Beirnaert 1962; **B2:**

Billinsky; **B2:** Thayer 1951; *also see* section **I**

theology of vocation: **A1:** Ple 1952; **A3:** Southard 1957; **B1:** Blizzard 1956c; **B1:** Marian; **B2:** Bier 1963; **B2:** Gratton; **B2:** Nabais 1955; **B2:** Nabais 1956; **I:** Bier 1953; **I:** Bier 1954a; **I:** Corcoran; **I:** Dondero; **I:** Hostie

therapy: **G:** Guthrie

   with clergy: **F:** Kobler; *also see* guidance and section **E**

thoughtfulness: **A2:** Darling

time: **A2:** Hepple; **B1:** Blizzard 1956a; **D:** Blizzard; **D:** Nichols; **G:** Koehler

underachievement: **A4:** Hunt, **F:** D'Arcy

uniformity: **D:** Evoy

values: **A1:** Dick; **A1:** Pugh; **A1:** Schroeder; **A4:** Kling; **A4:** Neal; **B2:** Maehr; **C:** Baldwin; **C:** Foster; **D:** Falk 1963; **D:** Hoyer; **G:** Scanzoni 1964; **G:** Scanzoni 1965

vocational, choice: **A1:** Dodson; **A1:** Ernst; **A1:** Geraud; **A1:** Hickman 1921; **A1:** Hickman 1923; **A1:** Strike; **A1:** Thorndike; **A1:** Whitlock 1959; **A1:** Whitlock 1961; **A1:** Whitlock 1963; **A2:** Alaimo; **A2:** Barrett; **A2:** Bowdern 1936; **A2:** Bowdern 1941; **A2:** Bowdern 1942; **A2:** Dougherty; **A2:** Evans; **A2:** Felton; **A2:** Fichter 1959; **A2:** Gaspar Mission Society; **A2:** Gilbert; **A2:** Herman; **A2:** Hertzberg; **A2:** Jamieson; **A2:** Johnson; **A2:** Kauffman; **A2:** Keightley; **A2:** May 1934a; **A2:** Sunday School Board; **A3:** Froyd; **A4:** Fichter 1960a; **B2:** Tageson; **B3:** Biot

   guidance: **A1:** Davis; **A2:** Smyth; **A3:** Ganss; **A3:** James; **A3:** Kemp; **A3:** Southard 1953; **A3:** Southard 1957; **H:** D'Arcy; **I:** Johnson; **I:** Ryan

   satisfaction: **A2:** Bossart; **B1:** Blizzard 1955b; **B1:** Blizzard 1956a; **B1:** Insleo; **B1:** Murphy; **B2:** Hodge; **B3:** Campbell 1963

vows: **B3:** Biot; **D:** De Milan; **D:** Hagmaier; **D:** Kelly

wives and families: **C:** Allen; *also see* section **G**